Being a Gracious Guest

Here are some guidelines for being the kind of guest who gets invited back:

- Stay home if you're sick. Simply call your host, explain the situation, and say thanks for the invitation.
- Respond promptly to the invitation and arrive promptly at the party. (Remember that arriving too early is as impolite as arriving late.)
- Dress appropriately. If you're unsure of what to wear, ask your host.
- Give your host a thoughtful and appropriate gift if the situation requires it. Suggestions include arranged flowers or plants, chocolates, wine, and books.
- Be self-sufficient at the party. Introduce yourself to the other guests and involve yourself in others' conversations. If you're not sure what to talk about, read up on current events beforehand.
- Drink alcohol in moderation, if at all.
- Be considerate about smoking. If you don't see an ashtray, refrain from smoking.
- Exit gracefully, thanking each host (if there is more than one) for a lovely party.
- Send a thank-you note to the host within a week of the event — the sooner the better.

Tasting Wine

After you order a bottle of wine, your server brings it to the table for your inspection. You then follow these steps:

1. **Verify that your server brought the correct wine.**

2. **Examine the seal and bring to your waiter's attention any sign of leakage or damage.**

3. **Feel the bottle with your hand to determine whether the wine seems to be at the correct temperature.**

   Your waiter then removes the seal, takes out the cork, and places it on the table next to you.

4. **Examine the cork to make sure that it's in good condition.**

   If the cork is dry and crumbly, air may have gotten into the wine and spoiled it.

   The waiter then pours a bit of wine into your glass.

5. **If you want to, gently swirl the wine in your glass to admire its color, and inhale the bouquet (the aroma of mature wine). Then taste the wine to make sure that it hasn't spoiled.**

6. **If the wine hasn't spoiled, make a comment such as "Excellent. Please serve it." If you don't think that the condition of the wine is acceptable, alert your waiter to the situation.**

Etiquette For Dummies®

Making Introductions

Introductions are more casual than they used to be, but a few rules persist:

- Always introduce the lower-ranking person to the higher-ranking person.
- Always present a man to a woman (in business situations, only if she holds a more prestigious position than he does).
- Out of respect, introduce the younger person to the older one.

Remembering Your Table Manners

- During the meal, keep both feet flat on the floor, or cross your feet at the ankles. Keep your shoes on!
- You may rest your hands up to your forearms on the table, but don't prop your elbows on the table.
- Sit up straight on at least three-quarters of your chair — away from the back of your chair. This way, you shouldn't have to bend over your food.
- In between courses, or anytime you want to rest, place both hands in your lap or place one hand in your lap and the other at the wrist on the edge of the table.
- Women, never place your handbag on the table or hang it on the back of your chair. If it's small enough, set it in the back of your chair, or set it on the floor slightly under your chair so that no one will trip over it.
- After you see the host or guest of honor do so, place your own napkin gently in your lap. If the napkin is large, fold it in half; if it's a smaller luncheon napkin, open it completely. In more upscale restaurants, your waiter will place your napkin on your lap for you.
- Remember that liquids are placed to the right above the plate, and solids to the left.
- Begin eating after your host does. If you're at a banquet or in a group dining situation, wait until all those around you are served the first course, and then begin to eat together.
- Start from the outside utensils and work inward with each course.
- Cut no more than two or three bits of food at a time.
- Use your napkin only to dab the corners of your mouth.
- After you finish a course, place your knife and fork side by side in the 4:00 (sometimes called the 10:20 o'clock) position on the plate, the blade of the knife facing in. Never push your plate or bowl away from you.
- If you have to leave the table during the meal, politely and quietly excuse yourself, lay your napkin on your chair, and leave without fanfare.
- When leaving the table at the end of a meal, place your napkin to the left of your plate. You don't have to fold it again, but leave it sitting neatly, with no soiled areas showing.

For Dummies: Bestselling Book Series for Beginners

Praise For Etiquette For Dummies

"This is a book for our times. *Etiquette For Dummies* has much to offer. Sue Fox's instructions and her down-to-earth tone — peppered with examples and humor — take away the fear of the way we approach etiquette in particular and life in general. A highly readable and invaluable book."

— Joie Gregory, The Right Fork, New York

"From office parties to extended families, e-mail to introductions, Sue Fox covers it all in this smart, sassy manners guide for the new millennium. Wise, funny, and practical, *Etiquette For Dummies* is just what we need to be on our best behavior."

— Alex J. Packer, Ph.D., author of *How Rude! The Teenagers' Guide to Good Manners, Proper Behavior, and Not Grossing People Out*

"Our social life affects our business attitude. *Etiquette For Dummies* has done a wonderful job of addressing the confusion that exists in today's family dynamics so we can become more understanding and respectful of our differences."

— Gloria Petersen, President, Global Protocol, Inc.

"This is not your mother's prissy etiquette book. *Etiquette For Dummies* is an engaging, clear-headed guide for doing the right thing in virtually every situation. Susan Fox performs a kind of alchemy, transforming dusty old rules into modern maxims for polished, courteous action. I am using *Etiquette For Dummies* in all of my seminars — it's the best introduction to etiquette I've seen."

— Perrin James Cunningham, President, *In Good Company, Inc.* (www.etiquettetraining.com); Instructor, Department of Philosophy, University of Colorado

"With its in-depth but lighthearted approach, Sue Fox's *Etiquette For Dummies* goes a long way in proving that even in today's rapidly changing society, some things remain the same. Good manners — whether in business or at home — never go out of style."

— Doug Merritt, CEO, Icarian Software

"This book is instructive, interesting, and philosophic. It is, in fact, one of my favorite books. I, a visiting professor from Peking University, have learned a great deal about Western etiquette. I am attracted not only by the contents of the book, but also by the talent, humor, and enthusiasm of the author."

— Hongxia Zhang, Associate Professor, Peking University, China

"Somehow, somewhere, all of us have blown a social or business interaction and realized . . . too late . . . what we should have done or said. This book will keep those gaffes to a minimum. But more than that, Sue Fox gives the reader priceless tools for polishing one's image and moving through our complex lives with an aura of class."

— Suzanne Saunders Shaw, Business Reporter, San Francisco

"*Etiquette For Dummies* could turn the Beverly Hillbillies into the Royal Family. It covers every area of etiquette imaginable while also addressing different cultures and issues of etiquette in the 21st century. I highly recommend it!"

— Kathy Johnson, CEO, Mentor Training, Inc.

"Rarely have I found a book that can truly claim that it has something for everyone — but this is one. Sue Fox delivers good old common-sense advice that can be used in the boardroom or the dining room. Its clear, straightforward style makes it a powerful guide, whether one is entertaining corporate executives or dealing with in-laws."

— George Everhart, Fujitsu PC Corporation

"An energetic and entertaining advance in the education of etiquette. Sue Fox's writing is fun, educational, and easy-to-use! An essential for anyone interested in preserving politeness in society."

— Tamera J. Friesen, Owner and Founder of *Everyday Etiquette*

"This book should be on every office manager's bookshelf. *Etiquette For Dummies* gives succinct, easy-to-find advice on everything from dressing appropriately for casual Fridays to successfully negotiating through the minefield of a business dinner. Sue also has an innate grasp of the gray areas between social and business situations, and the best ways of moving between them unscathed."

— Jamie Rapperport, CEO and President, OfficeClick.com

Praise For Sue Fox

"She helps demystify the rules of the table and social contact in general. She makes European knife handling as easy as downloading a file."

— *Vogue*

"Etiquette maven Sue Fox shows techies how to mind their manners."

— *ComputerWorld*

Etiquette FOR DUMMIES®

by Sue Fox

Wiley Publishing, Inc.

Etiquette For Dummies®

Published by
Wiley Publishing, Inc.
909 Third Avenue
New York, NY 10022
www.wiley.com

For general information on our other products and services or to obtain technical support, please contact our Customer Care Department within the U.S. at 800-762-2974, outside the U.S. at 317-572-3993, or fax 317-572-4002.

Wiley also publishes its books in a variety of electronic formats. Some content that appears in print may not be available in electronic books.

Library of Congress Cataloging-in-Publication Data:

Library of Congress Catalog Card No.: 99-66335

ISBN: 0-7645-5170-1

Manufactured in the United States of America

10 9 8 7 6

1B/RV/QR/QS/IN

About the Author

Sue Fox is the Founder and President of Etiquette Survival, Inc. (formerly The Workshoppe) and ESK Publishing Group (a California-based professional development and publishing company). She has provided group training and private consultations to business professionals, corporations, children, and educational institutions since 1995. She also has 20 other Etiquette Survival, Inc. consultants in business across the United States, Malaysia, Saudi Arabia, and the Philippines.

Fox is trained and certified by The Lett Group in Silver Spring, Maryland. She is the Executive Producer of *The Etiquette Survival Kit,* a 1997 series of educational videos and classroom curriculum that features dining and social etiquette for adults and teens. She is also a member of the editorial board of OfficeClick.com, an online service for administrative professionals, for which she writes the weekly "Mind Your Manners" column.

Etiquette Survival, Inc., has been featured in numerous radio and TV news stories, such as KQED, San Francisco; CNBC TV; KRON TV San Francisco; Knowledge TV; Mornings On 2; KOVR/Sacramento; and ABC World News. Its World Wide Web address is www.etiquettesurvival.com.

Fox and her business have also been written about in publications such as *Vogue, Newsweek, Fortune, Seventeen, Entrepreneur, ComputerWorld, Network World, Los Angeles Times, San Francisco Examiner, New York Times, San Jose Mercury News, San Jose Business Journal, The Sunday London Times, The London Telegraph, London Daily Express,* and *The Australian Financial News.* Articles on The Workshoppe (or Etiquette Survival, Inc.) have focused on Fox's unique approach to an "old-fashioned" subject.

Fox continually updates her etiquette, leadership, and professional presence programs designed for corporations, schools, educators, adults, teenagers, and children. Her goal is to educate the public for today's etiquette appropriate situations as well as those of tomorrow.

Prior to 1994, Fox was employed for 12 years in the high-tech industry, with 10 years of experience in event planning and in sales and marketing at Apple Computer, Inc. She spent the previous 5 years as a Realtor associate in residential real estate sales. She has additional background in image consulting and make-up artistry and 20 years of fashion modeling experience in TV and print.

Fox has been a volunteer for charitable organizations in the San Francisco Bay Area, such as The Boys and Girls Clubs of Santa Clara and Interplast, Palo Alto. She resides in Los Gatos, California, and is the mother of two sons, Stephen and Nathan.

Dedication

To my parents, Ray and Betty Swanson, for their lifelong love and support. And to my brother-in-law, John McKibbin, we miss you.

Author's Acknowledgements

This book could not have come together without many people's contributions and participation. First and foremost, I would like to thank and honor the exceptional and talented team at Hungry Minds. I am most grateful to my Acquisitions Editor, Holly McGuire, for her ongoing encouragement, valuable input, and generous advice throughout the preparation of this book. I'd also like to express my deep appreciation to Pam Mourouzis, my Project Editor, for her editorial brilliance, gentle guidance, amazing patience, and professionalism. You are an inspiration. Many thanks are due to editors Billie Williams and Kyle Looper, Acquisitions Coordinator Jonathan Malysiak, illustrator Liz Kurtzman, cartoonist Rich Tennant, and Project Coordinator Maridee Ennis.

My heartfelt thanks and gratitude go to Laura Johnston, whose writing talent and valuable contribution in defining my voice and tone made the completion of this book possible. I would also like to express my appreciation to talented writers Richard Molay and Lydia Bird, whose expertise, input, and humor were essential in shaping this book.

I owe a debt of gratitude to my mentors, Cynthia Lett and Emily Chatfield. Your combined wisdom, enthusiasm, practical knowledge, and friendship have been invaluable.

Thank you to my Etiquette Survival, Inc. consultants and colleagues Perrin Cunningham, Linda Wiggins, Donna Larkin, Jennifer Zacharis, Bonnie Reele, Jacqueline Lombard, Sondra Atkinson, Delia Barrows, Cindy Henderson, Barbra McFarland, Rebecca Black, Judith Booher, Tamera Freisen, and Sung Ling Lee for your support, friendship, and, most important, patience and understanding this past year. To my new friends, the teachers and students from Peking University, thank you for your endearing support and for the honor of teaching you "Western etiquette." And thanks to all my students and clients.

On a more personal note, I'd like to thank my family for their unconditional love and faith in me, especially this past year. To my terrific sons, Stephen and Nathan Fox; my parents, Betty and Ray Swanson; my sisters, Shirlee

McKibbin and Sandy Haynes, and their families, Kelly, Sam, Scott, Carrie, Tashia, and Taylor. To my brother, Rick Swanson, his wife Robyn, their daughter Amy, and my Aunt Doris. An enormous hug goes to Stephanie Haynes for her creative suggestions and support.

To my amazing friends and colleagues, Joie Gregory, Gloria Petersen, Michael Groom, Jackie Moghadom, Christine Montana, Valerie Foster, Ray Askew, and Scott Davis: Thank you for being there every step of the way and especially for reminding me to keep smiling.

Finally, to my Buddhist teacher, Thich Nhat Hanh, whose teachings on lovingkindness, joy, compassion, and the art of mindful living have enriched my life beyond belief.

Publisher's Acknowledgments

We're proud of this book; please send us your comments through our online registration form located at www.dummies.com/register.

Some of the people who helped bring this book to market include the following:

Acquisitions, Editorial, and Media Development

Senior Project Editor: Pamela Mourouzis

Acquisitions Editor: Holly McGuire

Copy Editor: Billie A. Williams

General Reviewer: Cynthia Lett, The Lett Group

Editorial Assistant: Carol Strickland

Production

Project Coordinator: Maridee V. Ennis

Layout and Graphics: Beth Brooks, Amy M. Adrian, Angela F. Hunckler, Kate Jenkins, Barry Offringa, Tracy Oliver, Jill Piscitelli, Brian Torwelle, Doug Rolison, Jacque Schneider, Maggie Ubertini, Dan Whetstine, Erin Zeltner

Special Art: Liz Kurtzman

Proofreaders: Laura Albert, John Greenough, Joanne Keaton, Marianne Santy, Rebecca Senninger

Indexer: Sherry Massey

Special Help
Lydia Bird, Emily Chatfield, Laura Johnston, Richard Molay

Publishing and Editorial for Consumer Dummies
Diane Graves Steele, Vice President and Publisher, Consumer Dummies
Joyce Pepple, Acquisitions Director, Consumer Dummies
Kristin A. Cocks, Product Development Director, Consumer Dummies
Michael Spring, Vice President and Publisher, Travel
Brice Gosnell, Publishing Director, Travel
Suzanne Jannetta, Editorial Director, Travel

Publishing for Technology Dummies
Richard Swadley, Vice President and Executive Group Publisher
Andy Cummings, Vice President and Publisher

Composition Services
Gerry Fahey, Vice President of Production Services
Debbie Stailey, Director of Composition Services

Contents at a Glance

Cartoons at a Glance

By Rich Tennant

Table of Contents

Introduction

● ●

Your time will come. When you least expect it, you'll receive an invitation to a banquet where each table setting involves more utensils than you have in your entire silverware drawer at home. Your company's annual holiday party will be designated semi-formal, and you won't even have a clean tie. You'll buy exactly four steaks for Sunday dinner with your in-laws, and they'll bring along two cousins you never even knew existed. Life is full of moments when you don't know exactly what to do.

Even the world's most mannerly people have uncertain moments. For example, there was a moment when President George Bush, the honored guest at a state dinner in Japan, had a sudden attack of illness and actually "lost his lunch" in front of everyone, including news photographers. One can only hope that he knew how to say "Oops, I'm sorry" in Japanese.

Even I can't escape awkward situations, and I teach etiquette for a living. Many years ago, when I was working for a large computer manufacturing company, I made a formal presentation to sales representatives and resellers. I wore a brand new sweater and skirt so that I would look my best. After my presentation was over, one of my coworkers leaned over and quietly advised me to remove the sales tag from under the arm of my sweater. Oh, no! Every time I had lifted my arm during the presentation, that tag had been clearly visible.

How did I get past that embarrassment? During our lunch break, I made a few jokes about the tag. I said I was grateful that it wasn't a red sale tag. Everyone laughed, and the tension was broken. I'm sure that my companions were grateful for the opportunity to laugh out loud after holding back their amusement during my presentation! The point is that I did my best to make the others feel comfortable. And that's a point that you'll hear again and again in this book. *Etiquette For Dummies* can help you find a way to put others at ease in almost any situation.

Etiquette: A Fancy Word for Getting Along with Others

Etiquette is such a fancy word that some people think it applies only to fancy situations, such as formal dinners and wedding receptions. Other people think that etiquette concerns itself with only minute details, such as the correct way to grasp a teacup at an afternoon social. In other words, etiquette is often regarded as something you turn on and off for special occasions. But that just isn't so.

Yes, etiquette deals with which fork to use for the salad course and concerns your behavior at cocktail receptions. But etiquette is a much broader issue. Etiquette is your key to surviving every human contact with your sense of humor and your self-esteem intact, and your reputation enhanced. Etiquette works in supermarket checkout lines, at family picnics, at company holiday parties, on the phone, online, and yes, at wedding receptions.

Poise is one of those old French words that gradually took on a new meaning in English. The root refers to weighing things, as you would with a scale. In the world of etiquette, poise is the process of evaluating a situation (weighing it) and responding in a way that moves things toward the desired outcome. Another way to think about poise is to associate it with the word *leadership*. When you take the lead in putting people at ease and making every situation pleasant, you exhibit real poise.

That's what politeness is all about: taking the lead, making guests feel welcome, taking the time to evaluate the needs and intentions of others, and behaving in a way that ensures a pleasant outcome. It works at formal dinner parties and it works in tense meetings at the office. Politeness works everywhere, all the time.

Remember that there's no such thing as a vacation from good manners. At home, your polite behavior helps everyone in your family develop self-esteem. On the job, good manners encourage others to work well with you. As you go about your errands and chores, polite contacts with others earn you pleasant and helpful responses. As Ralph Waldo Emerson wrote, "Your manners are always under examination, and by committees little suspected, awarding or denying you very high prizes when you least expect it."

About This Book

There's certainly no shortage of books loaded with the so-called rules of etiquette. This book contains rules, too, but I approach the subject from the perspective of an ordinary person faced with social situations that are just a bit challenging. If you have time to put up your feet and read this book from cover to cover, you'll come away with a working knowledge of etiquette in all its aspects. On the other hand, if you just received an invitation to a party and you're not sure how to dress or how to behave, you can turn to the appropriate section in this book, find the information you need, and head out to the party with confidence.

How This Book Is Organized

I've organized this book into parts and then chapters by specific topics and situations. You don't need to read any previous section to understand the one that interests you; just plunge in anywhere and get what you need. Following is a description of each part and what you can find in it.

- ✔ **Part I: Building Better Relationships:** As I said earlier, etiquette is all about putting others at ease. The result is that you build better relationships, whether it's with the members of your family, your coworkers, or your friends. This part walks you through each type of relationship, giving you advice about making all your relationships better. I also address the particulars of gender relations — an especially tricky area in modern times. Do you hold the door for her or don't you? Do you allow him to pay the tab or not? This part of the book has the answers.

- ✔ **Part II: Presenting Yourself Positively:** How you present yourself is just as much a part of etiquette as how you treat others. In this part, I tell you all about how to keep yourself neatly groomed, how to send the right messages with your body language, and how to get yourself through potentially embarrassing situations (such as a sudden attack of illness) with a minimum of awkwardness. And if you need to figure out what you should wear to a semi-formal or formal event, or you need to get to the bottom of this "business casual" thing, look no further than this part of the book.

- ✔ **Part III: Communicating with Care:** Good communication is essential to good relationships, and thus an essential part of etiquette. This part explains how to handle yourself gracefully on paper, on the telephone, online, and in face-to-face conversations. I also include a chapter on business communication and the particular issues associated with communicating in the workplace.

- ✔ **Part IV: Entertaining (And Being Entertained):** Many etiquette questions come up when you're planning to host a party or dinner. This part provides quite a bit of useful material for uncertain hosts who want to provide a good time for all guests. I also explain how to be a gracious guest who will definitely be invited back, and how to both give and receive with the best of manners.

- ✔ **Part V: Dining with Delight:** With people eating out so often these days, knowing the ins and outs of dining etiquette is especially important. This part covers dining in all its variations, from casual dining to very formal dining, business and social. I also include a chapter on wine and other beverages, because selecting, ordering, and tasting wine can be such an intimidating process.

✔ **Part VI: Conducting Yourself in Special Situations:** Special occasions are times that put many people into a panic, because "normal" behavior may no longer apply. The chapters in this part address those special situations, such as weddings, funerals, baptisms, and bar and bat mitzvahs. I also cover travel, both local and international, as well as the special etiquette that's required when you're interacting with someone who has a physical disability.

✔ **Part VII: The Part of Tens:** This part contains four quick chapters that contain small, easily digestible bits of information. Here, you can find tips on tipping, being a good guest, and teaching etiquette to children. You can also read about ten etiquette mistakes to avoid.

Icons Used in This Book

Every ...*For Dummies* book uses icons to help you navigate your way through the text and to point out particularly noteworthy information. Here's what the icons in this book look like and what they tell you:

This icon points out etiquette tips that can help you get through a particular situation with ease.

This icon highlights information that's important to remember.

This icon warns you of areas that can trip you up if you're not careful.

This icon points out faux pas to avoid at all costs.

Part I
Building Better Relationships

The 5th Wave · By Rich Tennant

"I always speak to the kids in a quiet and respectful way, but occasionally I wear this to add a little punctuation."

In this part . . .

One of the ultimate goals of proper etiquette is to make everyone around you feel at ease, so this part on building better relationships is an important part of this book. These chapters cover everything from your relationships with your children and other housemates to your relationships with your extended family, your friends, and your coworkers. Because the rules regarding behavior between men and women are ever-changing, this part also includes a chapter on gender-specific etiquette issues. Finally, you'll know whether to hold the door for (her or him)!

Chapter 1

Good Manners Begin at Home

- -

- -

*E*tiquette is often associated with experiences away from home. Before you prepare yourself for parties, dinners, and other social occasions, however, it's a good idea to put your own house in order. I offer a bare minimum of guidelines with the hope that you'll be inspired to think about and practice good manners every waking hour.

Practicing Everyday Good Behavior at Home

Practice is a word with several meanings. Music students know that practicing is a way to sharpen skills and get ready for public performances. Saying that a routine is "common practice" means that it is habitual behavior. Both meanings apply to good manners in the home. After you learn to do the right thing at home, you'll be fine out in the world. But there's an even better reason for etiquette at home: The whole family will get along better.

Building character and self-esteem by being courteous

Somebody once said that you need love most when you're most unlovable. That same idea applies to courtesy. In a world where people are often hurried, stressed out, or aggravated by some prior experience, being courteous isn't always easy. But that's when extending courtesy is most important and most appreciated. Your considerate behavior can have a magical effect on an otherwise difficult person, and your determination to do the right thing enhances your own self-esteem. Best of all, if you succeed in surviving a "good manners challenge," your self-confidence will soar.

There's no better place to practice good manners than in your own home. Treat your family with respect and courtesy, and all the difficulties of the outside world will be easier for them to bear. This is especially true for parents of teenagers, who are often placed in difficult peer situations outside in the "real world." Teenagers (and children) need more than lessons to learn how to behave. They need assurances that they are valued, good people. By praising and complimenting your children when they exhibit good manners, you give the world much more than a well-mannered human being. You give the world a person who has self-respect and respect for others.

Creating a safe haven

Time spent at home should be calm and peaceful, and home should be a refuge from the demands and pressures of the outside world. Simple expressions of politeness contribute to an environment of refuge from daily aggravations: "Please pass the potatoes." "Thanks for the glass of water." "I really appreciate your help in folding the laundry." "You look nice this morning." "I'm proud of your grade in biology." It looks a little corny on paper, but this approach can accomplish miracles at home. Do it. Say it. Be nice. Treat your family members as if they were honored guests, and their responses may surprise you. Courtesy is contagious.

Living up to expectations

Adults who live together, whether in marriage or in some other agreement, begin the arrangement with an expectation of compatibility. Unfortunately, as time passes, familiarity often leads to shortcuts in communication. Our advice here is to exercise *expressive* courtesy. Go ahead and *say* those nice things. Don't just enjoy a meal; *say* that you enjoyed it. Don't just feel that your spouse or significant other is more pleasant than the unfeeling clods outside; *say* so.

Behaving like a polite adult all the time isn't easy. Taking the lead in exercising common courtesies when you feel rotten isn't easy, either, but that's part of the burden of adulthood. Accept the burden. Do what's right. Live up to the expectations of everyone in your household, and you'll find yourself accomplishing things that you never thought possible.

Family etiquette do's and don'ts

When it comes to etiquette, I tried to teach my children some basic rules. Here are some of the most important ones. I encourage you to copy this page and put it up on the refrigerator!

- Always say please and thank you.
- Be responsible for your words and actions.
- Be polite when answering the phone.
- Keep your room tidy.
- Pick up after yourself.
- Do not leave your dirty dishes for others to clean up.
- Assist with family chores.
- Learn proper table manners and use them.
- Turn off the television at mealtime and when company is present.
- Agree to disagree courteously.

- Speak, don't shout.
- Be willing to share.
- Be a good listener.
- Do not open a closed door without knocking.
- Respect others' privacy.
- Do not eavesdrop, snoop, or read others' mail.
- Treat others' property with respect.
- Don't take others' belongings without asking.
- Be kind to yourself and others.
- Practice patience.
- Leave things nicer than the way you found them.
- Think before you speak.
- Leave the toilet seat down.

Modeling Good Manners for Your Children

Loving parents spend endless hours teaching their children skills such as speaking, reading, and tying their shoes — all essentials for future success. However, one of the ironies of parenthood is that while you focus on teaching the mechanics of a certain task, your child watches your every move in an effort to be *just like you*. Is your voice calm and well-modulated, or is it shrill? Are you patient with repeated failed attempts, or do you lose your temper?

Although teaching good manners to your children isn't difficult to do, the greatest challenge is to set a good example and point out the reasons for your behavior. The less you talk and the more you demonstrate, the more effective you are.

Life after a divorce

Sadly, current statistics show that more than 55 percent of American marriages end in divorce. The transition can be extremely difficult for children. Here are some tips to keep your family on an even keel, and to keep civility foremost in your new life on your own:

- Try to make life as normal as possible. Stick to routines as best you can, because consistency creates security for children. Keep mealtimes and bedtimes the same as before the divorce, for example.

- Resist the temptation to spoil children by allowing them to do things you'd normally prohibit them from doing. Stand firm, but remember to explain why you are refusing, and use an extra amount of compassion.

- Be willing to answer your children's questions honestly without sharing the negatives or gory details — keep these to yourself!

- Do not speak badly about the other parent in front of your children.

- Try not to hide new relationships from your children. Your children should learn to extend courtesy to new friends as they would toward other guests. However, don't expect them to welcome your new romantic interests with open arms.

- Never ask your children to side with one parent over the other. Make sure to continue family relationships with both sides of the family, including grandparents, aunts, uncles, and cousins.

- Do not attempt to get back on your kids' good side by buying them gifts.

- Do not ask your children to snoop or report back details of the other parent's comings and goings.

- Always be polite to your ex in front of your children.

You are a full-time teacher

There's no such thing as time off for bad behavior when you have children. Long before you think about teaching your kids some of the basics of good manners, they shape their own actions by watching and listening to you deal with telephone conversations, visitors, relatives, and so on. Parents are full-time role models for their children, and — without putting too much pressure on parents — the entire world depends on them to turn out civilized, polite members of the next generation.

Your kids will do what you do at the table

Children learn table manners, especially, from parental example. A very young child may be incapable of manipulating a knife and fork, but when the time comes to pick up a piece of silverware, that same youngster will know what to do by following your example. If you conduct yourself sensibly, your children will, too, as soon as they're able.

Call us "Mom and Dad," please!

Some parents feel that there's something close and chummy about encouraging their children to address them by their given names. Instead of "Mom," I hear some kids say "Helen." In my opinion, though, this practice is unwise. As a parent, you need to be the authority figure, and having your child call you by your first name throws confusion into that relationship. Stick with "Mom and Dad" instead.

This brings me to the rock-bottom foundation of etiquette. You know every one of these little "rules," but do you *always* follow them? Here's a list of just a few ways to set a good example for your youngsters:

- ✔ Come to the table on time, clean, and suitably dressed.
- ✔ Wait for everyone to be seated before starting the meal.
- ✔ If it is your custom to offer a blessing, do so as if you mean it.
- ✔ Ask for items to be passed rather than reaching for them.
- ✔ Take fair portions, considering the number of others at the table.
- ✔ Use a knife rather than the side of a fork to cut food.
- ✔ Take manageable bites.
- ✔ Do not speak with food in your mouth.
- ✔ Don't make a fuss over items you don't like.
- ✔ Wait until everyone has finished before leaving the table.
- ✔ Avoid confrontations and conflicts while dining.
- ✔ Express gratitude and satisfaction to the preparer of the meal.
- ✔ Deal with spills and accidents calmly.
- ✔ Follow the family rules that you invent. Be consistent.

You probably can think of many more items to add to this list, but the general idea is sound: Behave at home as you would in public, and your kids will make you proud when *they* meet the public.

Maintaining Household Harmony by Setting Expectations

The easiest way to maintain peace in your home is to make it clear to everyone what you expect from them in various situations. If you prepare children (and adults, too) for what they will encounter and explain to them what type of behavior is appropriate, you're bound to have fewer problems and squabbles. This section walks you through the various aspects of etiquette at home and helps you set the right expectations.

Dining out as a family

Preparations for eating in a restaurant should begin at home. Children may have a tough time in restaurants. The food is unfamiliar, and the surroundings are not at all as they are accustomed to at home. The seating may be uncomfortable, and your impatient kids are forced to wait for a server to bring things. Perhaps most challenging is visualizing the actual item from a menu description or an interpretation by an adult. Youngsters are often disappointed with the food they receive, not because it isn't well-prepared but because they were expecting something else.

If you understand the difficulties of being a kid in a restaurant, you're better equipped to ease your children into the world of dining out. In your role as a teacher, try to help your kids understand these basics of good restaurant behavior:

- ✔ Wait patiently to be seated.
- ✔ Wash hands before beginning the meal.
- ✔ Speak softly.
- ✔ Remain at the table (except for an escorted bathroom visit if necessary).

The best way to introduce children to the restaurant experience is to take them to a child-friendly establishment. A cafeteria is a good place to start. When youngsters can see the actual food items before making a commitment, they make better choices. A little guidance can keep them from concentrating on desserts.

To prevent temper tantrums in restaurants, talk to your children before leaving the house to let them know what to expect and what you expect from them. Setting their expectations beforehand helps you avoid upset and the need to discipline at the restaurant. Explain to them what type of food is on the menu before you leave, and discuss possible choices ahead of time, or whether they may have dessert. If you're going to a Mexican restaurant, let them know that they will not be having hot dogs! Doing so prevents power struggles during the meal.

Arrive at the restaurant prepared by bringing a quiet toy or crayons to keep children occupied. Don't expect the restaurant to provide these things to entertain your children. It's also important to remember that the waitstaff is there to provide you with food service, not janitorial service. If your little darlings choose to put more food on the table and floor than in their mouths, try to clean up as best you can before leaving.

A restaurant is not a playground for children. They should learn early that they are to remain at the table. Never leave them unsupervised or allow them to run wild around the restaurant — not even at child-friendly restaurants. Young children don't understand the difference between dining in a fine restaurant and dining in a coffee shop. If they're allowed to misbehave in one, why not in the other?

If your children are obviously disturbing other diners in the restaurant, take them out of the room until they calm down.

Using etiquette in your daily routine

Children — and the rest of us, for that matter — thrive on routine. It's comforting and stabilizing to know that certain events will happen at certain times every day, and to know what's expected of everyone.

Two of the most common complications to daily routine concern wakeup calls and lunch preparation during the school year. Kids often delay getting up, and countless parents mention the tedium of making sandwiches that won't get eaten at lunchtime.

A restaurant rehearsal for children

Here's a great way to turn play into a learning experience. Have a restaurant rehearsal with your children a day before you go out for dinner. Tell your kids that you're going to "play restaurant."

Have the children dress up and wait at the entrance to your dining room, and then usher them to the table. Have printed menus from which they can select a meal. Let them know that restaurant behavior means being quiet and well-behaved, so as not to disturb the other customers. Show everyone how to unfold their napkins and place them on their laps. Fill the water glasses, and then serve the meal. Encourage the correct usage of utensils and quiet demeanor.

Dealing with restaurant temper tantrums

Yes, you have good intentions. Yes, you want to make a restaurant meal a learning experience for your child. Yes, you understand all the problems that children have in restaurants. But what do you do if your little angel suddenly bursts into tears, has a screaming fit, throws food, or otherwise causes a commotion?

Your response depends on the kind of restaurant you're in and the kind of commotion your child is causing. If you happen to be in one of those barn-like places where toddlers are taken for birthday parties and pizza, you can try waiting for the storm to blow over. Many juvenile behavior problems can be eased by a timely application of food or drink or a trip to the bathroom.

On the other hand, if you happen to be in a pricey restaurant where affectionate couples are gazing into each other's eyes while toasting their love with expensive wine, you have to activate an alternate plan. Classy restaurants sell atmosphere as well as food, and a screaming kid cheats the other customers out of the experience they expect. Your best tactic is to scoop up the child, go outside into the fresh air, and do your best to explain that all the other people expect the room to be quiet. After taking in a few breaths of fresh air, try to find out what's bothering the child. You may be able to address the problem easily. Most noisy-kid-in-restaurant problems are based on hunger or fatigue.

If you can't pacify your child, your duty to the world at large is to remove the child from the premises. There's no justification for ruining the dining experience of 50 other adults just because your 3-year-old is having a bad evening.

One working mother came up with inspired solutions to both issues. As part of the "outfitting" for her children as they entered first grade, she gave each of them an inexpensive alarm clock and charged them with the responsibility of getting themselves up. It worked. A child can easily ignore a mother's sweet wake-up voice, but there's something about the sound of one's own alarm that works every time.

That same mother taught her kids to prepare and pack their own lunches. The rule was that Mother would purchase any lunch item requested by a child, but the children had to assemble their sandwiches (or whatever) the preceding evening and store them in the fridge. The children came up with some far-out concoctions in the beginning, but it wasn't long before things settled into a smooth routine.

To avoid problems in the morning, be prepared and follow these helpful tips:

- ✔ Have your children help you select their outfits the night before school.
- ✔ Make sure that your teenagers have their clothes ready before going to bed, even if it means that they need to wash and iron them.
- ✔ Have your kids put all their schoolwork and supplies in their backpacks before they go to bed.

✔ Prepare lunches or lay out money for buying lunch the evening before.

✔ Have children bathe or shower at night rather than in the morning.

✔ Make your children aware of what time they need to be ready in the morning.

✔ Make sure that your children complete their homework before bedtime. Rushing to finish in the morning only creates anxiety!

Knowing that how you use words means a lot

How you speak shows a lot about how much respect you have for yourself and others. In your family life, sticking to these principles helps maintain civility — and maybe your sanity, too:

✔ Teach your children to refer to other family members by name or title. In other words, when speaking of a third party, say "Sally," "Jimmy," "Mom," or "Grandpa" — not "she" or "he."

✔ When correcting or scolding your children, speak with them out of earshot — they'll appreciate your courtesy. Similarly, they'll glow with pride when you make sure that others overhear your words of praise.

Treating your guests as my guests

The adage "Your guest is my guest" applies equally to children and their parents. Whenever any family member has a visitor, others must extend all ordinary courtesies. This means a friendly greeting, an offer of refreshments suitable to the hour, enough space so that the friends can enjoy each other's company without interference, and a proper farewell.

Just as younger people should address grownups by title, grownups should address young guests by name. If you don't know their names, a self-introduction is in order:

"Hi. I'm Tommy's mother, Mrs. Vinson. What's your name?"

Better yet, the host can offer a voluntary introduction:

"Mom, I'd like you to meet my friend Alfred. Al, this is my mother, Mrs. Vinson."

Regardless of who takes the lead, the proper response is this:

"I'm pleased to meet you, Alfred. Have a nice time!"

Using courtesy regarding the telephone

After raising two sons, I could write an entire chapter about family courtesy and the telephone. When you pick up the phone and the call is for another person in the household, walk over to that person and give the message. Don't shout "Nathan! Phone!" at the top of your lungs.

Although identifying yourself to the answering party is considered polite, teenagers are especially sensitive about having their calls screened. Another common offense is to speak loudly and rudely when you want to use a phone that another person is currently using. Patience carries the moment and sidesteps bruised feelings. This goes for young children tugging on you or whining to get your attention while you're on the phone as well. Teach your children at an early age that when Mommy and Daddy are speaking to someone on the phone, they are not to be disturbed (unless for an emergency).

Divvying up household chores

Sharing the household chores is important in learning responsibility and respect for others and for a household. Each week or month, trade specific duties so that one child is not always responsible for the same chore. Doing so prevents boredom and teaches children the various jobs around the house.

The first rule of any well-mannered household should be to clean up after yourself. That goes for dishes, countertops, spills, toys, and dirty clothing. The cardinal rule in a household should be to always leave things the way they were found. By teaching your children early that you expect this of them, you'll have a happier life as a parent of teenagers.

A corollary to leaving things as you found them is that if it's empty, you throw it away or recycle it. Don't allow your children to put an empty milk carton back in the refrigerator with just a drop left, or a bag of chips back in the cupboard with just the crumbs! In the same vein, tell children that they're responsible for being good inventory clerks. If they eat or drink the last of something, they should tell the person who does the shopping. Parents can make this task easier by posting a list for needed items.

Using fair share as an expression of courtesy

For everyone in a household, the regular practice of doing your fair share, and not taking more than your fair share, is a large part of family etiquette. Sharing comes into play in many important ways, including the following situations.

Using the bathroom and the hot water

When bathrooms serve more than one person, and when a number of family members need to make themselves presentable for the day ahead, the etiquette of sharing space requires that you use the bathroom for only your fair share of time. After one or two chilling experiences, everyone should have a pretty good idea of how long the hot water will hold out. Limit your time in the shower or bath to allow for others who also need hot water.

Time in the bathroom means more than just hot water. When others must also use the bathroom, get in and out in the minimum time you need for your routine. Consider moving parts of your morning routine, such as blow-drying your hair or applying makeup, to a bedroom or other place outside the bathroom.

The first person into the bathroom has the advantage of a dry floor, unfogged mirrors, and a clean tub. Before you exit the bathroom, take a minute to wipe down counter surfaces and the floor, straighten out the floor mat, towel off the mirror, and do whatever else is needed to give the next person a reasonably presentable bathroom. If you use up the last bit of shampoo, soap, and so on, you're responsible for replacing them.

Housekeeping

Parents can do a great favor for future daughters-in-law and sons-in-law by teaching children to pick up after themselves and to do their fair share of the general housekeeping. Straightening a bed, putting dirty clothing into the hamper, placing dirty dishes in the dishwasher or rinsing them off in the sink, and putting away personal possessions before retiring for the night takes only an extra minute or two. Remember that a beneficial side effect comes from teaching children to do their share of the general housework: Other adults within earshot may get the idea as well.

Counting the cupcakes

When four adults sit down to a pie sliced into four pieces, it's clear that everyone will get one piece. Put four children in front of a dessert tray of four cupcakes, however, and the results are not as obvious. Children need to be taught how to measure objects — particularly desirable objects such as cupcakes — with their eyes and calculate their fair share.

Adults can provide guidance for kids by thinking out loud. When the kids dig into a platter of cooked shrimp, say something like, "Let's see, Jennifer, there are five of us, and I think six shrimp each will just about go around fairly." This idea works well with beverages, too. When three kids want fruit juice, place three clean glasses on the counter and make a show out of pouring equal portions. Your script can read, "Well, we didn't have enough for full glasses, but everyone got the same amount of juice."

Respecting Your Elders

Just as children have special needs and require special consideration, so do older people in your circle of relatives, friends, and coworkers. Nowadays, there are many more elderly people in our country, and the idea of designating a person as a senior citizen at age 55, 60, or 65 is rapidly falling by the wayside. Many folks in the workplace are beyond their 70th birthday, and knowing people who are in their 90s and beyond is becoming less unusual.

Senior citizens may have sharp minds and excellent professional skills, but as people age, they develop special needs. Consider those needs and accommodate older people, and you'll be rewarded with a much richer social life.

Many societies extend elaborate courtesies to parents and elders. In recent decades, American families have tended to be much less formal about such things. I think that there's a difference between informal and inconsiderate and that your treatment of elders falls under the umbrella of etiquette several ways.

Seniors at the dinner table

Think ahead and try to accommodate the accumulating mealtime difficulties that people suffer as they age. Plan your menus with the most senior guest(s) in mind. Older folks have difficulties chewing tough foods, don't get along very well with raw or crisp-cooked vegetables, usually dislike high-acid or very peppery foods, and may wish to avoid beverages containing caffeine. If they're diabetic, they can't eat foods that contain sugar. Go ahead and serve whatever you want, but make sure to include foods that will please your most senior guests.

Seating assignments should also reflect your considerate nature. Older folks may have a limited tolerance for sitting on hard dining room chairs. Provide a seat that allows easy escape from the table without disturbing others. And if you know that an older person has a hearing problem, seat him or her next to a relative who is sympathetic to the situation.

When age affects ability

A person in a wheelchair, walking with the assistance of a cane or walker, or affected by arthritis or other affliction of age always has the right-of-way. Your obligation as an able-bodied adult is to do what you can to help folks with limited mobility: Hold open the door, bring over the tray of hors d'oeuvres, volunteer to fetch a glass of water, do what you can to ease the way in and out of a car, carry packages or other burdens, and so on.

Another way to honor elders

The Chinese have a custom regarding seating arrangements, especially in restaurants. The most senior person present is always afforded the seat that faces the main entrance. If the entrance is not within sight, the honored position faces the main body of the restaurant.

When you think about it, this arrangement makes sense, because it allows the honored elder to see what's going on without a lot of twisting and turning. I think that this is a charming way to show respect for elder people, and I recommend it for all family gatherings.

You owe this courtesy to *every* senior citizen, not just to your own relatives. Keep your eyes open for a chance to help while you're out shopping, moving in and out of a theater, and so on. At a restaurant, volunteer to go through the salad bar. Help with menu selections if the person has a visual disability. Pass things without being asked. When speaking to an elder who has a hearing impairment, face the person so that your body language and facial expression help him or her understand.

A loss of mobility does not equal a loss of interest in normal activities. Plan to include elders in family outings. Courtesy to elders implies an effort on your part to do whatever is necessary to help them remain connected with the world of activity around them.

Family living with mixed generations

Even though no official definition of "the family" exists, most discussions assume that a family consists of a mother, a father, and their children. But many households have one or two grandparents in residence, and perhaps even a grandchild or two. If your household has mixed generations, you already know that grandparents have special sensitivities, as do teenagers and the very young. This household must be governed by the best possible manners on the part of all members.

Common courtesies are an absolute necessity. When grandparents need help from the kids, "please" and "thank you" are a lot more effective than brusque commands. The children must learn to give courteous greetings and farewells to the older folks: "See you later, Grandpa, I'm going to the library." "Hello, Grandma, I'm home from school." These simple messages help eliminate confusion as to who is present in the home.

All children need private space and possessions to call their own. This need becomes much more intense as kids become teenagers. Make sure that each family member has a room, or at least a piece of furniture, that is considered private. Many disputes arise when one person invades another's space, and learning how to respect another person's territory is an important part of good manners.

As you review the "courtesy climate" of your household, make sure that everyone understands your expectations regarding the following:

✔ **Bathrooms:** Time spent within; straightening up; resupplying paper, soap, towels, and so on.

✔ **Telephones:** Who answers, how to answer, how to summon another person to the phone, taking messages. Don't eavesdrop, and set reasonable time limitations.

✔ **The kitchen:** Making lists of shortages, doing routine chores and assignments, cleaning up after yourself, and taking the last drop of milk or juice.

✔ **Home entertainment:** Who controls the TV, how loud music may be played, what programs are suitable, and hours of use.

✔ **General housekeeping:** Assigned chores and personal responsibility.

✔ **Cost sharing:** Who pays for what and fair-share contributions to expenses.

✔ **Chain of command:** Issues between children and their grandparents.

✔ **Pet care:** Responsibility for providing food and water, brushing and combing, cleaning cages, and cleaning up "accidents."

Civilized discussion followed by general agreement can settle all these issues and head off friction that might otherwise arise.

There's no substitute for good manners within the home. Whenever the going starts to get a little rough, remember that everyone, from the youngest toddler to the most senior grandparent, has a need to be treated with respect and consideration. A short pause, a deep breath, and a determination to treat others with courtesy go a long way toward assuring smooth sailing.

Achieving Roommate Harmony

The etiquette of close quarters is just as important for those who are not related to you as it is for those who are. When two (or more) adults live together or share group living quarters, such as an apartment, college dorm room, or military barracks, even small courtesies make a big difference. These reminders will surely make life a lot easier for everyone involved:

✔ Respect each other's personal space. Never invade closets, drawers, lockers, and cabinets claimed by or assigned to another individual. Don't help yourself to the other's food. (This is also good advice for married couples.) Everyone needs a bit of private territory.

✔ Don't eavesdrop, snoop, or sort through each other's mail. Once again, the basic consideration is a person's private space.

✔ Appropriate greetings are important — "Good morning," "Good evening," and so on. Your failure to issue a greeting may be misinterpreted as a sign that you are angry.

✔ Courtesy includes cleanliness. Keep your space straightened up, keep your body and clothing clean, and pitch in with maintaining the common areas. When deodorant commercials mention "offending someone," the sponsors are combining hygiene with etiquette.

✔ Ordinary good manners are as important between roommates and good friends as they are in general social situations. Say such things as "Please," "Thank you," "You're welcome," and "You look nice."

✔ Set and respect agreements regarding use of laundry facilities, duration of showers, length of phone calls, loudness of stereos, visitor hours, and other domestic issues.

✔ Even if you're pretty sure that you know your roommate's attitude, try not to speak for him or her. When you field a phone call for the other and the caller asks a question intended for the absent one, take a message and promise a callback. Otherwise, your innocent good intentions could trigger a major conflict.

Showing Courtesy to Domestic Workers

In the old days, only the very wealthy had domestic workers helping out at home, but nowadays, when all the adults in many households work outside the home, it isn't unusual to have at least part-time help with the housekeeping. If you haven't thought about the courtesy issues involved, see if your behavior measures up to our list of guidelines:

✔ Be clear about duties and compensation. Have a frank conversation in the beginning about what the working hours and days are, what you want to be accomplished, how much you'll pay, and when and how you'll pay.

✔ Determine how the worker wishes to be addressed, and make sure that your children understand this point. Say how you wish to be addressed as well.

✔ Agree on details that may seem trivial at first but can grow into problems if not formalized. You don't need a formal contract, but you can write down your thoughts about the following issues and go over them with your prospective domestic worker:

- Personal telephone calls

- Time allowance for lunch

- Visits from the worker's relatives or friends

- Pay policy for holidays, sick days, and so on

- Requests for salary advances

- Contacts for various emergencies

- Responsibility for pet care, if any

✔ Tell the children to stay out from underfoot as the worker pursues his or her duties. Make sure that your children do not ask for special favors from your domestic worker. This kind of request puts the worker in an awkward situation and enables the child to take advantage.

Chapter 2

Extending Courtesy to Your Extended Family

. . . .

In This Chapter

▶ Deciding what to call your parents-in-law

▶ Dealing with all those new relatives

▶ Sorting out the confusion of stepfamilies

▶ Getting along by "balancing the books"

. . . .

*E*xtended family relationships often turn on the very first words out of your mouth. The way you initially address various relatives, in-laws, and family friends can have a lasting effect on them and can shape the future of your relationships. Unfortunately for the rule-makers, every family is unique. This chapter gives you some guidelines to keep you in safe territory until you figure out what works best in your own extended family.

Determining What to Call Your In-Laws

You've probably heard the old story about the woman who called her mother-in-law "you" until her first child was born, after which she used the name "Grandma." This little anecdote may seem harmless until you face the fact that names used in direct address are a very important consideration of courtesy.

If you can bring yourself to call your parents-in-law "Mom and Dad," they'll probably be pleased. In many families, parents consider sons-in-law and daughters-in-law to be as close to them as their own children, and they appreciate that affectionate regard in return. But some people find this practice difficult, at least at first.

The safest tactic is to confess your uncertainty and ask your parents-in-law how they wish to be addressed. And be prepared to honor their response. If they ask you to use their first names, do so. If your mother-in-law asks to be called "Mother Smith," so be it. If the answer is "Mom," call her "Mom." When everyone's parents are present, you may call your own parents "Mom and Dad" and your spouse's parents "Mother Jones and Father Jones."

In all cases, using a pronoun instead of an actual name is an absolute no-no. When the person is within earshot, using words such as *she* and *her* is definitely not courteous, and the more you use them, the more rude they seem.

For example, suppose you're all at the dinner table and your mother-in-law's water glass needs refilling. You call to your wife in the kitchen and say, "Janet, *she* needs some more water. When you come back, bring *her* a refill." This doesn't sound at all nice. Courtesy demands a proper name: "Janet, Mother Brown's water glass is empty. Please bring the pitcher when you return."

Addressing Grandparents Appropriately

The same suggestions about direct address apply to an even older generation. You can usually address your spouse's grandparents with their last names appended, as in "Grandma Smith" (unless there is no ambiguity, in which case you can call them simply "Grandma and Grandpa"). Some grandparents don't wish to "sound so old" to their adult grandchildren, though. Once again, ask directly what they prefer to be called. And please remember that grandparents are due a double measure of courtesy — first as honored relatives and again as senior citizens, as Chapter 1 discusses.

There are regional ways of addressing relatives, and there are titles that are peculiar to individual families. Some terms may sound strange to you if you were raised elsewhere, but if that's the way the family behaves, do your best to fit in and use those forms of address. For example, Jewish families often refer to grandparents as "Bubbie and Zaideh." Some families call parents "Mother and Father" and refer to grandparents as "Momma and Poppa." If a great-grandmother is present at a gathering, some families call her "Big Momma." The English language is weak when it comes to titles for various relatives, but a few other cultures have much more precise terms. Listen and learn.

Nowadays, it's not all that unusual for children to have four sets of grandparents. (This happens when grandparents on both sides divorce and then marry others.) Surprisingly, young children cope very well with this situation. Unless the various grandparents suggest names for themselves, have the children address them as "Grandpa Jones," "Grandma Murphy," "Grandpa Emerson," and so on. The formality eliminates confusion when referring to grandparents who are not present and reinforces identities in the minds of the children even when the grandparents are on the scene.

Interacting with Aunts, Uncles, Cousins, and Close Friends

You're on safer ground with aunts, uncles, cousins, and close friends. The rule is "Titles up and given names down." *Up* and *down* refer to age. For example, you address an older aunt as "Aunt Ida." A younger cousin is simply "Henry." If somebody prefers a different form of direct address, respect that person's request. Children, however, should always include titles when addressing relatives who are older than themselves.

When dealing with your spouse's relatives, the general rule is to use the title that your spouse would use. In other words, your husband's Aunt Irene is also your Aunt Irene, at least for the purposes of informal gatherings. At a more formal affair, when you're making introductions, your script would be, "Roger, I'd like you to meet Alice's aunt, Irene Smith. Aunt Irene, this is Roger Black." Roger's response would be, "I'm pleased to meet you, Ms. Smith." (Note the use of the unspecific *Ms.* when the person's marital state is not mentioned.)

What about a relative your own age? The custom varies from region to region. In some parts of the country, certain titles, such as Cousin, are appended to the names: "Why, Cousin Nancy! What a delight to see you again!" Another regionalism that you may encounter is the use of Brother and Sister when addressing in-laws. "Sister Sally, would you like another slice of pecan pie?" Keep your ears open for these customs when you're away from home. In general, though, first names are appropriate when dealing with relatives nearly the same age as yourself.

Remember that you always have a safe fallback position. When in doubt, you can confess your confusion by saying, "Honestly, I enjoy being with you, but I can't quite figure out what to call you. Please tell me what you prefer." This approach almost always works. If the answer happens to be, "You can call me whatever you wish, as long as you don't call me late to dinner," narrow the choices to "Uncle Bob," "Robby," or "Mr. Mason."

Sorting Out a Few Other Relationships

Reblended families and former spouses fall into a gray area with no firm rules. Second (and successive) marriages often bring a confusing collection of relatives to family gatherings, and people have a lot of uncertainty as to how to address all these people. The following sections give you some guidance.

Calling family friends "Aunt" and "Uncle"

Parents sometimes introduce adult friends of the family to children as "Uncles" and "Aunts." This is a term of affection rather than an actual genealogical designation, and it's generally harmless. You can also have your children address the adult friend of the family as "Mister Williams" rather than "Uncle Walt." If Walt wants your kids to address him as "Uncle," he'll tell them so.

There's one exception in which having a child call an adult friend of the family "Uncle" or "Aunt" is completely unacceptable. If a parent is separated or divorced and is having a romantic liaison with an adult "friend," or if the parent is still married and is having an affair with another person, children should never be encouraged to call that person "Aunt" or "Uncle."

Considering some of the horror stories printed in the daily newspapers, children should know for sure who is a genuine relative and who is not. In most cases, the practice is completely innocent, but for your own peace of mind, guide your children in sorting out actual relatives from others.

Ex-spouses

The ultimate test of your ability to maintain poise and good manners comes when an ex-spouse shows up for some plausible reason, perhaps to claim the kids for a visit. Even here, you should be on your best behavior. Address your spouse by first name. If an introduction is required, use this format: "This is my former husband, Jeffrey Allen. Jeffrey is Sam and Sylvia's father."

Note that you do not refer to the man as "Sam and Sylvia's *deadbeat* father." Reserve that sort of talk for conferences with your lawyer.

Stepchildren and other-custody offspring

If rules can be written for introducing and speaking about children from a previous marriage of your spouse, you can be sure that they won't work in your particular family situation. Children have very little control over the recoupling of their parents, and one of the ways they can assert themselves is to test your patience in this sensitive area. Begin with these conservative suggestions and see how things go.

Suppose your husband's ex-wife has custody of the children, and you get them every other weekend. How do you introduce the kids to your friends? Try, "I'd like you to meet Roger's son and daughter, Chad and Elizabeth." That's

TIP

When a family is not a traditional family

A great many households function like families but have no legally sanctioned family standing. There are men and women living together in very stable (but unmarried) relationships, devoted same-sex couples, and difficult-to-characterize communal arrangements.

If you're determined to exhibit perfect manners, you will accept and introduce members of these interesting "families" in exactly the manner they desire. Here are a couple of examples:

✔ "Good evening, Estelle. I'd like you to meet my son Joe and Joe's companion, Victor. Boys, this is my neighbor, Mrs. Greenberg."

✔ "Mother, please say hello to your grand-daughter's partner, Ramon Garcia."

the first stage. When you know for sure that things are okay between you and Chad and Elizabeth, you can experiment with, "And these are the children, Chad and Elizabeth." Talk it over with the kids before you refer to them as "our kids."

If the woman you married has a son from a prior relationship, I offer the same suggestion. Call him "Judy's son, Jeff" until you know for sure that you're on safe ground with the boy. Then go to "This is our son, Jerry."

Foster children deserve to have that specific title appended and made clear. One of the goals of the foster child program is the eventual reunification of natural parent and child, and foster children have a tough enough time without title confusion. Introduce a foster child as "my foster daughter, Maria." The same goes for what your foster children call you. Let them address you as "Daddy Sid" or "Momma Denise" rather than expecting them to call you "Mom" or "Dad." This is a flexible rule, however; if a child seems to need to call you Mom or Dad, let it be.

Adopted children are exactly the same as those who are dropped into your lap by your own personal stork. Forget all about the legal details. These are your real children, and you need make no reference to their adoption. If they want to talk about being adopted in later years, that's their business.

Half siblings and stepsiblings

Siblings who join the family from a stepparent's previous marriage are called stepbrothers and stepsisters, whereas siblings that result from a new marriage are half brothers and half sisters. Introduce your half siblings simply as "My brother Ralph" or "My sister Eloise" in general situations.

Being a successful stepfamily

When two people decide to remarry and bring children from previous marriages into the new marriage, several rules of conduct become crucial. Here are a few tips for newly blended families:

✔ Sort out your discipline styles. Issues to discuss include acceptable behavior and the consequences when children misbehave. Predictable rules make your children feel safe and secure.

✔ Decide on each child's duties and responsibilities. Together, work out jobs, expected behavior, and family etiquette. Assign chores so that children feel part of the household, not like guests in a stepparent's home.

✔ Set precise and specific rules about visitation by ex-spouses. Children need stability and predictability.

✔ Make sure that grandparents and other extended family members, if involved before the divorce, remain just as involved in the newly blended family. Grandparents and other extended family members may need to mourn the loss of the original nuclear family before they become part of the stepfamily.

✔ Maintain family rituals in your home as you wish, and adapt to new traditions in the stepfamily as they develop.

Avoiding the Unspeakable

Every family has ups and downs. You don't have to be a member of the British Royal Family to understand that every extended family experiences a steady stream of developments that challenge the patience and understanding of close relatives.

Most families have ways of containing divisive issues and sticking together. If a relative who's in a difficult position brings up the subject and wishes to discuss it, by all means lend a sympathetic ear. That's just one more way of showing that you care for your cousin or sister-in-law.

However, etiquette-wise, there's an even better way of showing your love. Bite your lip and do not inquire about rumors to the effect that

✔ Her unmarried daughter is pregnant.

✔ His recently married son is back living at home.

✔ Their college-student daughter wants to marry her girlfriend.

> ✔ Her uncle was indicted on a tax-evasion rap.
>
> ✔ His brother-in-law was elected to Congress.
>
> ✔ Joe's hardware store is going belly-up.

Gossiping is not good etiquette. Although hearing negative things about another individual may be unavoidable, repeating that information is not polite — and doing so can create particularly sticky situations within a family. Life is tough enough without some busybody forcing an unpleasant conversation!

Balancing the Books

Within every extended family, there is an elaborate system of keeping score. The details may not be written down anywhere, but you can bet that folks have a pretty good idea of where things stand regarding dinner invitations, birthday gifts, tradeoff baby-sitting, and other give-and-take situations. For the sake of peace in the family and for broader reasons of good manners, do your best to keep things on an even keel.

Invitations to meals, especially, should be equalized. They invite you, and then you invite them. It doesn't matter whether they invite you to a lunch and you invite them to a dinner, or you invite them to your home and they invite you to a restaurant — however you arrange it, meals must be reciprocated. Within your extended family, it isn't important to try to outdo your sisters-in-law when it comes to menu choices, but the effort of planning, preparing, and serving a meal and then cleaning up afterward should be distributed evenly over the course of a year.

Gifts, especially to children, should also be reciprocated. Although the value of the gift need not be the same, the thought that goes into the gift should be. If one of your daughter's cousins attends your child's birthday party and brings a gift that your child cherishes, try to send along something as thoughtful when the tables are turned.

The time will come when the younger generation grows up and marriages begin to take place. You can avoid a lot of bruised feelings by adhering to the family norm when it comes to wedding gift-giving. Different families have different practices, so if you're in doubt, ask an aunt or uncle for some friendly advice. (You can find more information about wedding gifts in Chapter 20.)

The perfect relative

A woman on Chicago's North Shore had a reputation for excellent manners and unusual consideration for others. After she died, her husband found a notebook containing records of every social event in which she was involved. She wrote down what she wore, who else was in attendance, what was served, and if there was gift-giving, what she gave or received. This was her way of keeping things balanced and never repeating a menu or outfit. Her friends and relatives didn't specifically notice the care with which she conducted herself, but everyone agreed that they always felt comfortable in her presence.

Dealing with Relatives from Day to Day

There may have been a time when everyone in a family lived in the same city and had frequent in-person contact, but nowadays, it's much more common for relatives to be scattered all over the country. Some children go many years without ever seeing, or even meeting, all their aunts, uncles, cousins, and grandparents. Building and maintaining good relationships with your extended family is more than an exercise in good manners; families lend strength and support when it's most needed and appreciated.

Sharing big news and participating in life events

Tell everyone in the family about births, graduations, engagements, marriages, special honors, and, sadly, deaths. A personal note is best, but a formal announcement is better than nothing.

A formal invitation to a life event, even if you do not intend to be there in person, calls for a note of congratulation and a gift. If the relative is a distant one and you do not ordinarily exchange gifts with that branch of the family, your gift can be modest, but giving any kind of gift will surely help cement relations.

Your attendance at special occasions is another way to express your pleasure at being part of the family. Likewise, the presence, support, and expressions of love of far-flung relatives can greatly ease the terrible sadness of a funeral.

Visiting and vacationing

When you travel to a distant city to visit relatives, a little bit of consideration can save you a lot of uncertainty. Keep these suggestions in mind as you plan a trip to see your grandparents, for example:

- ✔ Discuss the timing of your intended visit before you make definite plans. Be sure that the dates of your visit coincide with your relatives' agenda.

- ✔ Be definite and specific about arrival and departure dates. Don't stay longer than three days.

- ✔ Unless you know for sure that your relatives have adequate guest accommodations and expect that you will stay in their house, make reservations at a nearby hotel or motel. You can always cancel the reservations if Grandma insists that you stay with her.

- ✔ Do not expect to be waited on. As a houseguest, pick up after yourself, make your own bed, straighten up the bathroom, and so on.

- ✔ Pick up your fair share of the restaurant tabs, admission fees, and other entertainment costs. Don't make your visit a drain on your hosts' finances.

- ✔ Graciously participate in any social activities that your hosts plan.

- ✔ Keep your eyes open to the general décor of the house. After you return home, send a little thank-you gift to your hosts.

Making the holidays happy

Putting any extended family together in one place for the holidays is like turning on a pressure-cooker. Those qualities that you consider endearing in your cousin who lives hundreds of miles away can suddenly become intensely annoying after three days in one small house. Etiquette during the holidays is all about taking the high road, avoiding unnecessary conflict, and sharing good times.

Generally, the eldest capable members of a large family have first choice of hosting the major family holiday gathering each year — Thanksgiving, Christmas, Hanukkah, Passover, or Easter. Make sure to take travel, small children, cost, and distance into account when deciding where to stage the events.

If some members of your family have a conflict with other members, the best way to deal with the situation is to tell everyone that the holiday will go on as planned, everyone will be invited, and if certain people choose not to attend, the rest of the family will miss them.

Saying thank you

If you stop by your mother's house every week, sending a thank-you note is going overboard. For those normal family visits, saying thank you with a telephone call the next day is more appropriate. However, if a relative goes out of the way to be hospitable by hosting a holiday event or a vacation, or if you receive a gift, then a thank-you note is in order.

TIP

Surviving the holidays after a divorce

The holiday season can be particularly difficult for divorced adults and children. Expectations of picture-perfect family get-togethers create pressure and stress for everyone involved. In order to get kids and adults through the holidays with as little stress as possible, follow these tips:

✔ Keep all schedules the same whenever possible. If you must make changes, tell your children ahead of time or, better yet, allow them to participate in the decision-making. Doing so gives them a feeling of at least partial control over their lives and schedules. Reassure your child through words and actions that everything is going to be okay.

✔ Don't try to squelch fond memories of past holidays. A divorce does not eradicate memories, and in many cases, part of the fun of the holidays is reminiscing about past good times.

✔ When it comes time to give gifts, steer clear of any sort of competition with the other parent. Better yet, coordinate gift choices together. After you give the gifts, don't make restrictive rules about keeping gifts in one parent's home or the other. Children who receive gifts should be allowed to take them wherever they go — no strings attached. Help your children make or select gifts for their other parent. By doing so, you teach them to be thoughtful and generous.

Chapter 3

Building Relationships Up and Down the Corporate Ladder

Your success in getting along with others in your workplace has a major influence on your career success. You can have excellent job skills and good productivity, but if you don't fit in with the others and your colleagues find you difficult to work with, you'll have a much tougher time winning promotions and advancing up the corporate ladder.

There's another, equally important reason to pay attention to the relationships that you form with others in the company: For better or for worse, what goes on at work comprises the most significant portion of your social life. You spend more time with your coworkers than you do with friends outside of work, and in many instances, you spend more time at your job than you do with your family.

Yes, there is an etiquette for conduct on the job. Men and women in military service are drilled in the details of military courtesy and appreciate the freedom from uncertainty that those guidelines provide. The rules of courtesy in civilian life are not quite as rigid, but a code exists nevertheless. Incorporate the suggestions in this chapter, and you may find Monday mornings a lot less challenging.

Building Positive Relationships at Work

Outside of your family, you live your most important social life at work. That's where you spend most of your time, where you interact with the largest number of people, and where good manners can lead directly to raises, promotions, and a pleasant work environment. Business school may teach you how to draw a graph of sales results, but it seldom shows you how to use a company holiday party as a springboard to bigger and better responsibilities. Stay tuned. I'll tell you.

Relating to your boss

Is there still such a thing as a boss? In this era of *team leaders* and *group effort facilitators,* identifying the boss isn't always easy. But you're on pretty safe ground if you consider the person who writes your performance reviews and gives you suggestions for improving your productivity to be your boss.

Courtesy toward the boss begins with direct address. Your supervisor is always Mr. Jones or Ms. Edwards until the moment that Mr. Jones asks to be called Ed or Ms. Edwards gives you permission to call her Josie. Nine times out of ten, you can get away with unbidden informality, but that tenth time can be a career killer. Stay with the formal title until you're told to use the first name.

The most important courtesy that you can extend to your boss is to give your undivided attention. Take notes on his or her directions, ask intelligent questions, and be involved and responsive. All these things indicate respect.

Greet the boss as you would all fellow employees. When passing in the corridor for the first time of the day, say "Good morning" or whatever is appropriate to the hour. When departing for the day, say "Goodbye" or "Have a nice evening." If you and the boss are of the same sex and you happen to use the lavatory facilities at the same time, a simple nod of greeting is greeting enough.

In general, bosses issue invitations and subordinates respond. This means that your boss may invite you to take lunch with her, but you should be hesitant to initiate that same sort of suggestion. In the same vein, the boss should take the lead in the conversation. Subordinates should follow the tone and subject matter that the boss sets.

There's one more area where etiquette coincides with company rules and regulations: grievances. If you have any reason to complain about *anything* in the workplace, speak with your immediate supervisor. Nothing upsets a supervisor more than learning that a subordinate has lodged a complaint with someone else. If, for some reason, the outcome of your discussion does not satisfy you, ask your supervisor to advise you of the next step in the process. Going over the boss's head is one of the worst offenses you can commit on the job.

Connecting with your coworkers

Every work situation has its own set of practices and procedures. Look around and you'll see that folks in your department tend to dress alike, make similar arrangements for lunch, discuss certain topics at length and never mention other things, arrive and leave at certain times, and so on. There are countries where alikeness is part of the national character and is considered to be the very root of courtesy. That's not quite how things are in the United States, but even so, every workplace has established norms. If you decide to make a personal statement by standing out, be very sure that you know what you're doing and why you're doing it. Succeed in fitting in before you try to stand out.

Be alert to the special sensitivities and needs of your coworkers as well. As diversity in the workplace brings together people from different ethnic, cultural, religious, and national backgrounds, you need to have a much more tolerant and inclusive attitude than you do at home or within your private life. Keep the following suggestions in mind when relating to your coworkers:

- ✔ Learn the accepted terms for the ethnic groups, religions, and nationalities of your coworkers. Get rid of the slang and sometimes disparaging terms that you may have used in the past.

- ✔ Do not identify or refer to others by race or ethnic identity. People are people. Use names and titles and avoid other labels.

- ✔ Sexist terms are strictly taboo. A person is a sales representative, not a salesman or saleslady.

- ✔ Companies select job titles with great care, so use those titles. An administrative assistant is not a secretary, and an information systems specialist is not a computer jockey.

- ✔ Older, more experienced coworkers are owed respect for their tenure and expertise. In today's world, where very young people are often peers or even managers of older workers, you need to be watchful of your behavior in this area.

- ✔ Be alert to people's special needs. If one of your colleagues must be absent for a religious observance, for example, offer to cover his or her responsibilities for the day.

Always remember that your coworkers are a vital part of your social life and that good relationships on the job are paramount.

Dealing with an open environment

Today's office environment is often described as *open*. Instead of floor-to-ceiling walls with latching doors, people have cubicles with half-high dividers. Such an environment offers precious little privacy for personal telephone conversations or confidential chats with coworkers. It's safe to assume that your every utterance will be overheard, so don't say anything that you wouldn't want published in the company newspaper. And try to practice selective deafness; don't listen in on the activities taking place in the cubicles adjoining your own.

Extending courtesy to your subordinates

Libraries have shelves full of books offering management guidelines. The most important etiquette advice concerning your dealings with subordinates is this: *Praise in public, criticism in private.* Never let others know that you find it necessary to chew out Richard for forgetting to lock the cash box, but if a customer sends a note of thanks for Richard's kind assistance, read the letter to the whole work group.

The question of direct address and subordinates comes up often in the workplace. Your safest course of action is to ask this way: "May I call you Richard?" If Richard says that he prefers to be called by his nickname "Swiftie," then "Swiftie" it is. Regardless of what you call subordinates in private, always use titles (Mr., Mrs., and so on) whenever anyone else is within earshot.

One of the most important courtesies that you can extend to those who report to you concerns awards, praise, and other honors that come to you in the course of your work. If you're honored for your performance, be sure to mention the contributions of others who made your achievement possible. If a ceremony of sorts is held, name the names of those who helped. It's no accident that acceptance speeches at events such as the Academy Awards are the way they are. Share the glory of the moment with your whole team, and they'll be eager to help you be a winner in the future.

Remembering that strangers and newcomers deserve courtesy, too

A new face in the workplace calls for the courtesy of introductions and an expression of good wishes. If a third party has not taken care of introductions, take the initiative yourself. Here's a sample script:

> "Hello. My name is Jack Browne, and I'm responsible for computer maintenance. What would you like me to call you?"

In the event that a stranger appears in your workplace, approach the situation with both courteous behavior and a reasonable amount of caution. If your company gives identification badges to employees and visitors, look for a badge. Introduce yourself to the stranger and ask how you can help. Specific rules regarding security are usually outlined in a written document available to all employees; if your company provides such a document, follow company policy.

Handling Unfamiliar Situations

Countless unfamiliar situations arise in which you simply don't know how to behave: The boss asks you to escort an important shareholder through the facility. You're called to a high-level meeting involving managers several levels above you. A power failure knocks out the air conditioning in your office building and leaves everyone suffering from the heat and stale air. You get into a traffic accident while driving a customer to the airport.

Unfamiliar situations bring out the best in people who can behave as sensibly and gracefully as possible. Communication counts in these situations. Inform your supervisor at once. Inform the human resources office. Call plant security. Call the receptionist and ask for help. Remember, the people who have mastered the many details of etiquette seem to know everything, not because they actually *do* know everything but because they know what to do when they don't know what to do. In the business world, as in society at large, self-confidence and smoothness carry the day.

Confessing your ignorance

A business lunch or dinner gives you an opportunity to form stronger bonds with your colleagues, clients and managers. If you're caught off guard, remember that you're only a human being, and it's always appropriate to ask for help. Your coworkers and even your manager may be just as perplexed as you are — or they may be flattered by being asked to display their expertise. So if you're caught in a restaurant where the foods are strange and the table manners are foreign, confess your need for advice. Ask your host for help. If necessary, ask your host to order for you. If you *are* the host, ask your server for advice. (You can also find more information about business dining in Chapter 18.)

If you're handed a wine list and you have no idea what to order, give the wine list to your host and confess your uncertainty as to the best choice. If you *are* the host, ask your server for a recommendation. A good general rule is to keep the price of a bottle of wine somewhere in the neighborhood of the price of one person's complete meal. Don't show off with a super-expensive wine unless you really know what you're doing. (See Chapter 17 for more on wine etiquette.)

Are you headed out to eat with a guest who has special needs? Ask about his or her preferences first. You don't want to take a vegetarian to a steakhouse, and a person who follows Jewish or Islamic dietary laws won't enjoy a barbecue place. Remember that you can always phone ahead and ask the restaurant about provisions for people with special dietary needs.

In every situation, take the time to consider the comfort of others. Ask questions. Confess your uncertainty. People will appreciate your thoughtfulness.

Bridging the language gap

It's a small world, and business brings together people from all cultures. You may find yourself in a meeting with a foreign visitor, or you may find yourself sent off to a country with a language you don't understand. A language gap is a great opportunity for good manners to shine.

The best course of action is a little preparation. With as little as a single day of warning, you can obtain a phrase book and learn a few words of common courtesy — "Good morning," "Please," "Thank you," "I'm pleased to meet you," "My name is Adam Smith," and "Goodbye." Making an effort to communicate in another person's language shows your respect for that person.

Once you establish that you're friendly and interested in the needs of your foreign guests, things ease up considerably. Large companies almost always have at least one employee who can serve as an interpreter. Ask for assistance in locating someone who can help. (See Chapter 21 for more information about interacting with people from other cultures.)

Ducking the limelight

We've all been in meetings where we feel that we're in unfamiliar territory. Survive by taking a seat away from the conference table or, if that's not possible, by sitting as far as you can from the head of the table. Remain silent unless called upon, and if you don't have a useful response, defer to another, more knowledgeable attendee.

In any situation in which you really feel out of place or out of your depth, place yourself on the fringes of the group. Paste a pleasant expression on your face and be quiet. Others will probably be eager for the limelight and will appreciate the absence of competition.

Apologizing: The final fallback

You really did it. You spilled coffee on the carpet in your boss's office. You went though an entire meeting calling one of the participants by the wrong name. You broke the glass trophy that a coworker won at last year's golf tournament.

Don't try to make your official apology while other business is being conducted. Do your best to minimize the damage and, at the same time, continue with the business at hand. Wait for the meeting to end before you try to patch things up. Then express your apology in writing with a brief, sincere note:

> Dear Mr. Green,
>
> I deeply regret the disruption I caused and the damage I did when I upset the aquarium in your office. I have already contacted the tropical fish store, and they are prepared to repopulate the aquarium at my expense as soon as it is once again ready to receive new residents. If there is any additional damage, please bring it to my attention and I will do my best to make things right. Once again, I feel terrible about the incident, and I hope that you will find it possible to forgive me.
>
> Sincerely yours,
>
> James Miller

Note that such a letter is most effective when submitted immediately after the incident. The longer you wait to express your regrets, the less effective your gesture will be.

Exchanging Gifts in the Workplace

Gift-giving may be an important corporate tradition, depending on the company's policy. It is wonderful to give, and people enjoy giving presents. However, the plethora of corporate functions and gift-giving carry with them the danger of pratfalls. Say the wrong word or give an inappropriate gift, and the harm is done. I'm finding that more and more companies discourage gift-giving among employees, partly because the workforce is becoming more multicultural and partly because the working world may have gone overboard in the past with too many presents that were too extravagant. Some people can't afford this practice, and it creates a financial burden. It can cause people to worry and distract them from work that needs to be done.

That said, if no company policy forbids it, gift-giving is appropriate. Some companies encourage gift-giving at holiday parties; others leave the formalities up to individual departments.

The general rule when it comes to giving gifts to fellow employees is strict equality:

✔ If you're the boss and you distribute holiday or birthday gifts to your group, make sure to treat each person equally.

✔ If you bring souvenirs from a vacation or business trip, try to have the same item, or items of the same value, for everyone.

✔ When it comes to giving a gift to an employee, make sure that you don't single out someone or play favorites with a more expensive present. The one exception is the boss's administrator or assistant. Then the present can be something more substantial.

Going the opposite direction — a gift from an employee to a boss — etiquette questions become trickier. Giving your boss a gift is normally not necessary. Just because your boss gives you a gift doesn't mean that you have to reciprocate, either. It's appropriate for a secretary or an administrative assistant to give something to his or her boss, but if you're one of a manager's direct reports, you shouldn't do it.

Gifts given among colleagues of equal responsibility are fine, as long as they aren't too personal. Particularly when giving gifts to a coworker of the opposite sex, you don't want the gift to be too personal; under no circumstances do you want to imply an underlying meaning or message. Choose something very generic, or try to find out whether someone has a hobby or special interest.

Avoid giving women makeup or clothes. Perfume is a gray area. Bath salts or the interesting packages of spa products that many stores sell these days are fine. A bottle of wine is a good choice if you know that the recipient enjoys wine. At first thought, food items may seem like ideal gifts, but they can be difficult because of dietary issues. Jewelry is too personal. The best gifts are those that all can share — a luncheon or a fruit basket, for example.

Gift certificates get around a lot of problems. That's why they're very popular gifts from managers. A gift certificate to a restaurant, bookstore, or day spa is always welcome. Tickets to a cherished sporting event or concert bring joy as well.

Let the corporate culture dictate how much you spend on a gift — in some companies, employees spend in the neighborhood of $10 per gift, and in others, people spend much more. Again, be careful. I remember receiving an extravagant flower arrangement after working at a computer company for one week. It must have cost $200, and it led to a lot of gossip and suspicion. People asked me what I had done to deserve an arrangement that elaborate. The same dissent occurred when someone else was given emerald earrings. Business was booming at the company, and executives forgot the value of their generosity.

Contributing to group gifts

In some organizations, birthdays, weddings, anniversaries, and other celebrations seem to come up every other day. The hat is passed, the cards are signed, and shopping assignments are handed out. You have every right to ignore the incessant festivities at the office, but your fellow workers have the right to call you a wet blanket behind your back if you do so.

When your coworkers take up collections for various special events, you're better off putting your fair share into the pot. Once you decide to go along with the crowd, do so gracefully. A dollar here and there won't ruin your budget, and you'll avoid being identified as a party pooper.

If you're absolutely unable to participate in that sort of activity, just say so. Tell the collector that you're with the group in spirit but that your family (or other) obligations come first. Here, too, honesty and clear communication carry the day. Also, if you know that a coworker is in a similar situation, you may want to discreetly mention that fact to the person collecting the money.

Participating in gift exchanges

Many companies and departments sponsor holiday gift exchanges as well. As long as the parameters are clear, these exchanges should go smoothly. First, always specify a price range. Also, make sure to distribute information about the types of gifts that people should give, such as "a gag gift" or "something for a woman." As a participant in a gift exchange, stay within the price guidelines and use good taste in selecting a gift. Buy something that you'd be pleased to receive, and you'll be fine.

Gag gifts are dangerous. What may seem like a great idea at the store can prove embarrassing when unwrapped at a party. It often works out that the person with the least creative sense of humor winds up with the most outlandish gift. Don't risk this possibility. Stay within the bounds of good taste even when so-called funny gifts are the rule of the day.

Making charitable contributions

Only you know about your charitable activities. You may be active in a church project. You may be a generous supporter of a service club in your community. Your family situation may or may not permit additional charitable contributions. If your company passes around sign-up cards for major charitable fund drives, think about your situation before committing to anything.

In some organizations, top management is determined to make a good showing in community charities, and you may feel a lot of pressure to participate. Remember that a company suggestion for the amount of your contribution is just that — a suggestion. Try to give something, because even a modest contribution counts toward the percentage of employees who participate. It's good to be generous, but you don't need to put yourself into a tight financial squeeze just because your company suggests a certain level of giving.

If your company sponsors a collection of gifts for the needy, such as toys for children in strained circumstances, buy a new item and wrap it nicely. This applies to any price range, even if your budget limits you to a very modest contribution. Making a donation is a matter of courtesy and respect, even for folks you don't know and may never meet.

Enjoying Yourself at Office Parties

Office parties can open up considerable opportunities if you learn how to take advantage of them. Learn people's names. Do some networking. If you want to move to another department, prepare some small talk in advance to use with the head of that department. Don't spend all your time talking to one person — you want to circulate. Make good eye contact, give solid handshakes, and try to speak to people you haven't met before.

Company parties and picnics are almost always motivated by management's desire to give workers a good time, but they also function as an arena in which everyone's behavior can be observed. If you (and your companion) are appropriately dressed, you say a few polite words to your host(s), and you enjoy the food and drink in moderation, you'll never hear another word about the event. On the other hand, if you stand out by being dressed too formally or too informally, if you overindulge in alcoholic beverages to the point of misbehaving, or if your "party manners" are crude, your supervisors will remember your behavior.

Don't leave anything to chance. Ask your supervisor what to wear. Arrive on time. Go easy on food and drink. Circulate and chat with your fellow employees. Seek out the boss and express your appreciation for the party. And then, when things seem to be winding down, go home.

To go or not to go?

In a word, *go* to company holiday parties, picnics, and department gatherings. Invitations posted on the bulletin board or sent around as general memos are not really invitations; they are calculated efforts to build team spirit and accomplish other company goals. Although your lack of attendance may not be held against you, you do need to have a good excuse for not showing up. Of course, emergencies change the ground rules. You don't have to go to the company softball game if your child is at home with a fever, for example.

Some people are just shy and can't handle social events, especially with coworkers, around whom they may not feel entirely comfortable. If this is the case with you, simply tell your supervisor that you have a conflict, but think carefully about your career before you do so.

The rules change when a significant admission fee is involved. If a group is headed to a theater performance and the price of a ticket is more than you can comfortably afford, you can duck the event with a clear conscience.

The performance they'll remember forever

Company gatherings, such as parties and picnics, may appear to be informal events where everyone is on equal footing, but the same old rules of business behavior still apply. Here are some points to keep in mind when it comes to having a good time at company parties:

- ✔ Company holiday parties are not regular gatherings of friends. People are there taking notes, so to speak, so you have to mind your Ps and Qs. The boss may be wearing blue jeans and drinking beer, but you can't run up, pound her on the back, and bellow, "Great party, Susie!"

- ✔ Alcoholic beverages can help lubricate a great party, but you need to know your capacity. Your coworkers will soon forget who won the three-legged race, but they'll remember your alcohol-fueled misbehavior. A kind and considerate supervisor may quietly tell you that you've had enough. If and when you get that message, opportunity is knocking. Get somebody to take you home, and leave the party without so much as a dizzy farewell.

- ✔ You may find yourself trapped in a situation in which a supervisor or some other important person demonstrates an impressive capacity for alcohol. Try to remember that you are under no obligation to match the other person drink for drink. Keep your head. If necessary, quietly ask the server to provide you with a nonalcoholic beverage each time another round is served. And remember that there is never any shame in saying that you've reached your limit. If you don't drink alcohol, order whatever suits you, and don't bother making excuses or apologies.

> ✔ If someone behaves in an embarrassing or disgraceful manner, it's best to deal with it the next day, unless someone is being outrageously abusive. You have to bring the behavior to the perpetrator's attention. Be discreet, though, and avoid making a bigger deal out of it than it really is.

Pot-luck protocol

Don't panic if a dreaded pot-luck party has you trapped. Ask the person who made the arrangements what you should bring and how many people your dish should serve. Then assess your kitchen skills. If you can manage it, prepare something yourself. If not, order from a deli.

Above all, don't poison your colleagues. Hot food must stay hot, and cold food must stay cold. Make sure that there will be adequate oven or refrigerator space for your dish. When in doubt, ask.

Be careful when making comments regarding the food at a pot-luck function. If you try something that doesn't suit your tastes, just eat around it without saying anything. Score extra points by requesting the recipe for an item you like. Pitch in with the cleanup, too. And if the party is at a private residence, be especially careful to respect the furnishings.

Keeping the Secret of Blossoming Office Romance

Know your company's policies *before* you get into any situation involving more than ordinary day-to-day contact with another employee. Your employer may have rigid rules about fraternizing, and there may be special provisions designed to head off suspicions of harassment. The etiquette of office romances involves a combination of good judgment and discretion, but company rules are absolute.

It sometimes happens that folks who work together — or at least at the same company — develop romantic feelings for each other. If you find yourself involved in such a situation, do your best to keep your personal affairs to yourself. No matter how careful you think you are, your colleagues can easily pick up all these little clues:

> ✔ Frequent telephone calls back and forth
>
> ✔ Flower arrangements delivered to the workplace
>
> ✔ Frequent lunches together

   ✔ Arriving and departing in the same car

   ✔ Long chats in the corridors or at each other's desks

Assuming that you're both unencumbered and officially eligible, there's nothing shameful about a blossoming office romance. But some companies are extremely sensitive when it comes to fraternizing, and if your relationship persists, you should make that fact known to your supervisor. Until that moment arrives, keep your personal life totally separate from your activities at work.

One final note on the subject of workplace romances: Some companies have an extremely rigid attitude about "illicit" romances — affairs between people who are married to others. Yield to temptation of this sort, and you may find yourself out of a job or transferred to a remote location that's snowbound eight months out of the year. There is no etiquette for illicit romances — just sad consequences. Don't do it.

A Few Final Thoughts on You and Your Corporate Family

Threading your way through the strange social complexities of the workplace isn't always easy. There's an element of competition that doesn't exist outside the corporate environment. Workers who get along well with each other may suddenly find themselves competing for promotions, choice assignments, office space, or even job survival in the event of downsizing.

Through all the ups and downs of life on the job, let good manners be your trademark. Friendly greetings, cheerful participation in group activities, help for others when they need it, and a pleasant demeanor all contribute to your reputation as a whole person. When you practice good manners on the job, your coworkers will cheer whatever success you achieve and will be eager to put in a good word on your behalf if the need arises.

Chapter 4

Cultivating Friendships

In This Chapter

▶ Making new friends

▶ Keeping old friends

▶ Doing your share to keep your friendships vital

*O*ne of the keys to happiness is having good relationships. After family ties, the closest bonds you form are with friends. And whatever kinds of friends you have throughout your life — best friends, fast friends, friends through thick or thin — there's no doubt that having friends helps you through an awful lot on this planet.

Because no one is born with friends, you have to learn how to make them. You have to put energy into friendships to keep them. Whether you consider yourself an introvert, an extrovert, or something in between, you can learn how to meet and keep friends.

In this chapter, I let you in on the subtle etiquette to the process of forming nurturing friendships. I also show you ways to make your friendships rewarding for many years.

Widening Your Circle of Friends

New friends don't magically appear. And as life changes, old friends may move away, get married or divorced, or develop new interests with new circles of friends. Never fear! The opportunities for new friendships are all around you. Just a little bit of effort on your part can yield a rich harvest of satisfying new relationships.

If you want to meet people, you need to extend yourself beyond your comfort zone. That includes extending invitations as well as reaching out to new people. The following sections show you how.

Introducing yourself

Knowing someone's name is the starting point of a relationship. You may have a nodding acquaintance with a lot of friendly-looking people at church, at PTA meetings, or even at the supermarket, but you might not engage in conversation with those people for the simple reason that you don't know their names.

By simply introducing yourself, you can make the leap from a friendly nod to a genuine conversation. Although doing so may seem difficult, it doesn't have to be. Here are some ways to introduce yourself:

- ✔ "Hi. We keep nodding and smiling at each other, but I don't think I've ever really known your name. I'm Jane Johnson, and I live just around the corner. What's your name?"

- ✔ "I've been calling you Joe for weeks now, but I'm not really sure if that's the right name. Mine is Andrew Rich, and I work in accounting. Am I right about Joe?"

- ✔ "We seem to come to the cafeteria at the same time almost every day. My name is Jeff Johnson, and I'd sure like to know your name."

Remembering names is a challenge for everyone. One of the best ways to remember a person's name is to repeat the name aloud after he or she says it, and then repeat it when you say good-bye.

Making small talk

After you introduce yourself, keeping the conversation going takes just a little effort. When initiating conversations with new acquaintances, here are some effective conversation starters:

- ✔ At work, objects on a person's desk may provide fodder for small talk. Find an item to discuss — perhaps a rock used as a paperweight. Ask about it: "I see that you have an interesting rock on your desk. Does it have a story?" (Almost every rock on a person's desk has a story.) Or try something like, "I notice that you always use a fountain pen. Do you collect them?"

- ✔ At the supermarket, ask for guidance: "Is that cilantro? I've always liked the taste of it, but I never know what to do with it in my own cooking."

- ✔ In your apartment complex, you can try something like this: "I just moved in. Is there a jogging path/convenience store/mailbox nearby?"

Try to use an opening statement that the person can't answer with a simple yes or no. Give a person a chance to talk about a hobby, interest, or area of expertise, and you're on your way to building a new friendship.

TIP

The do's and don'ts of making small talk

✔ When you're at a social event, DO try to include everyone in the group in the conversation by asking various people questions and drawing out their opinions. ("Larry, you are so brave to have gone whitewater rafting down the Colorado River! Stacy, you said you're from Arizona. Have you ever been down that river?")

✔ DO stay current on world events and best-selling books so that you can bring up topics of interest to everyone.

✔ DON'T ask very personal questions. ("The last time we met, I could have sworn you had an engagement ring on your finger. What happened?")

✔ DO recognize when you're boring someone. (Telltale signs include looking at a watch, glancing around the room, and shifting uncomfortably in a chair.)

✔ DON'T use inappropriate language, such as slurs or curse words, and never tell a joke that you think may be even slightly off-color.

✔ DO recognize when talking business is or is not appropriate. Avoid company or industry jargon.

✔ DON'T bring up money-related topics (including how much someone makes in salary, how much someone stands to inherit from their great aunt, and even how much you think someone's hairstylist charges).

✔ If you've met a person previously at an event, DO bring up your mutual interest. ("I think we met a couple of months ago at the book-group meeting. Have you started the next novel on our list?")

✔ If you're dining, DO say something positive about the meal, host, or event.

Using leisure activities to meet potential friends

You meet new people when you get out of your house, break from your normal routine, and take part in activities that interest you. Once again, you need to push yourself slightly beyond your comfort zone. But I can practically guarantee that you'll be richly rewarded for taking this small risk. The following are some great places to meet potential friends:

✔ **Sports clubs, such as running groups, volleyball and softball teams, and exercise classes:** These groups bring together people with at least one common goal: to be active and fit. Playing together on a team or encouraging each other to run farther or faster is a great way to form lasting friendships — and maybe to meet the person of your dreams! I know a couple of 30-something runners who joined a marathon training group and found that they ran at the same pace. They wound up running together for a year, through rain and snow and sleet and heat. At the end of the training period, they realized that they were in step in both running and romance.

- **Committees and social groups organized by a church, temple, or other religious organization:** These groups can help you meet a wide variety of people, many of whom may live in your neighborhood.

- **Community service organizations:** These organizations enable you to give back to your community while widening your circle of acquaintances. Working together toward bettering your community may also make you feel more connected to your neighbors.

- **Continuing education classes:** If you take a class in a subject that really interests you — be it Italian cooking, a foreign language, flower arranging, architecture, or sailing — you'll find yourself in the company of others who have similar interests.

- **Neighborhood groups:** Gail, a client of mine, told me that when she moved to a new city, she joined a dog-walking group to meet friends. Not only has the group been a huge success in producing great friendships and traveling companions, but her dog always has companions and a place to stay when she's out of town!

New neighbors need your friendly greetings and welcoming words. They need your help in getting acclimated to their new neighborhood, and they want to feel at home. Take them a small "welcome to the neighborhood" gift, such as a jar of homemade jam, homemade cookies, or a bottle of wine. Invite them to accompany you on local errands, and explore your common interests. You won't form close friendships with every new neighbor, but you never know what may happen if you extend a welcoming hand.

Preserving Your Existing Friendships

Good friendships are the result of caring and hard work. Friendships are constantly changing and evolving, and good friends continually refine and renew the ties that connect them. I've learned that there are three prongs to maintaining friendships:

- When good fortune smiles on your friends, you help them celebrate.

- When bad news comes their way, you comfort them.

- When a special need arises, you do your best to help.

How do good manners affect your ability to keep friendships? A well-mannered person behaves nicely toward everyone, all the time, including the doorman, the mail carrier, the bus driver, the dry cleaner, and even the dentist. People who are kind and who have a good word and a smile for everyone they meet are loved and popular and build and maintain long-lasting, loyal friendships.

Keeping friendships in balance

Good manners include an effort to keep friendships balanced in terms of invitations extended, favors reciprocated, and kindnesses acknowledged. Friends don't keep written records, nor are friendships always exactly balanced, but most people have a general feel as to whether efforts to maintain friendships are being reciprocated.

Do your best to stay on an even keel in matters such as placing telephone calls, extending luncheon invitations, doing the driving, and suggesting activities to do together, such as an afternoon at a spa, a movie outing, or a fishing trip. A friendship can't thrive if one person alone takes all the initiative to keep the relationship going.

An invitation to your friend's house calls for a return invitation from you. When your friend grabs the check at lunch, remember the gesture and pick up the tab the next time you're out together. This general rule applies to most acts of friendship — a lift to the airport, a gift of homemade cookies, willingness to go along on a shopping trip, and so on. To be a good friend, be conscious of the kindnesses that your friends extend to you and reciprocate when you're able.

Nurturing your friendships through entertaining

The ability to entertain well is one of the greatest assets you can have as you seek to maintain friendships — and bring new friends into your life. In fact, making and keeping friends is one of the main reasons that people entertain. As I said at the beginning of this chapter, human beings are social animals and need to be with other people, and entertaining is one way to bring people together.

Whether you're entertaining because you're new in town, you'd like to return the favor for someone else, you want to honor a special person or mark a special occasion, or you just want to do something out of your normal routine, there's an art to organizing an event that everyone will want to attend.

The success of a party depends not only on the host's organization and creativity, but also on the guest list. It's essential that everyone enjoy each another. Remember that mixing your guests encourages conversation, so try to select an interesting and varied group. The goal is to make the event as enjoyable for you as it is for your guests.

Here are some events that your friends might love to attend:

- ✔ Hot chocolate and cookies after ice skating or sledding
- ✔ A trip to cut down your own Christmas tree, with homemade chili afterward
- ✔ A progressive dinner, in which the group has appetizers at the first house, the first course at the next home, an entree at the next, and so on, through dessert and coffee
- ✔ A glass of Champagne and a bite to eat after the theater to relax and discuss the play
- ✔ A Sunday evening family-style supper of spaghetti and meatballs
- ✔ A block party with your neighbors, which gives everyone an opportunity to meet new families or become reacquainted with old friends
- ✔ Tea on a Saturday afternoon
- ✔ A backyard potluck or picnic with badminton and croquet to celebrate the Fourth of July, Memorial Day, Labor Day, or the Summer Solstice
- ✔ Hot food after a college football game on a crisp fall afternoon
- ✔ When you're new to the neighborhood, an open house on a Saturday afternoon for the neighbors and their children
- ✔ A barbecue and cold drinks after an afternoon at the ballpark watching the local baseball team

By nurturing your friendships through entertaining, whether you host a grand feast or a casual dinner, the rewards are plenty — in the form of new friendships, closer friendships, or simply being invited to your friends' homes in return! (See Chapter 13 for more information about hosting an event.)

TIP

The do's and don'ts of maintaining friendships

- ✔ DO respect your friends' and neighbors' private lives. Don't show up on someone's doorstep without calling first (unless, of course, it's an emergency).

- ✔ DO use tact, the quick awareness of others' feelings. Be thoughtful about the remarks you make. An offhand remark such as, "You look tired today," can cause hurt feelings.

- ✔ DON'T make negative statements about a friend's spouse, children, relatives, pets, decorating, weight, or age.

- ✔ DO be sincere. You can be honest without being hurtful or telling people only what you think they want to hear.

- ✔ DO keep track of birthdays and anniversaries and remember to send cards.

- ✔ DO give as well as receive. Be available and supportive in times of distress and trouble — and ask your friends for help when you're in need.

- ✔ DO write thank-you notes for the kindnesses you receive.

- ✔ DON'T overburden your friends with constant complaining about your problems. Pay attention to signs that your complaints are dragging them down. If friends begin to avoid you, take it as a sign to lighten up.

- ✔ DON'T take your friends for granted. Having a casual, easygoing relationship doesn't mean taking advantage of someone's kindness or asking favors of their contacts or friends.

- ✔ DON'T borrow money from friends. They are not your bankers. Many good friendships have been ruined by disputes about money.

- ✔ DO cultivate your listening skills. Even if you don't always hear perfectly, it's important to "listen." Someone once told me a story that illustrates this point perfectly. A man was sitting in a restaurant and saw an elderly couple at a nearby table. He couldn't help noticing how much the couple were enjoying each other, holding hands and chatting. He approached the couple to ask if they where married and, if so, what was the secret to their obvious happiness together. The woman answered by saying that yes, they were indeed happily married, for over 60 years.

She said that during the Great Depression, shortly after they were married, both of them held down two or three jobs and were always exhausted when they got home. One evening, the woman told her husband she was so tired that even her "teeth" hurt. Her husband, being sympathetic and loving, said, "Sit down, dear. Relax, and I'll rub your 'feet' for you." The secret to their happy marriage? Her husband has continued this loving ritual by rubbing her feet every evening since then. Although he may not have heard perfectly, he certainly knew how to listen!

Chapter 5

Sorting Out Gender Relations

. . . .

In This Chapter

▶ Remembering that the rules may change, but basic politeness remains

▶ Understanding the new codes of behavior for men and women

▶ Delving into the dating game

. . . .

*E*normous changes have swept through society in recent decades, and many of the "rules" regarding the behavior of men and women toward each other have evolved. What *hasn't* changed is the importance of putting others at ease, making them feel comfortable, and assuring that their needs are met.

When you act with respect and consideration, you react appropriately to every situation. As in other areas of etiquette, common sense reigns. People help each other when help is needed. When a person, man or woman, is burdened with packages and is trying to make his or her way out the door, whoever is nearby should step ahead of that person and open and hold the door. Doing so is simple human kindness. Today, a woman hails her own cab, puts on her own coat, and orders her own meal. That doesn't mean, however, that if a woman is struggling to get into a cab in the rain or is having trouble getting her coat on, a man shouldn't offer assistance. These are the common courtesies of our era.

Men need not think that extending equality to women should include skipping common courtesies, or that doing so makes a man "less of a man." And women shouldn't feel that the achievement of workplace equality requires them to abandon their femininity and imitate the behavior of unmannerly men.

It's understandable that men and women are confused by changes in traditional etiquette. What hasn't changed is that men and women should be gracious to one other. Etiquette between the sexes means give and take.

Staying Current and Polite at the Same Time

Women fly fighter planes, serve as police officers, fight fires, repair heavy machinery, drive race cars, ride Harleys, and rule countries. In short, women can do every job that men do. Is there any reason for men to continue to open doors for them, offer them seats on subway trains, and offer to carry their heavy packages? In a word, yes. Common courtesy toward another human being shows a regard for the other person's comfort and safety. And no man should be surprised if a woman returns at least a few of those same courtesies when the situation calls for it. When you practice the "new rules" of courtesy, you're making a gesture of respect.

Equal rights did not revoke the need for thoughtful conduct of ladies and gentlemen toward each other. If for no other reason, common courtesies help ease the strains of everyday life. When it's understood that a gentleman holds open a door and a lady goes first, women should accept graciously. And if a man spent just one day walking around in high heels, he certainly would appreciate a seat on a crowded bus.

For men

Just in case you're not familiar with these demonstrations of gentlemanly courtesy, please make these rules a part of your routine behavior.

- ✔ When walking along the city streets with a woman, walk to her left (closer to the street) to keep her from being splashed. If you're in a potentially unsafe neighborhood, walk on the building side to prevent her from being mugged.

- ✔ When entering an elevator in the company of a woman, go first to clear the way. When exiting, the person closest to the door goes first, regardless of gender, and holds the door open for the others.

- ✔ Precede women when walking down stairs.

- ✔ If two people are sharing an umbrella, the taller person — usually the man (but not always!) — should hold it.

- ✔ Take off your hat (even if it's a baseball cap) indoors.

- ✔ In a theater, allow a woman to walk ahead of you into the row. You sit on the aisle. If you're in a group of two or more couples, the women sit between the men.

✔ In a restaurant, you lead the way if you're the host. If the woman is the host, she leads.

✔ If your female companion has a heavy package and your hands are free, offer to carry the package.

✔ In any unfamiliar building or situation, open the door first and look before inviting your female companion to go ahead.

✔ Walk around to the passenger side and open the car door for your female companion. Look inside the car before you open the door to make sure that an unwanted intruder is not hiding in the backseat.

✔ After parking a car in unfamiliar territory, walk around and open the car door for your female companion. Look all around the car before opening the door.

✔ When using public transportation, defer to older persons, male or female. It is not necessary for you to give up your seat to an able-bodied woman, although the gesture is almost always appreciated.

✔ Rise when a woman enters or leaves a room or leaves or returns to the table. (The woman will usually exclaim, "Oh, don't get up" — but not until after you have already gotten up!)

✔ If you are a woman's dinner guest, relax and be her guest. Her invitation implies that she will pay the tab, and she should be allowed to do so.

✔ When dealing with a woman who is unable to accept a man's courtesies gracefully, consider her unpleasantness as a failing on her part, not on yours.

✔ Hang up a woman's coat for her.

✔ Hold a woman's chair and help to seat her. (In some restaurants, the maitre d' does the seating. In this case, stand until she is seated.)

✔ Serve a woman first, before serving yourself.

✔ If you're telling a group of men a joke or story that you wouldn't be comfortable sharing with a woman, it's better not to tell it. Most people have experienced this scenario: A man is chatting with other men, perhaps telling an off-color joke, when a woman approaches the group. Suddenly, everyone stops talking, and there's dead silence. Sudden silence in the presence of a woman is rudeness with a capital R. The lesson? Keep all public conversations suitable for a mixed audience.

Women can accept these courtesies with a gracious smile, a "thank you," and an inner satisfaction in receiving just a bit of extra consideration for their comfort.

Certain behavior that was once thought to be polite has faded into the mists of time. At a restaurant, for example, a woman is fully capable of declaring her wishes to the servers. She may also pick up the tab or order the wine, depending on which party issued the invitation or which one has the company expense account.

For women

A woman of good manners knows how to carry herself gracefully. That includes knowing how to accept common courtesies extended by men. Allow a man to be a gentleman and accept his courtesies with a gracious "thank you" — that includes courtesies that may seem a bit dated. You may accept the offer of a seat on the subway and allow a man to order for you in a restaurant, if that's what he does. If a man indicates that you, his female companion, should go first into an elevator, go ahead and go first. A man's attempt at gentlemanly behavior should be encouraged, even if he's a little behind the times.

Here are some other tips for women:

✔ Not only should you open your own doors, but you should also hold doors open for others, male or female.

✔ Regardless of the situational awkwardness, never give up your personal safety. Don't let yourself out of a man's car in a dimly lit parking garage, for example. If the man doesn't offer, tell him that you'll wait for him to come around. Likewise, don't be a passenger in a car whose driver has had too much to drink, and feel free to insist that the man slow down if you think he's driving too fast (the same goes for men!).

✔ Never feel pressured to behave like ill-mannered men just to fit in. You don't have to pretend to be amused by foul language, off-color jokes, or X-rated films.

Purging Sexism from Your Vocabulary

People may think that their attitudes are modern, but sometimes their mouths reveal otherwise! Make a conscious effort to speak inclusively, without letting sexist terms creep into your vocabulary — and listen to the things that slip out of your mouth without your thinking about them.

Often, sexist language comes up when referring to third parties. ***Remember:*** The world of adults consists of men and women. Adult women are not girls, dames, chicks, or babes. They are women. Period.

Job titles are another major category in which many people need to modernize their language. Occupations are nonsexist. Firefighters, police officers, mail carriers, camera operators, and other such workers deserve gender neutrality. This is an important area because it affects the career potential of every young person who aspires to be a neurosurgeon or pilot as opposed to the equally important job of nurse or flight attendant.

Dating in the 21st Century

Dating among adults is a process of searching for a person you love and want to be with for a long, long time — perhaps forever! If you're a high school or college student, you probably know plenty about dating. You may have a bit of difficulty finding the "right" person for you, but at least you know how to behave. You have the advantage over older folks who, for one reason or another, are just getting back to the dating scene after being away for some time. Still, everyone needs to be reminded from time to time of the proper way to ask for a date, behave on the date, and follow up if you're interested in pursuing a relationship.

Understanding what passes for a date these days

A date is two people meeting at a certain time and place for the purpose of enjoying an activity together. Beyond that loose definition, anything goes. It's a date when a potential romantic partner asks you to meet for coffee for half an hour during the workday; it's also a date when you're invited to accompany someone to a cocktail party. A date may be a jog in the park or opening night at the opera.

 Women no longer need to sit home and wait for the phone to ring. One of the new rules of dating is that women can take the initiative as well as men. That said, asking someone out on a date can be nerve-wracking for both men and women — but at least the pressure isn't always on the man these days.

Going out on a date enables you to get to know a person one-on-one, and if you show yourself to your best advantage, that person will get to know you and to like you. An ideal date allows you to have some peace and quiet together — as well as some fun — so that you can focus on each other. Rather than being stressed out by the prospect of a date, view it as an opportunity to show off your best qualities — your intelligence, wit, kindheartedness, and creativity.

Asking for a date

Say you're at a cocktail party and an attractive person catches your eye. You introduce yourself, the two of you chat, and you find that you want to get to know the person better. Now what? Ask if you may call to schedule a get-together. A day or two later, summon up your courage and call to ask for a date.

When you're gearing up to ask for a date, expect the worst and hope for the best, as they say. The person you ask may well have another social engagement, have a heavy workload, or be involved with someone else. That person simply may not want to go out with you. Whatever happens, try to remember that getting turned down for a date is not a major rejection, or even a judgment on you — it happens to everyone at one time or another. Keep your goal in sight: to find a person who wants to be with you. If you look long enough, you'll find that person. There are lots of fish in the sea!

 When proposing a date, try to come up with an idea that's so creative, so fun, and so appealing that no person in his or her right mind would refuse. By making the date *sound* terrifically exciting, you can make the other person excited to accompany you. How do you come up with one of these fantastic ideas? Keep up with the latest happenings in your area. Think of creative themes. For example:

- ✔ You can get tickets to a baseball game and propose an afternoon at the ballpark with all the trimmings — hot dogs, peanuts, and Cracker Jacks, with a drink at your favorite ballpark-area bar afterward.

- ✔ You can go see an intriguing foreign film followed by dinner at your favorite corresponding Italian/French/Chinese restaurant.

- ✔ You can have dinner at your favorite French bistro followed by an evening of jazz.

- ✔ You can stop at a soul food restaurant on your way to a blues club.

Although most people simply call and ask for a date, a written invitation may make your offer stand out. Writing enables you to set the right tone without running the risk of stuttering, sounding nervous, or tripping over words. Besides, it's easier for someone to turn you down immediately over the phone than to consider the invitation and call you especially to decline. Make sure that your letter or e-mail message is casual in tone, is amusing in style, and describes a wonderful event that you have planned. Here's an example:

Dear John,

It was such a pleasure to meet you in class last week — it's so great to meet a fellow Shakespeare fanatic. I would love to hear more about your views on Macbeth. Since you mentioned that you often work on Saturday afternoons, why don't we take a coffee break together this Saturday at 3 p.m.? There's the most charming new coffee house in our neighborhood called The Third Coast. We can grab some comfy chairs, relax, and chat while we watch the world go by.

Give me a call at my office, 555-1212. I hope you can make it!

Sincerely,

Allison

If you decide to call rather than write, your invitation should be time-specific, event-specific, and sincere. Here are two good examples:

- "Would you like to join me Saturday evening for dinner at my favorite Italian restaurant and a movie? I would be thrilled to have your company."
- "I've got two tickets to Friday's symphony performance, and I'd be so pleased to have you accompany me. There's a wonderful Champagne party after the concert in the orchestra hall."

Here's the wrong way to ask someone for a date over the phone:

"You wanna do something this weekend?"

Why is this wrong? The object of your attention doesn't know what kind of *something* you have in mind, and the word *weekend* can mean anything from a Friday night movie to three nights in Las Vegas.

Accepting or declining a date

You should be considerate when accepting or declining a date; honesty is the best policy. If you've already committed to another social engagement for that evening, simply say so with a simple "I'm sorry, but I already have other plans." Never try to cancel a previously scheduled engagement for a date. If you welcome the invitation but are simply busy, you can add, "I would love to see you some other time."

If you never, ever want to have a date with this person, say firmly but pleasantly, "No, thank you, I'm not available." Theoretically, you should only have to say this once, but sometimes you need to repeat the exercise once or twice to get the point across. Be kind to the other person — someday you may be in his or her shoes!

Knowing what to expect on a date

Whether the man or the woman does the asking, you can reasonably expect a few things once you accept an invitation for a date:

- A date should be kept, even if a more enticing offer comes along.

- You should be given enough advance notice to get ready for the date. Three days beforehand is the minimum. So, to ask someone out for Saturday night, you should call by Wednesday at the latest.

- The person who asks for a date should take the other's interests into account when suggesting an activity. If the person you're inviting out is a sports writer, attending a basketball game may be an excellent activity to do together. Tickets to a political debate may not be as interesting to that person.

- Sexual favors should not be expected from either person.

- Plans should not change at the last minute.

- Both people should dress appropriately and use good personal hygiene.

- The date should start on time.

- You should kiss on the first date only if both partners want to.

- Both people should make the best of a date if things don't go as planned, without complaining, yawning, or otherwise acting unhappy.

- The invitee should thank the other person at the end of the date, whether it's to compliment the planning of the date or to show that you enjoyed the person's company.

- The invitee should write or call with a thank-you the next day.

- Neither person on the date should gossip about the date with a third party afterward.

Knowing how to behave on a date

These rules of conduct would hold fast in almost any part of life, but they're particularly important when you're out with someone new and you're eager to make a good impression. Here's how to show yourself to your best advantage:

✔ Be thoughtful of the other person's feelings, space, and property.

✔ Don't make sarcastic comments that degrade anyone else.

✔ Don't boast.

✔ Don't drop names.

✔ Keep your promises.

✔ Don't talk about how much something costs.

✔ Never gossip or repeat a rumor.

✔ Go out of your way to put your date at ease.

✔ Always have cash or a credit card with you, even if you don't expect to pay.

✔ Say please, thank you, and you're welcome.

A female friend of mine recently had a luncheon date with a new man. He chose a casual restaurant with a salad bar. When she went up to fill her salad plate, he said, "They have some good watermelon up there. Want to bring me some?" This man clearly did not know how to show himself to his best advantage. Not only did he show that he was inconsiderate and lazy, but he also demonstrated a lack of respect for the woman. Needless to say, they did not go out again.

Picking up the tab

The traditional rule that the man always pays has been replaced by greater equality. Every couple in an ongoing relationship work out their own financial arrangements. In general, however, when it comes to a first date, the person who issues the invitation picks up the tab. If one person says to the other, "Let's go out," that indicates that both will share the cost equally. If one of them asks, "May I take you out?" it means that the partner who is asking intends to pay the full cost.

After the first date, the couple can split the cost of dining and entertainment as they see fit. Nothing prevents a couple from agreeing beforehand to split expenses; this practice is common among plenty of people, from students to older folks on fixed incomes.

Even if you are the invitee, it is polite to offer to pay your share when the bill arrives. Your date will appreciate the gesture.

If you're on a limited budget, there's an answer to the dilemma of dating without spending lavish amounts of money: Substitute creativity for big spending. You can suggest a trip to see a new exhibit at the museum, followed by a picnic lunch, a lecture, or a recital at a local college. The right person will

Public displays of affection

When you're on a date, it's nice to show that you care for each other. However, it's not nice to subject the rest of the world to a major make-out session. Long, drawn-out kisses and holding each other are fine in private, but in public this behavior is rude and distracting to others. When you meet, though, it's perfectly acceptable to kiss, whether it's a kiss on both cheeks, a kiss on one cheek, or a (brief) kiss on the lips. Hand-holding is also perfectly appropriate.

Couples should also avoid "hanging" on each other. Not only can it appear to be a sign of clinginess or insecurity on the part of one of the partners, but it may make outsiders uncomfortable.

appreciate your creativity and thoughtfulness in arranging such a date, even if it doesn't involve roses, wine, and caviar.

Waiting for the phone to ring: Telephone etiquette

The telephone can seem like tricky business when it comes to dating. And today, it's not just the phone itself you have to deal with — you must cope with answering machines, pagers, and other technological wonders. The following sections can help you through telephone trauma. (See Chapter 9 for even more on phone etiquette.)

Calling at work

Business phones are meant to serve the business, not your social life. If you phone a new love interest at her or his work location, make sure that you have a good reason for the daytime call, and keep it short. Begin by asking if the timing is convenient. Then say what you have to say, get the response you need, and promise to chat at length after working hours.

Answering machine and voice mail etiquette

Are you surprised to find out that there is an etiquette to using an answering machine? Well, consider this: Anyone with access to the machine can play the messages. And anyone within earshot of the machine can listen to messages as they are recorded. Suppose you leave a *really* personal message on your sweetie's machine, and her mother from out of town just happens to be staying in her apartment for the weekend. The phone rings, the machine picks up the call, and your amplified voice echoes through the apartment as your prospective mother-in-law learns a heck of a lot about her daughter's private activities. Kids, especially, love to check out the messages on Mom's answering machine.

Voice mail is usually more difficult for outsiders to access, but don't take a chance.

Leave squeaky-clean messages. State your name your affiliation (if appropriate), your phone number, and the best time to return the call. If necessary, leave information about where you can be reached. But don't trust an answering machine to be private. And while we're on the subject, don't trust e-mail, fax machines, or cellular phones to be private. Communicate as if the world were listening.

To beep or not to beep?

Calling another person's pager is a liberty that only those with a genuine emergency or with a genuinely intimate relationship should take. In the initial stages of getting to know somebody, pagers are better left unbeeped.

Coming clean about vital facts

There's a lot of stuff that nice people didn't discuss prior to the time when TV commercials dealt with every affliction known to humankind. Even now, you may have a number of little skeletons in your closet that you're not ready to share with the latest light of your life. But you simply must declare a few facts before your relationship moves from dinner to breakfast:

- ✔ If you harbor any sexually transmitted disease, you must say so. Even if it is held in check and is in remission by medication, you have to confess. This is best done during a quiet moment together, with honesty and kindness — something along the lines of, "I'm very attracted to you, and before our relationship becomes more intimate, there's something we should discuss."

- ✔ If you're going to start a sexual relationship, it's important to discuss the risk of HIV as well as sexually transmitted diseases, and what you both are going to do about it. That means raising the issue of taking an HIV test and using condoms. It's only proper to have that discussion if you're intimate enough to be talking about having sex.

- ✔ If you're married, you have to 'fess up. You may be legally separated, you may be dreadfully unhappy, or your spouse may be on foreign assignment for the next two years, but your marital status is a matter of public record, and you must not keep it a secret.

As for the 100 other little details that might send a new lover running, you have to listen to your conscience. In general, you owe it to the other one to come clean about really important facts.

Knowing when to cease and desist

It's terribly difficult to like someone romantically and find that your affection is not returned, but etiquette demands that you accede to those wishes by withdrawing in a dignified way. This means no late-night phone calls, no long letters, and no begging or pleading. On the other hand, the uninterested party should be firm but polite and unwavering in his or her statement that he or she has no interest in a relationship.

If you call someone repeatedly and the person does not return your calls, your repeated failure to reach the object of your intentions is a good indication that your feelings are not reciprocated. If the calling is all one-way on your part, stop calling — it wasn't meant to be.

Particularly for those getting back into dating after an absence (because of divorce or the death of a spouse), dating is stressful. Many people give up after an initial rejection. Don't give up. If you run into a person who doesn't reciprocate your interest, don't take it personally. It happens to everyone at some point. Keep trying, and sooner or later you'll hit upon the right chemistry with a special someone.

Part II
Presenting Yourself Positively

The 5th Wave   By Rich Tennant

"Oh, quit looking so uncomfortable! It's a pool party! You can't wear a cape and formal wear to a pool party!"

In this part . . .

*T*he way you present yourself, from your body language
to your attire, says a lot about the amount of self-
respect and self-confidence you have. This part guides
you through grooming, posture, and other body language,
and the tricky situations that come up every now and
then, such as suddenly feeling queasy or spilling a glass of
something all over everything. These are the things that
others use to form a first impression of you, and you want
it to be a good one. I also include a whole chapter on
dressing right for the occasion, whether it's a formal affair
or a meeting at an office where the employees dress in
business casual attire.

Chapter 6

Your Most Important Presentation: Yourself

In This Chapter

▶ Looking at your wardrobe, your gestures, and your posture

▶ Striking a pose with the correct body language

▶ Handling awkward or unexpected situations with grace

*T*he word *etiquette* is so often used to describe the things you say to others that people tend to overlook some mighty important details that have nothing at all to do with words. If you haven't thought about the effects of your wardrobe and body language on others, you'll come away from this chapter with a lot of new insights.

How you cope with unexpected little surprises and personal emergencies also can have a big effect on those around you. Do the sensible thing, smoothly, and nobody will think twice about your difficulty. This chapter's second purpose is to help you plan ahead and cope with the unexpected.

Understanding Why Looks Are Important

How you dress, groom yourself, and handle yourself in public are all part of your "packaging." Like a product, you can present yourself to be your most appealing. And you can present yourself differently according to the time and place. For example, your appearance should differ depending on your geographic area — how you dress and act in Rocky Mountain National Park in Colorado, say, as opposed to Midtown Manhattan.

Yes, you should wear what you like. However, you should also learn to set aside your personal preferences about clothing in favor of the most effective and appropriate clothes for a given situation. Just because you love wearing shorts and sports sandals doesn't mean that you should wear them to the opera in Paris.

Psychologists say that most people form impressions of others in the first four minutes, and that 80 percent of the impression is based on nonverbal signs. In other words, what comes out of your mouth has very little to do with how people judge you. And once you make a first impression, getting people to change that judgment is very difficult.

That said, I would love to have a nickel for every time I misjudged someone based on my first impression! You should always behave kindly toward everyone, whatever you judge them to be on your first meeting. However, when you're meeting new people, you don't always get a second chance, so do your best to present yourself in the best possible light every time.

A well-mannered person always considers the impression communicated by clothing, body language, and grooming. You always need to be thinking about what your appearance says about you.

Never pretend to be anything you aren't. There's a huge difference between dressing appropriately for an occasion and being a fake. You should not be uncomfortable or present an image that isn't you, but you should present the best *you* you possibly can.

People would rather associate with a person who is successful than with one who is not. And people respect others who visibly care about themselves and show respect for their roles in life. Even though some professions have gone more casual, I still like to see my doctor, accountant, lawyer, real estate agent, and advertising consultant appear neat and well put together. And I'm sure that others feel the same way about me. Who would want to work with an etiquette consultant whose clothes are fraying at the edges or whose mascara is smudged all over her eyes?

Although dressing well and grooming yourself properly show that you respect yourself, those things alone do not ensure your success, either socially or professionally. You also need to demonstrate a positive attitude in everything you do.

Planning Your Wardrobe

What you wear and how you wear it can communicate just as clearly as the words you speak. The messages you provide through your wardrobe are an important part of the manners you display in public.

First, it's important to wear clothing that is appropriate, of the best quality you can afford, and in good taste. It isn't how many outfits you have or the labels you wear that count, but how you care for your clothing and put it together with style. Most important is that your clothing reflect your positive attitude toward yourself, your work, and others.

Begin by thinking about your profession, your place of work, and your leisure time. If your work life and your "play" life are very different, separate your work wardrobe from your leisure wardrobe. Does your work wardrobe present a confident, well-groomed image? Are the clothes suitable for the type of work you do? Do you have clothes that can take you from your work to a social engagement? Are your leisure clothes also neat, even if they're casual? Are they in good repair, without stains or tears?

Once you've thought it through, it's time to venture into your closet.

Working with your existing wardrobe

Every once in a while, closets need a spring cleaning — whatever the season. Each year, try on your clothes in front of a full-length mirror. If you've gained weight, make sure that your clothes aren't stretching or pulling. No matter how much you suck in your stomach in front of the mirror, in real life people tend to relax. If you've lost weight and your clothes are hanging on you, you can have them taken in. If you can't have your clothes altered properly to accommodate a weight gain or loss, donate them to charity.

If pant legs or skirts are too wide, they can be altered to be narrower, if that is the style. Unfortunately, if they are narrow and the style is the opposite, that can't be easily changed. You can avoid some of these problems by never buying extremes in fashion for your basic wardrobe. Check your existing wardrobe (including ties) for large, bold patterns; checks; florals; and geometric patterns. These types of patterns generally do not wear well with time.

Color is something you should also look at in a wardrobe review. Although that lime-green leisure suit may have been all the rage in the 1970s, it's probably not going to convey the same impression decades later. Save it for a 1970s theme party!

Also take a look at the type of fabrics you have in your closet. Wool, silk, and cotton are always in style, whereas blends and new fabrics that include Lycra are also coming into their own. Even polyester has made a comeback, although it shouldn't be your first choice for business clothing. Natural fabrics cost more and are expensive to maintain, but they make beautiful, high-quality garments. Combinations of cotton, wool, silk, and synthetics are a good compromise because they combine a good appearance and fairly low-maintenance care.

While you're going through your closet, make sure that all your clothes are properly cleaned and pressed. Shine your shoes, brush your suede garments, and have any rundown shoes resoled. Then go through your clothes and hang them so that outfits are together and easy to reach. Don't hesitate to give away clothes that don't make your cut. Admit your mistakes and move on!

Adding new items to your wardrobe

Consider the following points when adding to your wardrobe:

- ✔ If you don't like to shop, simply shop twice a year — once for spring and summer and once for fall and winter. Purchase well-made classics that will last for several years and that you can mix and match with other items to create new outfits.

- ✔ Trendy clothing is fun to have, but make sure to balance it with long-lasting, classically styled items. Consider putting together a trendy shirt and a classic pair of wool pants, for example, for an updated and stylish look. You may want to spend more for the classics and less for the trendy items, which you won't be able to wear as long.

- ✔ Remember that new accessories, such as scarves and ties, can make old outfits seem new. If you don't have the money to purchase new garments, pick up a couple of accessories to freshen your look.

- ✔ At work, keep the trendiness to a minimum. You can alter the length of your skirt or sleeve or the style of your collar, for example, but you don't want to wear anything too out-there. If you yearn to express yourself with your clothing, purchase some trendy accessories that you can pair with your business basics.

- ✔ Know your company's dress code and the norms of attire in your industry. Even if your office is a casual one, make sure that you purchase neat, good-quality garments so that you present a professional image. If your office is more conservative and requires you to wear business suits, stick to more conservative clothing that isn't too flashy.

- ✔ Don't purchase an item if it doesn't fit you well. More than likely, you won't wear it, and the money will have been wasted. Consider how comfortable the article of clothing is, too — no one likes to wear clothing that is too constricting or is itchy.

- ✔ Choose garments that suit you in style and color. For example, dark colors and simple lines are more flattering to heavier people.

- ✔ Be wary about purchasing something if you're not sure where you'll wear it. Finding a bargain or an item that you just adore is great, but it's of no use to you if it sits in your closet untouched for years.

If a garment is made of a very fragile fabric, of a very light color, don't buy it for work. It will be very high-maintenance in terms of dry cleaning and special care. And if you live in a rainy or snowy climate, skip the light-colored shoes and boots.

Dressing tips for women

✔ Make sure that your clothes fit you properly. Clothing that is too big, too small, too short, or too long is not flattering. If an item is too large for you, a tailor may be able to take it in.

✔ Dress according to your body type. As you've probably already figured out, certain styles complement your figure, and others do not flatter you at all. If you need help determining what styles are best for you, consult a salesperson at an upscale department store.

✔ Find a color palette that suits you. Although there are no strict rules about who can wear which colors, you should know which colors are most flattering to you. Also make sure to have a variety of neutral-colored items of clothing that you can mix and match with bright-colored garments.

✔ Avoid loud colors at the office. If you simply must wear bright colors, limit them to accessories, such as a bright scarf or a colored blouse under a neutral suit.

✔ Dress tastefully. Yes, you have the right to look like a woman, but please refrain from wearing very short skirts, low-cut blouses and dresses, sheer clothing, and the like, especially at work.

✔ Make sure that your undergarments do not show through your clothing. Purchase a variety of undergarments to suit your various outfits, such as strapless and convertible-strap bras and slips in a variety of lengths.

✔ Coordinate your pantyhose with your outfit, and make sure that they fit properly. In business situations, stick to sheer, flesh-colored stockings.

✔ Remember that shoes can tell people a lot about you. For comfort and style reasons, it's better to spend a little extra on a good pair of shoes that go with a variety of outfits than to purchase several cheaper pairs that won't last. Keep the heel at a low or medium height. At work, make sure to wear shoes that cover your toes — simple flats or pumps are best.

✔ Accessorize well, but in moderation. Tasteful earrings and perhaps a necklace or lapel pin can really accentuate an outfit. A lovely scarf can add a splash of color. If you wear a watch, make sure that it is of good quality— sport watches and watches with worn-out bands are appropriate only for the most casual occasions.

✔ Make sure that your purse is appropriate to the season and the dressiness of your outfit. For example, if you're wearing a navy blue business suit with brown pumps, you should not carry a black fabric handbag. Also discard any purses that are worn out or torn.

✔ Don't carry several bags at once, such as a purse, a briefcase, and a tote bag. Carry one bag that can accommodate all the items that you need to carry in it — or, at most, two bags.

Dressing tips for men

✔ Don't get into a rut and wear the same thing every day just because you're male. You can vary your look by wearing different shades and fabrics, for example.

✔ Choose separates, such as sport coats and pants, that you can mix and match easily. That way, you can create several different outfits from just a few articles.

✔ Find clothing in colors that are flattering to you. White dress shirts may be the norm, for example, but you may look better in a subtle cream shade. The same goes for suits, which come in a wide range of neutral shades. You may be surprised at how much better you look in one shade of gray than in another.

✔ Your clothing should fit you well. Don't buy something if it doesn't fit quite right — if the pants are a little too snug around your waist, for example, or if the shirt collar doesn't lie quite right. Remember that too big is no better than too small.

✔ Choose jacket and pant styles that flatter you. If you're thin, you might try a double-breasted jacket and flat-front pants to make yourself look broader. Conversely, if you're on the heavy side, you might opt for a vest and pants with pleats.

✔ When you purchase dress shirts, make sure that the tails are long enough to be tucked in and stay there.

✔ Select your ties carefully. If you're not confident in your taste in ties, go for subtle colors and conservative patterns. As a rule, novelty ties are not appropriate in a business setting.

✔ Coordinate your belts and shoes with each other and with your outfit. Belt and shoes should be the same color (unless you're wearing casual clothing with tennis shoes). Also, make sure that your belts and shoes are in good repair, and keep your shoes shined.

✔ If you choose to wear jewelry, make sure that it's tasteful. Flashy jewelry does not enhance your business image.

Dressing appropriately for the occasion

Overdressing can be an accident. You may have been misinformed about the situation, or you may have misunderstood someone's advice. But if you wear a full a business suit to a beach party, you're telling the others that you don't wish to participate in their idea of fun. And if you show up wearing a cocktail dress and a lot of fancy jewelry for an afternoon bridge party with neighbors, your friends will feel you're telling them that you are better than they are.

Underdressing sends just as strong a message. When you wear blue jeans and a sweatshirt to a symphony concert, you're telling everyone around you that you place a low value on the evening's entertainment and that you have little respect for the other members of the audience.

And here's a message for those people who say that they have "gotten beyond the artifice of clothing and personal grooming": You generally look terrible, and whenever a gathering is planned, you don't receive an invitation. Only best-selling authors, Nobel Prize–winning scientists, and movie stars can afford to ignore the situational dress code. On them, the inappropriate attire looks charmingly eccentric. On you, it will look like you have no respect for others. Proper clothing, clean and neatly pressed garments, well-matched accessories, and just the right touch in a necktie or some jewelry is a sign that you are in tune with whatever is going on.

The key is to *ask* about the proper attire. If you're going to a party, ask the host. If you're attending a theatrical performance, call the ticket office. Chapter 7 includes more detailed information about dressing for various occasions.

Getting into Good Grooming

Although having appropriate clothing is very important, being clean, well-groomed, and well-cared-for is even more important. Some people dress in the latest styles and the right colors, yet they are not socially successful or successful in business. Why? They may not be properly groomed: Their shoulders are dotted with dandruff, they have ring-around-the-collar, or they have greasy hair or bad breath.

If you use the following checklist, you're sure to be in good stead grooming-wise:

✔ Make sure to bathe or shower and to apply a deodorant/antiperspirant (be careful not to get it on your clothes!) every day.

✔ Brush your teeth after you eat — or if you can't, suck on a breath mint to freshen your breath. If you have yellowed or stained teeth, use a whitening toothpaste or talk to your dentist about further steps that you can take.

✔ Be subtle with scents. Apply perfume, cologne, or aftershave sparingly, keeping in mind that you become accustomed to the scent, so it may be harder for you to detect on yourself. Remember, too, that hair-care products, deodorants, and so on also contain perfumes, so make sure that the products you use don't have clashing scents.

✔ Shampoo and condition your hair often to keep it looking fresh and grease-free. Have it trimmed regularly and keep it neatly groomed. Use products that keep hair in place if you need to, but don't overdo it — if your hair doesn't move, you've probably used too much hairspray, mousse, or gel.

Grooming tips for women

✔ Take good care of the skin on your face, keeping it clean and well moisturized. If you have problems with excess oil, use an oil-free powder to cut down on the shine.

✔ TUse makeup to enhance your features and give yourself a finished look, but use it sparingly. Heavy makeup can look cheap, and it's certainly not appropriate in an office setting.

✔ TGetting lipstick all over your cup or napkin is a big faux pas. To avoid this problem, make sure to blot your lipstick after you apply it. Also check your teeth to make sure that no lipstick has found its way onto them.

✔ TKeep your fingernails trimmed to a reasonable length, and make sure to file them regularly. If you polish your nails, choose a color that isn't too bright or flashy, unless you're going out for the evening.

✔ TFind a hairstyle that flatters your face and that you can maintain fairly easily. Make sure to keep your look up-to-date, too — try modifying your style every few years.

✔ TIf you color your hair, either to enhance your features or to cover gray, use a color that works with your skin tone, and don't do anything too drastic. The idea is to make yourself look better, not to make it obvious that you spend lots of money at your hair salon.

Understanding the messages sent by scents

In addition to their obvious utilitarian value, perfumes can communicate powerful messages. There's a vast difference between the message sent by a light floral scent and the message sent by a heavy, musky scent. The lighter floral perfumes are much more suitable for general wear during the day. The message is neutral — you simply smell nice. If you're headed for a large-audience gathering in a closed room, do your companions a favor and stick with something light. If you're going out for a night on the town, you may choose a slightly heavier scent.

TIP

Dealing with coworker's body odor

Dealing with a coworker whose natural body odor is overwhelming or unpleasant can be difficult. The least hurtful remedy is probably a direct, one-on-one approach where nobody else can overhear the conversation. Try to steer things in a neutral direction: "I know that people are often unable to sense certain things about themselves, so I hope you won't mind it if I tell you that the deodorant you're using just isn't working. It's probably time to switch brands." This approach is much kinder than leaving a stick of deodorant or a bar of soap on the person's desk or chair, as if the whole office were in on the humiliation.

Perfumes and colognes, too, can cause problems. These magical potions enable men and women to create an artificial atmosphere around their bodies, with scents that are anything from lightly floral to heavily musky. Unfortunately, that "atmosphere" might interfere with the nice, fresh air that you're used to breathing, and the scent can be nauseating.

In an office setting, if you need to tell someone that his or her aftershave lotion, cologne, or perfume is making you sick, you can usually handle it simply by telling the person that you could breathe easier if the perfume level in the office were a little lower. This approach worked in the days of cigarette smoking, and there's no reason why it won't work in this situation.

Grooming tips for men

- ✔ You may think that skin care is just for women, but healthy-looking skin is an asset for anyone. Wash your face regularly, and use a moisturizer if your skin tends to be dry. If you have problems with acne or you have a wart or mole that you'd like to have removed, consult a dermatologist.

- ✔ Keep your hair well-trimmed, clean, and neatly styled. That goes for facial hair, too! Make sure to shave any excess hair off the back of your neck between haircuts.

- ✔ Remove any hair that sticks out of your ears or nostrils.

- ✔ Keep your nails short, and file away any jagged edges. Check under your nails for dirt if you've been working in the yard or around the house, and promptly remove any dirt that you find.

Paying Attention to Your Body Language and Posture

Whole books have been written about body language. Psychology students can spend a semester learning how to read small gestures. Jury selection consultants think that they can separate the bleeding hearts from the executioners by watching how members of the jury pool stand, sit, and fidget. I'll skip the shrink-talk and go straight to the good advice:

- ✔ The person with whom you are currently speaking is the whole world. Don't let your eyes wander in search of someone else in the room. If you wish to disengage yourself, wait for a reasonable opening in the conversation and then be honest. Say that you have to greet an old friend or risk hurting his feelings. Promise to return (but don't say when).

- ✔ In groups, as in poker games, your facial expressions can betray your inner thoughts. Keep this in mind as you circulate at a party. When your supervisor hands out a new assignment, look enthusiastic. When you meet people at a social event, smile and look pleased to meet them.

- ✔ Folding your arms in front of your chest can be an innocent part of your normal fidgeting or a sign of rejection. The risk that people will assume the latter is high enough that you should avoid folding your arms.

- ✔ The signs of impatience — tapping your fingernails on a table or desk, tapping your toe on the floor, looking up at the ceiling, sighing repeatedly, looking at your watch every few seconds — are pretty easy to pick up. Teenagers are very skilled at indicating impatience, especially when an adult is trying to give them some good advice about good manners. It doesn't hurt to check yourself every few minutes to make sure that you aren't shouting something with your body that you wouldn't dare whisper with your voice.

Your body language communicates your feelings about others and about the social situation in which you are participating. Your posture communicates your feelings about yourself. It's no accident that cadets in military schools and recruits in military boot camps are drilled constantly on posture. After enough training and encouragement, service personnel stand straight and confidently, looking for all the world like competent defenders of life, liberty, and the pursuit of happiness.

When you stand with a slouch or sit with a slump, you're telling others that you don't feel confident and you'd like to be left alone. When your head is erect, your gaze is outward, and your backbone is as straight as Mother Nature made possible, you are inviting others to meet with you on equal terms. Mother was right; stand up straight!

Gesundheit! Coping with Things That Sneak Up on You

You are dressed correctly for the situation. Your posture and body language demonstrate that you are eager to participate in the festivities. Everything is going your way. Then, right in the middle of, say, a toast to the new bride and groom, you knock over a full glass of Champagne and the bubbly is headed straight for the bride's mother. What do you do?

This section is dedicated to life's unexpected unpleasantness. Read it several times over if you happen to be accident-prone.

Dealing with sneezes, indigestion, and other biological manifestations

Ah, the sneeze: anything from a gentle, ladylike puff of air to a moist explosion that could wake the dead. Herewith is a checklist of sneeze-coping strategies:

- ✔ Always carry a handkerchief or a small package of tissues. Reach for them at the first hint of a sneeze coming on.

- ✔ Forestall a sneeze at a critical moment (such as a priest's blessing over a newlywed couple) by pressing your extended index finger flat and firmly against your upper lip, just under your nostrils. This technique really works, but only temporarily.

- ✔ Sneeze gently. Practice sneezing without vocalizing.

- ✔ Turn away from those close at hand. When seated, try to bend toward the floor.

- ✔ If a sneezing fit seizes you, excuse yourself from the room.

- ✔ If you have no other way to cope and absolutely have to use your table napkin to catch a sneeze, fold the napkin inward, wrap it in a second, unused napkin, and signal a waiter to request two replacement napkins. Say that you were forced to use the napkin for personal purposes so that it can be disposed of properly.

Indigestion has two meanings. Literally, the word refers to physical discomfort from something you have eaten. More commonly, in social situations, indigestion is just a polite synonym for belching. It happens to everyone occasionally, but belching can be embarrassing at a banquet, especially if you are seated at the head table near a microphone.

If you feel a belch coming on, use your napkin to cover your mouth, turn away from others, and forgo the pleasure of making a noise that would delight an 8-year-old. Loud belching is an acquired skill that can be unlearned in favor of quiet belching.

Among the gems of folk wisdom passed along from mother to daughter, these suggestions apply to belching:

- ✔ All carbonated beverages pose some risk of generating a belch. Seltzer water is a particularly wicked offender. If you want to lessen your risk, stay away from carbonated drinks.

- ✔ Small sips of water are less risky than large gulps.

- ✔ Good sitting posture tends to lessen the risk of a large belch sneaking up on you.

- ✔ If you are speaking to someone and an unexpected belch befalls you, say "Excuse me" and go right on with your conversation. Any statement you make in an attempt to mitigate the happenstance will only make it worse.

- ✔ In some Asian cultures, belching is accepted as a sign of pleasure. Supposedly, the belch means that the food was delicious. Allow Asians to follow their own customs, but please remain true to Western manners yourself.

A human body that is determined to generate gas will not always limit itself to belching. If you are afflicted with any advanced manifestations, simply excuse yourself from the party until your system calms down.

Feeling carsick, queasy, or just plain woozy

There's a reason the word *carsick* was invented, just as there's a reason for those little white bags in airliner seat pockets. People do get sick once in a while, and occasionally even the most well-mannered person in the world has to toss her cookies.

I recommend rapid movement toward the bathroom and the conclusion of your upset in total privacy. You have absolutely no reason to report on your adventures after you regain your composure and rejoin the group.

In an automobile, be extremely direct in addressing the driver. We recommend, "Pull over right now; I have to throw up." Any other message is likely to be misinterpreted.

As a last resort, when trapped by circumstance and absolutely doomed to the ravages of your upset, turn away from the group, grab a napkin or handkerchief, and trust in the sympathetic understanding of the others.

Spilling the water or tipping the salt

What you do about dinner table catastrophes depends on the severity of the problem, where you are, and what's going on. Everyone has spilled a glass of water or wine, tipped over the salt shaker, or splashed soup onto the tablecloth. This is another of those categories of surprise that test your ability to think rapidly and minimize the social consequences. Keep the following tips in mind, and you'll get through the catastrophe with a minimum of upset:

✔ Above all, do not utter an expletive. Having ice cubes and water flowing all over the table is bad enough without the echo of your ill-considered curse hanging in the air.

✔ When liquid is spilled, your first thought should be for the protection of your clothing and that of others close by. Use your napkin as a dam to prevent the flow of water or wine onto your companion's lap.

✔ If waiters are present, allow the staff to take care of the cleanup details. Just move far enough away from the table to give them working room. Above all, do not call attention to the mishap.

✔ Assess the damage. If your clothing has been dampened but you are not too uncomfortable to continue with the meal, remain with the party. If your clothing is soaked, make your apologies and leave.

✔ As the host of a party in your home, do what you can to help a spill-dampened guest remain with the group. Offer an emergency change using your own clean clothing (if sizes match) or bring out an attractive robe. Yes, this is a tug-of-war between a guest with an impulse to leave and a host insisting that the dampened guest stay on. If there is a reasonable makeshift remedy, the guest should stay at the party.

✔ There are, in some circumstances, quick-thinking men who are willing to rush to the rescue of a woman dampened by a careless spill. Well motivated though he may be, a gentleman should not mop off a lady's dampened clothing with a handy napkin. In the excitement of the rescue, unwanted familiarities may ensue. In other words, hands off, guys.

✔ For less threatening spills, such as salt, croutons, hard rolls, and the like, remember to use clean silverware when repositioning edible items. Once again, if a serving staff is present, just signal a waiter and allow the staff to take care of the situation.

Avoiding Accidents That You Don't Have to Have

Dozens of little misfortunes befall people who fail to plan ahead, think ahead, or observe a few "social safety" rules. As you run down the following list, make a few mental notes to spare yourself some future moment of agony:

- ✔ **Look before you reach.** A banquet setting with several wine glasses plus a water goblet is an obstacle course just waiting to trap a careless guest. Resign yourself to the fact that you cannot safely reach for your water while regaling your table-mates with anecdotes from your trip to Brazil.

- ✔ **Chew or speak; don't attempt to do both simultaneously.** The food may be delicious and the company stimulating, but you have to take turns enjoying each. You are inviting disaster if you try to speak before your mouth is totally clear of food.

- ✔ **Do not try to eat a buffet meal while standing.** A passerby may collide with you and send your food all over your outfit and the floor. There's no way to cut your food while balancing the plate. You can't possibly use your napkin properly. Sit down with your dish or refrain from eating.

- ✔ **Never make a negative comment about the party to a stranger.** The stranger may turn out to be the host's mother.

Chapter 7

Dressing Right for Every Occasion

. . . .

. . . .

*W*hat you wear reveals a lot of information to the world:

- ✔ How you feel about yourself

- ✔ What you do for a living (Think of the Village People!)

- ✔ Where you may be spending your day (Are you wearing practical shorts and running shoes with a camera around your neck, or wearing a pin-striped suit and carrying a briefcase?)

- ✔ In the case of special occasions, what type of event you're attending

Every environment and every situation has a dress code. You don't have to do much decision-making if you work as an astronaut, professional boxer, firefighter, or salvage diver, for example. But you may need a word or two of guidance if you're headed for your first day of work in a high-rise office down-town, or if an invitation reads "black-tie attire." The general guidelines that I give in this chapter can help you dress properly for whatever occasion you are attending. I work my way through the most relaxed fashion day — casual day, for example — to "white tie," the ultimate in formality, clearing up confusion and helping you avoid fashion faux pas every step of the way.

Getting a Sense of the Situation

Sense is the key word when it comes to deciding what attire is appropriate for a particular situation. Your own common sense should be a pretty good guide. A factory has a different dress code than a business office, for exam-ple. You may be a punch press operator during the early shift and a car salesman in the evening. You may be called upon to escort your son's kindergarten class to the zoo one day and address the Rotary Club the next day. In these situations, you can use your common sense to sort out the wardrobe requirements for each environment.

The level of difficulty rises when it comes to dressing for a special event. In these cases, it is certainly appropriate to ask the host what would be proper attire (in case it's not specified in the invitation, either verbally or written).

Sorting out the meaning of "casual"

Even if you have a good understanding of the official definitions of such terms as *formal, semi-formal, business casual, informal,* and *casual,* the person who wrote the invitation or decided on the dress code may have had something else in mind. Later in this chapter, I have a thorough discussion of formal and semi-formal dress; this section tackles the tricky term *casual* and its even trickier cousin, *business casual.*

Most people use the term *casual* to describe their weekend wardrobes. The difficulty arises when your employer declares a "Casual Friday" or you get an invitation to a "casual" event. Here are abbreviated explanations of these two terms as they apply to most business and social occasions:

✔ **Business casual** varies from company to company but generally allows men to wear button-down shirts, without a tie, and khaki pants. Women can wear neat pants, a shirt, and a cardigan sweater, for example. Whatever your company's rules may be, make sure to stay well within the boundaries.

On the very first "casual Friday" declared by a public relations firm I know well, a female vice president showed up for work in leopard-print pants with a black sweater and loads of jangly costume jewelry. Although the woman didn't outwardly violate the "business casual" specifications — pants and sweaters for women were fine — the way she interpreted it made everyone in the office uncomfortable, and her superior had to have a private conversation with her.

✔ **Casual,** as the term is used on invitations, generally calls for sport coats for men. Open-necked shirts are fine, as neckties are not required. Women can wear informal pant suits or long or short skirts with blouses or sweaters. If the affair turns out to be more casual than you guessed, men may be permitted to remove their jackets.

No matter what the occasion, military personnel on active duty are always permitted to wear their specified uniform of the day. Officers have formal uniforms and follow military dress code rules.

You never know who will ring the doorbell

Every once in a while, the newspaper personal advice columns carry a question about doing housework in the altogether. The answer is always along the lines of "Different strokes for different folks" or "You can do whatever you wish in your own residence." If you agree, I hope that you don't get an unexpected delivery, a surprise visit from your preschool child's teacher, or a drop-in from Aunt Ida, who just happened to be in the neighborhood.

Do yourself and the world a favor: Put on reasonably presentable clothes as soon as you get moving on days when you don't work. You'll feel a lot better about yourself if you have to run out to the supermarket or receive a surprise visit.

Be aware that casual at the office does not mean the same thing as casual at home. Well-worn tennis shoes, raggedy blue jeans, and tee-shirts with wise-guy messages are for playing outside, not working in an office. Even if you're not wearing a business suit, your attire should reflect that you respect yourself and your coworkers.

Beyond that, you may want to consider a few subtleties that can affect your choice of outfit. For example, to impress your boss, wear an outfit that suits the projects at hand. You can do desk work and computer work in neat slacks and a well-pressed shirt or blouse. In other words, for the purposes of your career, treat Casual Day as if it were an ordinary day without a necktie or business suit.

Dealing with unexpected wardrobe clashes

Everyone has been caught in an unexpected wardrobe clash. A good example of this is when a high-ranking government official visits a community hit by a flood. The senator or cabinet member is dressed in a conservative business suit, and everyone else is filling sandbags and helping older folks into rowboats. Next thing you know, the VIP is wading in knee-deep water, hoisting a sandbag for the photographers and looking noble in a sopping wet jacket and tie. A perfect case of shrugging off concerns about proper dress and behaving correctly for the situation.

Maintaining your poise is a lot harder when the clash is in the opposite direction. For whatever reason, you're wearing your most casual outfit when you get trapped in a high-level committee meeting. Etiquette demands that the others ignore your improper clothing. Let etiquette rule the moment. Make a short comment about not having expected to attend the function, and then hold your head high.

Planning for after-work engagements

After-work engagements often bring about tricky wardrobe questions, particularly for women. Men can easily move from the office to a cocktail party in the same suit and tie, provided the shirt and tie have made it through the day without becoming overly wrinkled or stained. For women, however, what is dazzling at an after-hours "happy hour" date is usually unsuitable for general office wear.

The solution is to bring along alternate clothing, such as a dressy top or sweater to pair with the skirt from the suit you're wearing to the office that day, protected by a garment bag and stored in your car or in a closet in the office used by employees only. A dressier pair of shoes, a change of jewelry or the addition of a scarf, and a more dramatic shade of lipstick can completely change your daytime look. When the workday is done, simply find a private place to transform yourself. With a little advance planning, you can find clever ways to blend your business and after-hours wardrobes.

Balancing Good Taste with Forward Fashion

One of the biggest areas of confusion when it comes to wardrobe is finding a balance between what's in fashion and what's good taste. One common error is to mistake "flashy" for "fashionable." Being the arbiter of good taste is a tough job, but somebody has to leaf through all those full-page, full-color ads from fashion houses and cosmetics companies and help ordinary citizens decide what's right for heading off to a niece's wedding or a department picnic. (Those TV shots of models sashaying down runways are exhibits of the outer limits of the imaginations of a handful of designers who don't really expect their "show garments" to become standards in a typical office or social environment.)

Pointing out the bear traps of dressing is a lot easier than making up a list of the right stuff. Try to remember a few of these pointers the next time you're having trouble making up your mind about what to wear:

- **Stay within the economic range of the group.** By all means attend the PTA meeting, but don't show up in your full-length mink.

- **Accessorize appropriately.** You may have a drawer full of accessory jewelry, but you don't have to wear all of it at once. And save the family treasures for a genuine dress-up affair. A huge diamond ring looks a bit out of place at the beach.

Body art and other adornments

Body art is a fancy term for tattoos. There was a time when only tough guys who rode motorcycles had tattoos, but nowadays lots of kindly grandmothers are riding motorcycles, and plenty of people have tattoos on various parts of their bodies.

Although getting a tattoo is a personal choice, it's important to know when displaying it might make people uncomfortable. If you work in a creative field, such as advertising, graphic design, or Web design, you may well fit in just fine. A law firm, however, is likely to be another story.

Before getting a tattoo, carefully consider the future implications. Even if you're a college student now and you can't fathom wearing a suit every day, you might thank yourself someday if you choose to put your tattoo in a place that wouldn't be seen when you wear business clothing.

Similarly, earrings used to be a fashion accessory limited to girls and women and, well, earlobes. Then piercing extended to other parts of the body, and to men as equally as women. Again, body piercing is a personal choice, but your guiding consideration must be your long-range future. Something that appeals to you while you are a high school student may seem quite out of place when you become president of, say, a multinational publishing company.

✔ **Get fashion advice from an "expert" you trust.** Ask the sales clerk in a large department store for guidance. See if your hairdresser has a suggestion for that special reception. Ask what other people in the same group intend to wear.

✔ **Be sensitive to regional differences.** While you'll generally blend in wearing all black clothing in Manhattan, you may feel like a fish out of water wearing that outfit in Omaha. Particularly when traveling to a far-away social affair, do some careful questioning about suitable attire.

✔ **Be careful to respect local standards of fashion and modesty, especially in countries other than your own.** If you're going to be remembered for showing something, let it be the latest dance step rather than an eye-popping outfit. When in doubt, and when headed to a high-level affair overseas, check with the U.S. embassy in that country for advice.

✔ **Don't avoid social events just because you "don't have a thing to wear."** Check out thrift shops. Check with rental wear agencies. Wear your nicest outfit as many times as necessary. Anyone can spend money; prove that *you* can have a good time without going into debt.

Regardless of your wardrobe difficulties, remember that they invited *you*, not your outfit.

Top Hat and White Gloves: Formal and Semi-Formal Occasions

If everyone used the same terms to refer to the same standards of dress and conduct, social events would be much less confusing. When it comes to attire, the three main categories of formality are *formal, semi-formal,* and *casual,* but that doesn't even begin to describe all the variants that you're likely to encounter.

There's nothing more disconcerting than discovering that you've dressed incorrectly for a function. If you receive an invitation that gives no indication of dress requirements, telephone your host and ask.

A considerate host will help guests sort out the confusion by adding a few extra words to the invitation. If you have a question about proper dress, by all means contact the host, confess your uncertainty, and get some official guidance. And remember to include your escort in that inquiry. Gentlemen, especially, are most appreciated when they can tell their dates the specific facts regarding what to wear.

 Use the material in this section as a starting point for your wardrobe selection and your expectations of the "flavor" of the affair, and remember that your best efforts to conform will carry the day. Whether the invitation specifies formal, semi-formal, or casual, the purpose of the event is to provide a good time for all who attend. Put on your party duds, get there on time, and enjoy yourself.

What exactly does semi-formal mean?

For men:

- Good-quality dark suit
- White shirt and dark tie
- Dark socks and black shoes

The muddled world of informal

The invitation says "informal." What does that mean? Unfortunately, hosts often interpret the term differently. Strictly speaking, though, informal implies dark suits for gentlemen and cocktail dresses for ladies.

For women:

- ✔ Ballet or cocktail-length dress in a nice fabric such as crepe, silk, or brocade; a dressy suit (sometimes called a "cocktail" or "theater" suit, that is made of wool or crepe with rhinestone buttons, for example, or satin or velvet); or a long skirt or long dress

- ✔ Accessories, which can include a small cocktail bag that is beaded or made of silk, satin, or brocade and dressy sandals or pumps

Note: Active duty military personnel and others on duty in any of the uniformed services are always permitted to wear their dress uniforms to social affairs, regardless of the degree of formality.

The rigid rules of formal occasions

Formal affairs include both "black-tie" and "white-tie" evenings. Unless you move in high government or diplomatic circles, your chances of dealing with a full white-tie occasion may be slim. Big-city award ceremonies and charitable fundraisers sometimes are designated as formal, but many of those affairs actually fall into the semi-formal category.

In most social circles, a notation of *formal* implies tuxedos for gentlemen and formal gowns for ladies. If the formal occasion is related to your professional life, play it safe. Colorful ties and cummerbunds are not businesslike, and neither are low-cut, slinky, sexy dresses. Remember, at a business function, good taste and decorum are essential to your reputation.

When it comes to formal occasions, there are considerations for hosts and there are considerations for guests. When everyone is reading from the same script, the event is sure to be a smashing success.

Making sure that formal means formal

Be very careful about using the word *formal* on an invitation or reading it when you open your mail. Formal attire is the prevailing uniform of the head waiter in a fancy restaurant or the conductor of a symphony orchestra. Formal is what you see at the weddings of princes and princesses. If you know for sure that the occasion is formal, visit a company in the formal wear rental business and take notes. You'll probably have to rent an outfit — or at the very least, a few items to round out your wardrobe.

As a good host, try to be specific in your invitation. If you wish to see gentlemen in tuxedos, "Dinner Jackets and Formals" may help your guests understand your intentions.

Disaster: Your outfit is wrong!

What do you do if you show up at a fancy dinner in a business suit and find that all other men are wearing tuxedos? Here are a few suggestions:

✔ In a large hotel, run down to the concierge or the bell captain and beg for help. Big hotels have resources to handle most emergencies, including emergency formal wear.

✔ In a large hotel or restaurant, find the catering manager. There may be a waiter's jacket that fits you.

If you get help, be prepared to tip generously for the assistance.

✔ If you can't turn things around in a few minutes, give up and take your date to a nice restaurant. You don't want to have 1,000 correctly dressed couples remembering you as the oddball.

Note to men: *Never* attempt to convince a woman to attend an affair for which she is not properly attired, not even if your career depends on it. Rock stars, published poets, and a few other dignitaries can sometimes get away with far-out or improper dress, but ordinary citizens will only suffer.

Knowing the right thing to wear for a black-tie affair

For men:

- ✔ Tuxedo (dinner jacket)
- ✔ White dress shirt, cuff links, and studs
- ✔ Cummerbund and bow tie
- ✔ Black silk socks
- ✔ Black patent leather shoes

For women:

- ✔ Long, short, or three-quarter-length evening gown
- ✔ Sheer hose
- ✔ Peau-de-soie pumps (that is, heavy silk or silk-like material), dressy high heels, or evening sandals

The right thing to wear for a white-tie affair

For men:

- ✔ Tailcoat of black wool and silk
- ✔ White wing shirt, cuff links, and studs
- ✔ White bow tie

> ✔ White cummerbund or white vest
>
> ✔ Black patent shoes or dress oxfords with black silk hose
>
> ✔ White gloves (optional)
>
> ✔ Black silk top hat (optional)

For women:

> ✔ Full-skirted, floor-length grand ball gown or long, straight gown
>
> ✔ Sheer hose
>
> ✔ Peau-de-soie pumps, dressy high heels, or evening sandals
>
> ✔ Long, white gloves (optional)
>
> ✔ A wrap (optional)
>
> ✔ Jewelry

Plan ahead for wardrobe rental

Say that you don't happen to own a tuxedo or formal outfit. You're going to rent the right wardrobe. Remember that making arrangements takes time, and try to factor in at least a day or two to accommodate unforeseen emergencies. Two weeks is not an unreasonable lead time for renting an outfit. Citywide affairs may require you to make arrangements a full month in advance.

The tuxedo: Variations on a theme

The tuxedo is named after the Tuxedo Park Country Club of New York, where it was first introduced in 1886. The Oxford English Dictionary defines *tuxedo* this way: "In full, tuxedo coat, jacket. A short jacket without tails, for formal wear; a dinner-jacket."

Bravo for the dictionary. But if a tuxedo qualifies as formal wear, how would you categorize a jacket with tails? The same listing in the dictionary quotes a writer in 1925 as saying, "Dress coats and tuxedo jackets were removed." What in the world is a *dress coat*?

Nowadays, the word *tuxedo* implies a dinner jacket with prominent lapels, trousers with a silken stripe down the side, a white shirt fastened with decorative "studs," a bow tie, and a vest or a wide sash called a *cummerbund*. But even within this description, there are jackets and bow ties of various colors, cummerbunds and vests in decorative fabrics, and dress shirts with a variety of collars. The only constant seems to be the shoes, which are traditionally black and glossy.

Women sometimes forget that rental companies also provide dresses for formal occasions. Instead of making a large investment in something that you'll wear only once, it may be more sensible to rent a perfectly gorgeous dress for the evening or to purchase a gown from an upscale consignment shop.

If you plan to purchase a fancy dress from a well-respected store, tell the sales representative the name of the affair you will be attending. High-class stores will make sure that no two women attending the same event show up in the same outfit.

Confess your unfamiliarity to the clerk at the rental establishment. Describe the event. Bring along the invitation. Then accept the expert's suggestions. Unless you're a veteran at this sort of thing, don't get too creative with far-out colors or patterns. Usually, the store personnel will know about formal events in town and will have a good feel for the best outfit.

While you're engaged in negotiations with the rental agency, make sure that you find out when the outfit must be returned and what extra charges will be assessed for spilled soup, scuffed shoes, and the like.

Rental agencies also sell outfits. If you find yourself invited to several formal functions, it may be sensible to purchase a wardrobe.

Never bypass the rental agency's offer to let you try on your outfit. They'll make sure that it fits right and will alter it for you if it doesn't. There's nothing worse than pulling on a pair of striped trousers at the last minute and discovering that you can't zip 'em up!

Formal attire: Don't get creative!

As a member of a wedding party, an honored guest at the head table, one of the presenters at an award ceremony, or one of the select few at any truly formal affair, follow the instructions of the host or the event chairman. Go to the specified rental agency, be on time for group fittings, and conform. And no matter how strange the outfit may feel, pretend that you've been dressing that way all your life. There's nothing that hurts the ears of a host more than a casual reference to a "monkey suit."

Part III

Communicating with Care

The 5th Wave   By Rich Tennant

Dear Joe and Heather,

Please excuse the hospital stationery, but I wanted to thank you for inviting me to your inline skating/backyard trampoline/pommel horse party...

In this part . . .

You just can't avoid communicating with others. And whether you're small-talking with new acquaintances, writing thank-you notes to family and friends, composing business letters, or e-mailing to strangers who live across the globe, each mode of communication has its own set of etiquette guidelines. The chapters in this part can help you navigate your way through any form of communication with your manners intact. I even include detailed information about new technologies (think of cellular phones, pagers, Internet chat rooms, and the like) to help you mind your manners in these perhaps unfamiliar waters.

Chapter 8

Communicating in the Business World

*N*ot only is clear communication one of the best ways to ensure that your career advances, but it also ensures that your office is a pleasant place to work and that everyone functions efficiently. Pleasant, clear communication that takes the rules of etiquette into account helps to create a positive environment in which people can work to their full potential, without the confusion and unintentional errors that miscommunication engenders.

In this chapter, you can discover how to make your point in business clearly and concisely. You can find out how to communicate to a group while following the formal courtesies of conferences and meetings. I describe the latest etiquette do's and don'ts of electronic business communications, including the phone and e-mail. Finally, you'll see how the written word can still be the best way to accomplish many of your business goals.

Meeting and Greeting

Generally speaking, in formal business situations, your host meets, greets, and introduces you to other guests. In less formal situations, people frequently don the role of host for their immediate circle and facilitate introductions. In business situations, introductions may have been made at the beginning of a business meeting much earlier in the day, and it may be necessary to make reintroductions before beginning a meal. If you enter into a circle where introductions have already been made, it is always appropriate to introduce yourself.

Making introductions

In social situations, a man is traditionally introduced to a woman. Not so in the business world! In business, introductions are based on a person's rank and position in a company. Whether that person is a man or woman, young or old, makes no difference. Whoever is the highest-ranking person is introduced to everyone else in order of their position.

The only exception is when you're dealing with a client. In that situation, you always introduce the client first, even if the person from your company ranks higher than your client. For example, you would introduce a vice president of your client's company, Nina Duseja, to the president of your company, Chris Berenson, in this way: "Ms. Duseja, I'd like you to meet the president of Acme Graphics, Chris Berenson."

When you're introducing two people who are of equal rank in the corporate hierarchy, introduce the one you know less well to the one you know better.

If you're in a group and you're making many introductions, it's helpful to give people a little bit of information about each other to help them start a conversation. You don't want to introduce two people and then walk away, leaving them with no information about each other's position or how they might relate to each other. You might say, "Mr. Shaffer, I'd like to introduce Guy Morel, president of XYZ Shipping. Mr. Morel, I think I mentioned once that Mr. Shaffer is the president of our company and used to serve on the international shipping council as well."

In a large group, introduce one person to a few people at a time. This way, you won't overwhelm anyone with too many new names and faces.

There are always situations in which you need to introduce yourself. For example, if you're passing through your company's lobby and you see a new member of your client's company, you should stop and introduce yourself and your role. You might extend your hand and say, "Hi, I'm Mike Samuels. I'm the account executive on the Stainless Steel Council business and wanted to stop to introduce myself." At that point, the new member of your client's company should introduce herself as well: "Hi, Mike. I'm Sandy Durkin, and I just started with the Council on Monday. How do you do?"

When you're leading a meeting, it's more efficient to introduce people around the table or allow each person to introduce himself or herself to the group. Say you're in charge of the first meeting of a planning committee for the

Girl Scouts. You have a disparate group of people, all volunteers, coming from all sorts of backgrounds. In order for the committee to work efficiently, everyone needs to know one another, including each person's profession and how he or she will contribute to the committee. As leader of the meeting, your place is to begin with introductions:

> "I'd like to welcome everyone to the first session of the Girl Scout Council's planning committee. We have an exciting task before us, which is to lay out the activities that our scout troops will be tackling this year. We're going to need each of your talents and energy to accomplish this task. On my left is Michelle Palko, who is a graphic designer and will be helping us put together our brochure when we have the year's activities laid out. Next to her is Stacey Jordan, who is a camping guide and knows a lot about outdoor activities in our area. . . ."

One of the greatest fears about making introductions is forgetting a person's name — either when you're about to introduce that person or after you were introduced minutes before and you completely blank out when it's time to take leave of that person. The second greatest fear is mispronouncing a person's name. The third is hearing a name but not understanding it. Don't panic. Don't mutter or try to duck out of the conversation or the opportunity to introduce two people. These things happen all the time.

Everyone has problems remembering names now and again. However, if you have *a lot* of trouble with names or are in a job that requires you to remember lots of names (a minister or rabbi, for example), you might try repeating the person's name a few times to yourself after you're introduced. Or you might use the person's name immediately in the conversation after an introduction. It also helps to turn around and introduce the new person to someone you know.

If you heard the name but you didn't understand it, simply ask the person to repeat the name. If you have a name that's easily mispronounced, you might jump in and help the person making the introduction. It's helpful to find something that your name rhymes with or something people can visualize. Should you mispronounce someone's name, simply apologize, ask for the correct pronunciation, repeat the name, and continue with your introduction.

If — *quelle horreur!* — you forget someone's name when you're about to make an introduction, don't make a scene. Simply say, "I've momentarily forgotten your name." The person should jump in and say, "It's Bob Clinton." You can say, "Of course, Bob. I'd like to introduce Cheryl Damien . . . ." It's only a big deal if you make it a big deal.

If you've been introduced to someone previously, allow yourself to be reintroduced if you're not recognized. Don't make an issue out of it. Never walk up to someone and ask, "Remember me?" Always stop and reintroduce yourself.

Business card etiquette

Americans can thank the Japanese for the lesson in business card etiquette. For decades, the custom was to accept a person's business card in the course of introductions, glance at it, and slide it into a shirt pocket. Then Japanese business people began to make frequent appearances in American circles, showing us how to make a great impression by establishing business card–reading protocol. In the United States, we're not quite as formal as our Asian tutors, but think of the way this ritual can play out in your next formal meeting:

1. When handed a business card, read it as if it were a best-selling novel.

2. Say the name out loud: "Alfred B. Marquez. Did I say it correctly?"

3. Acknowledge the company: "We're very pleased to have an opportunity to do business with a company as well-respected as Widgets International."

4. Mention the job title: "You must have a great deal to do as the manager of engineering. I, too, am an engineer."

This process beats the daylights out of taking the other person's business card and slipping it into your pocket. You may not get around to all the details of this little ritual, but at the very least, take the time to read everything on the card and express your gratitude for the information. And remember to treat the card as a gift — don't deface it in front of the giver.

Using titles

Titles are very important when you're making introductions in a business situation, because the title puts the person into context for others — is this a marketing person, a salesperson, an engineer, or an accountant? This information is critical to everyone's comfort with one another.

Never assume that you can call someone by his or her first name automatically. You should use a person's title until you're invited to use the first name; stick with Mr., Ms., Dr., and General. If you're not sure which variation — Mrs., Miss, or Ms. — a woman prefers, just ask. However, if you know that the woman is a physician, a Ph.D., or a military officer, use the appropriate title.

Of course, people often begin using first names very quickly, especially in the U.S. This practice is fine, but still, make sure that the person invites you to do so first. Let the host or your superior set the example and follow his or her lead. When in doubt, err on the side of formality.

Shaking hands and making eye contact: Nonverbal communication

In this fast-paced, high-tech world, people tend to forget the importance of simple human contact and kindnesses, such as remembering people's names, trying to make a good first impression, and greeting people with a firm handshake.

When you are introduced to someone, you should always stand and shake hands. A handshake is the physical greeting that goes with the verbal introduction. Not shaking hands is a clear form of rejection and is very insulting to the other person. In America, it's expected that you will offer a firm (but not bone-crushing) handshake and that you will make eye contact. A firm handshake with good eye contact communicates self-confidence.

If nametags are worn, they should be placed on the right shoulder, because that's where your eye goes when you shake hands.

It's important that both men and women to learn when to shake hands and how to shake hands confidently, as the handshake is used in both social and business situations. You are expected to shake hands in the following situations:

✔ When meeting someone and when saying good-bye

✔ When renewing an acquaintance

✔ When someone enters your home or office

✔ When greeting a host and being introduced to people

✔ When meeting someone you already know outside your work or home

✔ When ending a transaction or leaving a business or social event

For an appropriate handshake in American etiquette — for men *and* women — you should grip the other person's hand so that the webs of your thumbs meet. Shake firmly just a couple of times and end the handshake cleanly, before the introduction is over. You perform this motion from the elbow, not the shoulder. A good handshake is held for three or four seconds.

In some situations, shaking hands can be awkward. If you are introduced to someone when your hands are full or you are carrying files or other packages, for example, don't try to rearrange everything. Simply nod your head as you respond to the introduction. If you're having cocktails, hold your drink in your left hand while introductions are going around. Later on, you can switch to your right hand. You don't want to fumble with your drink or offer someone a wet or cold hand to shake! If you're wearing gloves as part of formal attire, always remove them before shaking hands. (The same goes for wearing gloves outdoors — you should take them off unless the weather is bitterly cold.)

Avoiding other body contact

In business situations in the U.S., body contact beyond handshakes is inappropriate, regardless of the closeness of the relationship you have with an individual. You and your friend at work may feel comfortable hugging or exchanging a kiss, but this behavior may (and often does) make others uncomfortable. And physical contact with someone in the workplace who is not an intimate friend easily may be construed as harassment.

Excessive physical contact includes patting, hugging, putting an arm around the shoulder, kissing, holding hands, or touching any part of a person's body for emphasis. Don't do any of these in any business situation.

Good morning!

The world of courteous behavior reserves a special corner for actions that are "nice." Etiquette does not require you to issue a friendly greeting to everyone you encounter, but most people, including perfect strangers, consider those greetings to be unexpected and, well, *nice*.

In a hotel, for example, as you make your way toward your first appointment, you can certainly give a friendly nod and a "Good morning" to the people you pass on your way to the elevator. Once inside the elevator, a cheerful "Good morning" is a lot nicer than a silent scowl. The hotel doorman will appreciate your greeting along with, perhaps, a comment on the weather. And when you enter a taxi, saying "Good morning" sounds a lot nicer than just sliding into the back seat and barking out, "Grand Central Station."

On the job, these timely greetings humanize the workplace. Once you've said "Good morning" to a person, you've paved the way for a silent nod as you pass each other several more times that day.

Using the other person's name, if you know it, makes a greeting much more effective. The president of your company may say "Good morning" right back to you, but you'll feel much better if she says "Good morning, Leonard." Remembering names is a lot like playing golf. The more you practice, the better you'll do. Try to use names as often as you can. And speak up. A mumbled greeting is almost as bad as no greeting at all.

When you don't use a person's name because you don't *know* the person's name, say this: "You know, we've been greeting each other for a long time, but I don't think we were ever introduced. My name is Joe Smith. What's yours?"

Addressing Your Staff, Your Colleagues, and Your Boss

If you have a staff, it's your job to make it clear how everyone should address each other. Whether you decide to use Mr. and Ms. or to operate on a first-name basis, setting ground rules helps to establish cordial and respectful relationships.

If you're a junior person on staff and you're unsure how to address your superiors, always err on the side of formality until you're informed otherwise. It's better to call your boss Mr. Jones and sound respectful than to automatically assume that you can call him Doug and risk looking presumptuous. Even if you've been invited to use a first name, don't assume too much coziness with your boss. In American business, relationships are based on rank, and rank should always be observed and acknowledged.

In a group of outsiders, a boss should always acknowledge the presence of staff members and make sure that they're introduced to the group. If you're introducing a client to your administrative assistant, make sure to introduce the client in the same way that the client should be addressed. For example, if you expect your assistant to call your client "Mrs. Fox," you should introduce her as such. Use your assistant's last name as well, even if you normally use his or her first name.

Yes, people like to be informal in the U.S. Still, you should avoid using nicknames in business settings. You may well make Sparky look unprofessional in front of a client or superior.

Mannerly Survival at Meetings and Conferences

Meetings and conferences may masquerade as a chance to update the status of a project or a chance to catch up on industry developments, but they're really used as a way to learn about and measure other people. That's why it's important to communicate by using all the right verbal and nonverbal signals. This section tells you what those signals are and how to use them.

How to succeed in business by being a great conversationalist

In business, as in social situations, people appreciate someone who knows how to make the conversation flow pleasantly. How can you become one of them?

✔ Limit your conversation during business hours. (It's fine to chat all you like after work.)

✔ Do not succumb to conversation faux pas by dropping names or discussing who you saw in the boss's office.

✔ Don't brag about your dream three-month assignment in Hawaii.

✔ Don't ask about another person's age, weight, or personal possessions, such as clothing or jewelry.

✔ Speak clearly and use proper grammar (but don't be a nuisance by correcting everyone else's mistakes). Don't use cliches or slang.

Whatever you say, remember that a business conversation is never kept in confidence. If you don't want something to be passed along, don't say it — and if you do, don't be shocked if it comes back to haunt you.

Speaking up at a meeting

Meetings provide you with an opportunity to shine in front of your superiors and your peers. Here are some tips that can help you do so:

✔ Always think before you speak, and weigh your words carefully.

✔ Don't interrupt when someone else is speaking, no matter how wrong you think that person may be or how important you consider your addition to the discussion.

✔ Always smile at colleagues and be friendly and open.

✔ Avoid confrontations and harsh words. It's always better to use positive language. Instead of, "You're wrong. If you took time to read the report, you would know . . . ," say , "I disagree because it seems to me that . . . ."

✔ Be gracious in acknowledging your coworkers' contributions by using the word *we* when referring to your department or company's work and position. Remember that if you take credit for things when they're going well, you must take the blame if they take a downturn.

One of the big etiquette faux pas in business today is acting rushed. This is particularly evident in a meeting, when people look at their watches, clearly distracted, which means that they're not listening. If you're that pressed for time, you should decline the meeting invitation.

Going beyond the words you use

You can demonstrate your good manners in quite a few ways. When you go beyond the words you use and pay attention to the other details of meetings and conferences, you impress others with your sensitivity and consideration. If you haven't thought about the following details, try to imagine the effect that they have on you and others in a meeting setting:

- **Seating height:** Equal eyes mean equal people. That's just a cute way of saying that differences in seating height reinforce differences in authority. When the boss sits up on a platform and everyone else must look up, the meeting is definitely not a gathering of equals. Look around at "eye height" and make sure that no one has an odd chair that sits low.

- **Blinding light coming in through windows:** Being blinded by the light is especially problematic in one-on-one meetings. If one person has to deal with direct sunlight coming in through a window and the other has his or her back to the light, the squinter is at a disadvantage. Good manners call for you to pay attention to details of lighting.

- **A desk as a barrier:** Many executives have comfortable chairs in their offices and conduct conversations while all parties are seated informally. When you sit behind your desk and deal with others, you may be sending a signal that you wish to remain distanced from the other parties. Think about this when you hold a meeting in your office.

- **Refreshments:** Offer to provide coffee, water, or some other ordinary on-the-job refreshment for everyone at the meeting, or forgo a refreshment for yourself.

- **Interruptions:** Try not to take telephone calls during meetings. Switch your pager to vibrate. Wave off others coming toward you for your signature. You're much more effective when you can concentrate on the business at hand.

Talking Business: The Telephone

So many of us work in front of a computer screen all day that we tend to forget the usual social graces — which include things we learned as children, such as how to answer and make telephone calls politely.

Every time you make or receive a telephone call at work, you're representing your company. And many times, the first contact a person has with a company is over the telephone, so the impression you make on the phone may be a lasting one. Therefore, you want to sound professional. This section gives you some tips on answering and placing business calls.

Answering your own telephone

The phone rings so often these days that it's easy to slide into bad habits, such as picking up the phone and answering with a brusque "Yeah?" Even if the phone seems to ring every five minutes, you must be professional each time you pick it up.

Because the telephone limits you to sending only verbal communication signals, you need to make sure that those signals are loud and clear. You have to convey both your personality and your attitude to the listener through your voice alone. Speaking in a flat, monotonous voice makes you sound bored or depressed. Speaking too loudly and trying to inject too many inflections, on the other hand, may make you seem anxious. The ideal telephone voice communicates self-confidence and assurance.

This may seem hard to believe, but how you look when you answer the phone strongly affects how you sound to the person on the other end of the line. If you're slumped over paperwork at your desk, you will sound closed-off and preoccupied. If you're leaning back in your chair with your feet up on your desk, you will sound very relaxed (perhaps *too* relaxed). If you sit up straight in your chair with your feet squarely on the floor, you will sound "together," and that energy will come across over the telephone. When answering the phone, try to sound enthusiastic (or at least alert).

Smiling as you answer the phone is reflected in your tone of voice. Try it and see how positively people react.

Try not to let your phone ring on and on — you should answer it after two rings at most. Doing so makes you appear efficient, and the caller will feel important if you answer immediately. Always identify yourself with your name and department, plus a warm greeting for your caller.

Never use slang or words that are inappropriate to business, such as *honey, dear,* and *sweetheart.* Articulate properly (for example, say "yes" instead of "yeah"), and don't mumble into the phone.

When a call is for someone else

If a caller has reached the wrong person, assist him or her in getting to the right party. Don't shout for the intended recipient of the call, and don't slam down the phone. If you can't find the person, don't leave the caller waiting; take and deliver a message.

Answering someone else's telephone

These days, most phones seem to be answered by voice mail. It's wonderful to get a voice on the other end of the line! If you answer someone else's telephone, you should follow some special rules of etiquette:

✔ **Answer as promptly as possible.** Give the name of the person whose phone you're answering and then yours: "Ms. Kaufmann's office, Crystal White speaking."

✔ **If the person is unavailable, take down the caller's name, telephone number, and message.** Say something like this: "I'm sorry, Ms. Kaufmann is unavailable at the moment. May I take your name and number so that she can call you back?" When you take a message, check the spelling of the person's name and company to make sure that it's accurate. On the message, note the date as well.

✔ **Don't screen calls.** Doing so is terribly rude. If the person is unavailable, say so immediately. There's nothing more awful than asking for a caller's name, putting the caller on hold, and then coming back on the line to say, "I'm sorry, Ms. Kaufmann is out of the office." The caller will know that you're screening calls. If someone doesn't want to take calls, he or she should be "in a meeting" or "away from the office."

✔ **If the person is in but is on another line, ask the caller if he or she would like to hold.** Make sure to check back with the caller every 20 seconds so that you don't leave him or her hanging on endlessly. If the wait is going to be longer than a minute, let the caller know and suggest that the person return the call at a later time.

Unfortunately, you may have to handle a rude or angry caller from time to time. Do your best to defuse the situation by being courteous. Let an angry person calm down before trying to discuss the situation, and don't lose your own temper. Know, however, that you have every right to hang up on someone who uses profanity.

If you find yourself on the line with a caller who talks on and on, you may take the initiative to end the call by summarizing the point of the call and thanking the person for calling. You might say, "I will make sure to have Ms. Kaufmann call you back when she returns from New York tomorrow, and I'll let her know that you'd like a copy of that video. It's been a pleasure speaking with you, Mr. Talbot."

Or simply say that you're busy — politely tell the person that you have a project deadline, for example. Remember, this is business time, not social time, and you don't have to feel guilty about cutting social conversations short. (This goes for someone stopping by your office to chat, too.)

Other quick telephone tips

- If you dial a wrong number, apologize and hang up.

- Do not eat, drink, smoke, or shuffle papers when on the phone.

- Speak directly into the mouthpiece.

- When your administrative assistant makes a call for you and the person is in, be on the line when he or she picks up the phone.

- When answering a call and speaking on the phone, smile. Even though smiling may seem awkward, your voice is actually more pleasant when you smile while talking.

Placing a call

When you make a call, identify yourself and your company affiliation immediately: "Hello, this is Samuel Dixon from Lion Management." Don't feel put out if you're asked to state your business. Just explain succinctly: "I'm calling Ms. Cartland regarding the photo shoot that we have scheduled for tomorrow."

If someone calls you while you're waiting for your first call to go through, tell the caller that you will call him or her back. The person you called always has priority. You can say to the second caller, "Hello, Bill, I'm on the other line. May I get back to you in just a few minutes?" This way, poor Bill isn't left listening to a dead receiver on the other line.

If the person you're calling is unavailable, leave your name, company name, and telephone number. Unless you have a very common surname, it's considerate to spell your name. If you've tried to reach this person previously, ask when would be a good time to call. However, it's not appropriate to ask where the person is.

Make sure to end the call on a strong, positive note, because people remember longest what they hear last.

If you get a person's voice mail, give the date, the time you called, your name, your phone number, and a short message. Here's a good example: "Hi, Jim, this is Shirley Jones at Xenex Company. It's Wednesday at noon and I'm calling to check on the status of our paper order. Please call me at 555-1212. Thanks!"

Even though good etiquette requires you to return all phone calls on the day they were received, do not call back on the same day if the person you're trying to reach doesn't return your call. The only exception to this rule is if the situation is an emergency.

CAUTION

Personal calls

Avoid making personal phone calls at work. If you absolutely *must* make a personal call, keep it short.

When making a personal call to a friend who's at work, consider the time of day. When your friend answers the phone, ask if this is a convenient time to call, and offer to call back at a better time if it isn't. Also, be very polite to anyone who answers the phone when you call a friend's place of business. Remember, how you act reflects on your friend and can affect his or her business reputation.

Handling faxes, voice mail, and e-mail

First faxes, and then voice mail and e-mail, radically changed how people do business. Along with the good things that these technologies brought came new etiquette pitfalls.

You need to remember one common warning about these means of communication: What you say or write can easily be accessed by someone else. Although it's uncommon that a business associate might listen in on your business call, accessing your voice mail may be easy. Someone else can easily pick up your fax messages, and it's easy to read a computer screen over someone else's shoulder. Although there's nothing wrong with sending information back and forth as long as the information is work-related and would not cause problems if other people read it, keep these points in mind:

✔ Write or voice whatever you put into an easily accessible message in business language and tone, keeping in mind that it could be read or heard by someone other than the person for whom it was intended.

✔ If you receive or intercept a message that is intended for someone else, ignore it. Let your good manners stop you from reading or listening any further. Do not repeat any of the information to anyone. If it happens again, notify the parties involved that their messages are being directed incorrectly.

✔ When you send a confidential fax, notify the receiver that the message is coming through so that he or she, or a designate, can be there to pick it up.

✔ Be very careful what you write in e-mail. E-mail messages are often misinterpreted because e-mail allows for no inflections, facial expressions, and so on, and also because people often write messages hastily and fail to phrase the information clearly. Make sure to word your e-mail messages very carefully to minimize this problem. (See Chapter 12 for more information about e-mail etiquette.)

Corresponding in Business Situations

Just like a solid handshake or good phone skills, business correspondence can tell people a lot about you. Anything that you mail out for business is a reflection on your company, so make sure that you do correspond professionally. Follow these simple rules of business correspondence:

- Get the spelling and grammar right. This is perhaps the most important part of sending written correspondence. Choose your words carefully, and be sure to double-check the spelling of the recipient's name, company name, and address, as well as the recipient's title. There's nothing worse than sending your biggest client a thank-you note only to realize after you send it that you spelled his or her name incorrectly!

- Type the letter. To be professional, business letters must be legible. Although the letter itself should be typed, you should sign it by hand, in ink.

- Place the date on the upper right side, with your address either centered on the page or after a space and below the date. Place the recipient's name and address on the left side of the page.

- If you don't know the gender or name of the person to whom you're directing your letter, the appropriate salutation is "Ladies and Gentlemen" or "Dear Madam or Sir."

- When addressing a known person, use the right choice of the following salutations, and end the salutation with a colon rather than a comma:

  - Dear Mr. Jones:

  - Dear Ms. Leiderkranz:

  - Dear Dr. Johnson:

  - Dear General Benning:

When to write, and when to phone?

Write a note in these situations:

- To thank someone

- To acknowledge a gift

- To congratulate someone (on a promotion, on a marriage, or upon acquiring an advanced degree, for example)

- To convey condolences

- To thank someone for a luncheon or dinner invitation

In these situations, a phone call is sufficient:

- To acknowledge an associate's birthday

- To schedule or change a meeting

✔ The most widely appropriate closing line is "Yours truly." Traditionally, "Sincerely" is reserved for social letters.

✔ Whether you save it on your hard drive or in a filing cabinet, make sure to save a copy of the letter for yourself.

The following sections give you some specifics on business letters, from the stationery you write them on to the information you enclose with them.

Selecting stationery

Whatever their business purpose, write your notes on quality 5 x 7 notepaper printed with your company name and your name in small, embossed letters. You can use cream, taupe, or gray paper — nothing bright and flashy unless you're in the entertainment or fashion business. Do *not* write business letters or notes on hotel stationery. Take your own stationery with you or wait until you're back in the office.

All business letters and notes should be signed by hand. Letters with stamped signatures indicate mass production or a lack of interest in the recipient.

Never use company stationery for your own personal business. Likewise, you should make no references to your company affiliation on your personal stationery, although you may use titles such as Attorney at Law or Ph.D.

Using names and titles

In business, you can usually use just the first and last name with no title — for example, Joe Smith. When you're writing to more traditional companies, though, use the more formal form:

✔ **Unmarried women:** Ms.

✔ **Married women:** Mrs. used with the first name and last name ("Mrs. Jane Smith," not "Mrs. Jack Smith") or Ms.

✔ **Widows:** Mrs. used with the first and last name

✔ **Men:** Mr.

When you use a professional title in business correspondence, place it after the surname ("Joe Smith, M.D." or "Jill Black, Ph.D."), except in the salutation ("Dear Dr. Black:").

Business cards

In addition to using your business card as a means of introduction, you can include it as part of your business correspondence. For example, if you're sending flowers or a gift in a business situation, you might attach your card and personalize it with a note on the back. Or you can use your business card when forwarding material or a resume (not your own) to someone. Once again, personalize it with a note.

Because the way people prefer to be addressed is changing these days, it's wise to telephone the office of the person you're writing to and ask how that person prefers to be addressed. For example, some women may insist on Ms., while others may prefer Mrs.

If a businesswoman marries and uses her husband's name or combines both names, she should send announcements to that effect to those with whom she regularly does business.

Sending out business announcement cards

If you have important business news, it is proper to print and mail announcement cards. A card gets the recipient's attention and can effectively announce a change of address, a new phone number, new appointments, or a promotion.

Use good-quality paper stock, with the message either printed or engraved. When putting together the mailing, you may add a personal note if you wish, written on quality 5 x 7 note paper with your company name and your name in small, embossed letters. Envelopes should be typewritten, handwritten, or printed on a word processor. Never use labels!

Business announcements need not be acknowledged by the recipients. However, in the case of a promotion, sending a note of congratulations to the newly promoted person is good etiquette.

Remembering the importance of thank-you notes

Sending thank-you notes is so important — in business as well as in your personal life. Sending a thank-you note not only makes you look good, but it also shows that you respect the person who did something kind for you. Simply *saying* thank you is not enough! You must put your gratitude in writing.

Holiday cards

Holiday cards sent out by businesses have a dual purpose: to greet clients and to remind them of the company's products and services. These cards are usually printed with the name of the firm, but you should sign them in ink and include a brief personal greeting.

If you send a holiday card to a business associate's home, include the spouse on the envelope. If you send a card to the associate's office, you can address it to the client alone.

Writing a thank-you note takes a few minutes at the most and should be done promptly — within 24 hours of receiving a gift or attending an event. Two to three lines is a perfectly acceptable length — you don't need to write several paragraphs. The best thank-you note is short and sweet. Although it may seem like a chore at first, writing thank-you notes will become second nature to you once you get in the habit of doing so. (See Chapter 11 for more on writing thank-you notes.)

If you're feeling at a loss for words in starting a thank-you note, try writing the words "What a (wonderful luncheon, fantastic evening at the theater, thoughtful gift)." The rest of the words should flow from there. Try not to start off with "Thank you"; mention the event or gift or make a general comment first.

The Many Uses of Memos

Yes, there is an etiquette of memos. There are ways to be polite when writing and addressing memos, and there are ways to be overtly hostile. Your skill in choosing the right way to communicate business information will have an important bearing on how you get along with others in your organization.

Should you write a memo or something else?

A memo is a written communication, printed out in hard copy and circulated within an organization. Memos become part of the permanent archives of many individuals and departments, and they last forever. This "permanent" aspect means that memos should be composed with great care. Memos can be used as part of legal proceedings, they can end up in personnel files, they can lead to or discourage promotions, and they can have unintended effects on a wide range of people and projects.

The easiest way to communicate with a coworker is to speak directly with him or her. Memos are best used under these circumstances:

✔ Several, or many, people need the information, and you want everyone to get an identical message. Examples include a schedule of events for the coming week, the agenda for an upcoming meeting, a new policy guideline, a progress report or update, or general departmental instructions to be followed during a supervisor's absence.

✔ An employee has performed well in some assignment, and you wish to make your praise known to the entire department.

✔ New guidelines regarding compliance with company rules or government regulations have been mandated, and everyone needs to be informed of the changes and requirements.

Common courtesy calls for you to include everyone affected by the information in your memo. That same courtesy requires you to submit a copy of your memo to your supervisor. Your memo should have a clear indication of the subject and a list of all recipients.

Your memo may last forever. Study your words carefully before you circulate the memo, and make sure that your comments are impartial, brief, and to the point.

Never direct a memo upward in the chain of command without approval from your supervisor. An example of poor memo etiquette would be a note from an engineering aide to the president of the company.

E-mail instead of hard copy?

In organizations with local area networks and e-mail capabilities, ordinary advisories to coworkers can be communicated through e-mail. This practice saves paper and time, but it also carries some special hazards that must be understood:

✔ E-mail is *never* private. The recipient can forward your message at the touch of a key. Supervisors can obtain access to all e-mail within their departments. Somewhere within the information system, a permanent record of all e-mail is maintained, and even years later, the messages can be used in legal proceedings.

✔ E-mail can be "eavesdropped" by unethical coworkers who obtain the access codes of others or take advantage of a person's temporary absence and scroll through that person's electronic files.

✔ Under certain circumstances, e-mail can be "hacked" by outsiders who may misuse the information for malevolent purposes.

However, there's nothing wrong with sending information back and forth to coworkers, as long as it genuinely affects their responsibilities and would not cause problems if it were read by unintended parties.

Telephone instead of memos?

A brief phone conversation is suitable for many, if not most, communications at work. Phone calls are particularly suited to informal matters such as lunch dates, meeting postponements, and questions that arise in the course of the day. However, memos provide you with a written record of your correspondence, which can be helpful if you need to review the information at a later date.

Structuring your memos properly

Your employer may have a list of rules or suggestions regarding internal memos. If not, here's a handy rundown of memo etiquette:

✔ Include in the header the date you send out the memo, a clear subject line, and a list of recipients.

When writing memos, as when addressing people in person, be sure to use a suitable form of address. If you're on a first-name basis with someone mentioned in your memo, use the person's full name to help others who are on the circulation list. Instead of "Dan," make it "Dan Demming."

✔ Include everyone who needs the information in your memo, plus your supervisor.

✔ Position your memo by presenting a brief background statement — something like, "I've been asked about the situation with our pending order from ABC Machinery. Here's what I know," or perhaps, "I've been asked some questions about staggered lunch hours. This is the way we're going to schedule lunches for the month of June."

✔ Present the information clearly and briefly. Try to make everything fit on one side of a single sheet of paper.

✔ Finish with a cordial statement — something like, "I hope this clears up any confusion," or, "When I learn more about the situation, I'll let everyone know."

Don't yield to the temptation of using a memo as a weapon. Yes, you can probably think of a way to write a nasty memo to a coworker and copy others, but you'll regret it. Your workplace should be a place of cooperation, not an arena for animosity. Long after a conflict has been resolved and good relations have been restored, those ill-considered memos remain in folders, files, and long-term memories. If you have a conflict with a coworker, discuss it first with that person. If you have a more serious problem, discuss it in private with your supervisor. Keep the warfare out of memos (as well as e-mail).

If you must advise your supervisor of a problem, include a suggestion for action. For example, if the copying machine suffers frequent breakdowns, you can suggest the purchase of a new machine and include an estimate of the cost. Supervisors love it when they can hand-write a simple "OK" on your memo, circle your suggestion, and send the memo back to you.

Chapter 9

The New Telephone Etiquette

Technology is changing the rules of telephone etiquette so rapidly that many people don't know what's right or wrong anymore. In the not-too-distant past, telephone etiquette involved answering the phone and taking a written message. Today, technology not only has multiplied our communication options but also has made the number of opportunities for making an etiquette faux pas greater.

Before cell phones came into existence, for example, you had to use a pay phone or wait until you got home to make a call. Before answering machines and Caller ID were widely available, you had to answer your phone and talk to people you didn't necessarily want to talk to. But this is not the case any longer. Today, you can make (or ignore) calls almost anywhere, anytime — and you may be unsure of what etiquette rules now apply.

This chapter explains not only how to answer the phone courteously, but also how to answer critical questions of modern life, such as: Is it inconsiderate to screen calls, or should you answer no matter what? Where and when may you use your cellular phone? Can you call a friend back if the person's number appears on your Caller ID box, but he or she did not leave a message?

Making Calls

The telephone seems to bring out either the best or the worst in people. If people are looking for an opportunity to be rude and unmannerly, the telephone lets them do just that. On the other hand, you can bring out the very best in the person on the other end of the line by going the extra mile in courtesy. You can reinforce your friendships and social contacts by exercising your very best manners, and you can do a world of good for your company by handling callers with sympathy, consideration, and a genuine determination to help.

Follow these steps for a successful phone call:

1. **Think ahead about what you want to achieve before you place the call.**

   Will you actually reserve a flight if the price is right and the schedule is convenient? Will you agree to make reservations if the other party approves of your restaurant recommendation? If you decide *before calling* what you want to settle upon, your phone conversations will be brief, effective, and satisfying to both parties.

2. **Adopt a pleasant tone with the person who answers the call.**

   When you make a call, your voice should sound warm, cheerful, and upbeat. Your pronunciation should be clear. Make an effort to sound pleasing to the person you're calling. Sound glad to speak with the person who answers your call. Even if the purpose of your call is unpleasant (such as to make a complaint to a store), sounding pleasant gets the conversation off on the right foot and makes the recipient of the call more inclined to help you in an equally pleasant manner.

3. **Establish the identity of the other party.**

   When you get another person on the line, establish the identity of the other party before moving to the business at hand: "Good morning. Is this Mr. O'Malley?" If the answer is a flat "No," you might say, "My name is Ed Anderson. To whom am I speaking?" Have a piece of paper handy and write down the person's name. That information may come in handy during the remainder of the conversation, or perhaps later, when you speak with someone else.

   Once in a while, you reach someone who has not adopted good manners as a way of life. At your first opportunity, ask for that person's name. If you get a generic answer like, "This is the floor nurse," say, "That's wonderful. I understand there are many nurses on the sixth floor. May I have your name?"

4. **Identify yourself and your reason for calling.**

   Just as you want to know whom you're speaking with, the other party wants to know who you are and what you want. Settle this issue before you're asked. Say something such as, "This is Mike Morgan, and I need some help getting your brand of paint off my mother-in-law's curtains," or, "Hi. My name is Brenda Beeman, and I'd like to order a case of wine."

5. **Inquire considerately whether the timing of the call is convenient.**

   No matter whom you call or what time of day it is, begin your conversation by asking, "Is this a convenient time to talk?" If it isn't, volunteer to call back at a better time. Folks who have call waiting appreciate this little courtesy.

6. **Take notes during the conversation.**

You can exchange a great deal of information in the course of a telephone conversation. Get in the habit of keeping a notepad near every telephone and making notes as you chat. Otherwise, names, dates, model numbers, phone numbers, addresses, and the like can get scrambled if you try to keep everything in your head. Don't trust your memory. Jot it down.

7. **Achieve closure.**

When you have finished the business at hand and things have worked out well, say so: "Thanks for helping me. I really appreciate it" or "Thanks for changing my appointment. I'll see you next Tuesday at 11 a.m." Then end the conversation. Just say "Good-bye" and hang up.

Receiving Calls

Receiving calls is the delicate flip side of making calls. The human relations skills that you can bring to bear may cheer up a grouch or deal effectively with a nuisance. The following sections walk you through the various aspects of receiving a call with the utmost of courtesy.

Answering a call

If at all possible, you should answer your home telephone before it rings a fourth time. If you pick up the phone after four rings, the caller may expect to be transferred to an answering machine or voice-mail system or worry that you're in the middle of something and don't have time to talk. Portable phones that enable you to move around the house make it much easier to reach a phone quickly.

When you answer, make sure to identify yourself and your household: "Hello, Johnston residence, Joan speaking." If you live alone, a cheery "Hello" is appropriate. For safety's sake, never give out your number if someone asks, "What number is this?" Instead, ask what number the person is trying to call.

If you get a call from an unknown voice and you hear, "Hello, who is this?" you can say, "This is Charlie. To whom would you like to speak?" Give enough information for a genuine friend to verify that he or she dialed the right number, but no more.

Taking the world's fastest importance test

Your behavior when the telephone rings can amount to the world's fastest indication of how you feel about the importance of others. Study this list of scenarios and remember it, and you'll avoid a lot of unintended hard feelings:

- ✔ **You're having a face-to-face conversation with another person — a family member, neighbor, or guest — about an important topic. The phone rings and you say, "Excuse me," and pick it up.** You've just indicated that an unknown call from the outside may be more important than the face-to-face conversation. If you're expecting a truly important call, tell your companion ahead of time. Otherwise, let voice mail or your answering machine pick up the call.

- ✔ **You're on the phone with someone and the call-waiting tone chimes in your ear. You say, "Excuse me," and flash over to the other call.** You've just told the first party that whoever is calling on the other line may be more important.

- ✔ **In a call-waiting situation, you decide that the second call is more important than the first one, and you ring off the first call with a promise to "get right back."** The message? Call number two is more important than call number one.

Special circumstances may force you to engage in any of these rude behaviors from time to time. You may have to be slightly unmannerly to one person in order to avoid a worse offense to another, for example. Only you can judge the situation, but your choice to let a telephone call interrupt other business will inevitably cause hurt feelings. In almost every situation, good etiquette says to let it ring.

If you must pick up call waiting, be conscious of how long you leave the other person on hold. If you'll be any longer than a few seconds, offer to call the second caller back and resume your first conversation.

Ridding yourself of nuisances

Nuisances come in several guises. There are salespeople who call while you're trying to enjoy dinner with your family. There are repeated wrong numbers. There are heavy breathers who phone in the middle of the night. There are kids who dial numbers at random and giggle. The following sections advise you on how to deal with these nuisances.

Dinnertime sales calls

You do not owe any consideration to sales solicitations made during the dinner hour or later in the evening. However, as a polite person, you can't bring yourself to be unmannerly no matter what the provocation. Just wait for the first opening and say, "Thanks, but I'm not interested. Good-bye." And with that, hang up the telephone.

Truly obnoxious sales callers do not require any conversation. If a caller is rude or harassing to you, you're within your rights to hang up the phone without a single word of explanation. However, you may want to ask to be removed from the calling list before you hang up so that you don't have to deal with callers from that organization again.

What you may *not* do is curse the caller and slam down the phone angrily. This behavior sets a terrible example for your children.

Repeated wrong numbers

If you frequently get wrong-number calls, discuss the problem with your phone company. The cause may be a typo in the phone book that lists your number instead of the correct one. The ultimate solution is to request a new telephone number, but if all the mistaken calls seem to be connected to the same voice, try letting your answering machine take over for a week or so.

Prank calls and other nuisances

The easiest way to deal with nuisance calls is to let your answering machine or voice-mail system do the work. Nuisance callers are quickly discouraged when they can't reach an actual human being. If you happen to pick up a nuisance call, just hang up the phone without comment.

Every telephone company has a department that deals with nuisance calls and other telephone offenses. By all means, call the phone company, ask for the appropriate department, and describe your problem. The phone company has many resources to help you.

Your unlisted number — revealed!

Nowadays, you can get a gadget from the phone company that accepts calls only from the numbers you program. If you have an unlisted number and find that strangers are calling you anyway, the temporary use of such a device may make the problem go away. Otherwise, you may need a new unlisted number. Here again, you do not owe any courtesy to a telephone trespasser, but you shouldn't curse and slam, either. One rude action does not justify another rude action.

Dealing with threats

There's absolutely no difference between a telephoned threat and an in-person threat. Never take it upon yourself to decide that a telephoned threat is just a prank. If you receive a threatening call, write down all the details, keep the caller on the line by asking how to turn away the threatened action, and then, immediately after the conversation ends, alert your supervisor (if you're at work) or the police. If you are in charge at work and others are at risk, alert the police at once and take whatever action will guard everyone's safety.

Handling a sudden disconnect

Suppose you're chatting with a friend, and suddenly the connection is broken. You wait five seconds and then dial the other party. You get a busy signal because the other party is also trying to dial you. This goes on for a long time.

When a sudden disconnect happens to you, remember this rule: The original caller is the one who should attempt to re-establish a conversation, even if the cause was the called party accidentally leaning on a phone button.

Teaching Telephone Etiquette to Children

There's a gray area between child psychology and etiquette for children. Telephone usage falls into this uncertain area. On the one hand, you want your children to learn how to communicate effectively, but on the other hand, you don't want them to take over the phone as their own personal property. There comes a time in every toddler's life when he or she falls in love with the telephone and looks forward to every opportunity to use it. A bit later on, when your child becomes a teenager, the love affair may become an obsession. And that can cause major headaches for you, the parent.

Safety is also involved. Every child who is old enough to manage it should know how to dial 9-1-1 and stay on the line. Don't overlook your responsibility to teach your children when and how to dial 9-1-1.

Safety issues for children who are home alone

When children are in junior high school and beyond, they're sometimes left at home alone between the time school ends and the time parents finish working. If your children are home alone and a stranger calls and asks, "Is your mother home?" the child should always answer, "I'm sorry, but she is unable to come to the phone right now. May I have your name and number? I will have her call you as soon as she is free." No further answers are necessary, even if the stranger presses for further information about what the mother is doing or when she will be free.

It's a good idea to practice this technique with your child, calling at a rehearsed time and pushing the child for information. Teach your children to be polite but firm.

Here are some suggestions regarding children, phone etiquette, and phone safety:

- **Do not inflict toddlers on others via the phone.** When Grandma calls, don't put your 2-year-old on the line. You may think that it's cute, but Granny may not be thrilled to get an earful of silence when checking in from London.

- **Discuss with other parents your desires regarding child-to-child calling times.** Establish the best time of day and a maximum duration for calls between kids, and then enforce the rules.

- **Teach children to answer the phone by saying, "Good afternoon, Miller residence."** (Have them substitute your last name, of course.) Also teach them not to get into conversations with strangers.

- **Teach children how to take a message.** If a child is old enough to answer the phone, the child is old enough to take a name and number and promise a callback.

- **Make sure that teenagers participate in equal access to telephones in the same way that they participate in equal dessert at dinnertime.** It's fair to establish a time limit for each call and a between-call time interval. Otherwise, you won't receive incoming calls for anyone else in the house.

- **Don't worry if your Sally dials up her friend Roger to arrange a meeting at the mall.** The old business about girls not calling boys has pretty much disappeared.

- **Examine your monthly telephone bills carefully.** You may discover that one of your children is using the phone in a way that displeases you. Kids tell each other about little scams and pranks that they can play with the phone. Discuss exceptional charges and notations with the child.

The telephone company has elaborate means by which it can detect these types of infractions, and it will contact the subscriber with full details. If you learn of your child's telephone misconduct from the phone company, be prepared to take stern measures to prevent such behavior in the future.

✔ **If your children have their own line, consider placing limits on it.** Your telephone company can provide useful limits on a telephone line to keep your children — and your phone bills — safe. For example, you can arrange to block all outgoing 900-number calls and all long-distance calls. In other words, the youngster can use the telephone only for local calls.

Phone Etiquette for Guests in Your House

What do you do when guests in your house need to use your telephone? It depends on the guest and the situation. There are no concrete rules here, but this section provides some thoughts to help you decide on the best course of action for the situation.

Personal houseguests

The hospitality of your house includes permission for your guests to use your telephone for ordinary purposes, such as checking with the baby-sitter, letting the folks back home know that they arrived safely, and confirming airline reservations. Your guests will usually ask for permission and offer to pay you for the call(s). Grant the permission and refuse the money.

As a guest, you must always ask permission to use the telephone. Put lengthy long-distance calls on your credit card or charge them to the party you're calling. In most cases, though, your host will encourage you to direct-dial a call home to let folks know that you arrived safely.

In the event that you discover, when your bill arrives, that a guest in your house ran up a high charge (say by making calls to a distant continent), by all means make a copy of the bill, circle the items in question, and send it off to the guest with a written notation to this effect: "I sure hope these are expenses your company can handle!"

If a guest ties up your telephone for a very long business call, that guest is exhibiting poor manners. But a guest is a guest. There's nothing you can do about the situation except to read a book or trim the hedges until the caller finishes.

Contractors and other workers

It happens all the time: An energetic worker is putting down a new tile floor in your kitchen when his beeper goes off and he asks you if he can use your phone for a minute. You say, "Of course," and walk out of the room. Next thing you know, the tile man is on his fifth call, you have no idea who he is calling, and the day isn't getting any younger.

One call to the home office is nothing to get worked up about. But any excessive time spent using your phone is definitely not acceptable. Just tell the contractor that you need your telephone to be free, and you hope that he can keep his calls to a minimum.

Tussling with Technology

For better or worse, voice mail, answering machines, beepers, and cellular phones are a part of the modern world. In many cases, this is definitely for the better. If you're in an emergency situation on the road, for example, a cellular phone can be a lifesaver. When used properly and with consideration, voice mail can save you time. The following sections show you how to get the knack of the latest communication technologies.

Voice mail and answering machines

As recently as the 1970s, many etiquette experts considered answering machines to be insulting. But today, two-thirds of homes in the United States have them, and of those, many use them to screen calls.

It's easy to understand why some people found answering machines and voice mail difficult to handle. You've probably been in a situation in which you desperately wanted to speak with a human being, but instead you got a recorded message asking you to leave a message after the tone. Or, in the case of voice-mail systems, you get a mechanical voice saying, "Press 1 if you have red hair, and press 2 if you have fallen arches." Infuriating!

When confronted with these situations, especially in business, keep in mind that the person you called probably didn't have anything to do with creating the telephone system. It may have been designed and purchased by a cost-control expert who promised management that it would save money in the long run. So don't blame the manager of customer service. And don't take out your frustrations by leaving a nasty message. Just go with the flow — leave a pleasant message and wait for a callback.

When you get connected with voice mail or an answering machine, leave a simple message. Speak distinctly and clearly. Don't mumble or say "ummm" repeatedly. Identify yourself, slowly give a phone number where you can be reached, say why you're calling, wish the person well, and say good-bye.

If you dial an incorrect number and an answering device comes on, don't just hang up. The polite thing to do is to leave a message apologizing for the mistake. Doing so eliminates the possibility of a callback from someone who has Caller ID or some other callback feature.

If you own an answering machine, make your message as brief as possible. A simple "You've reached the Jones residence. We can't come to the phone right now, but if you leave a message at the beep, we'll get back to you" will do. Make sure that your voice sounds pleasant and cheerful (try smiling as you're recording the message). Don't speak too loudly or use a shrill tone of voice.

There's no need for a long speech, a recitation of a "hysterical" joke, or a taped musical interlude from your favorite rap artist. Your Aunt Selma who phones you from across the country doesn't want to pay long-distance fees while listening to an unnecessary speech. Get straight to the point.

Cellular phones

Countless articles have appeared in newspapers and magazines regarding the proper — and improper — use of cellular telephones. Today, cellular phones are being used in many situations once reserved for conventional wired telephones. But nothing about a cellular telephone excuses the user from good telephone manners. Although most people don't mean to be rude, they get into a sort of bubble while talking on the phone, and they may seem to forget the people around them.

I was at the movies recently when I heard a cellular phone ring. A woman pulled the phone out of her purse and began talking. I turned to her and said, "Excuse me!" She glared back as though I was rude for interrupting her conversation. First, you should not have your ringer turned on in a theater, but if you forget to turn it off and it rings, you should leave and talk in the lobby or turn the phone off and not answer the call.

Here are some other tips for using a cellular phone with the best of manners:

> ✔ Turn off the phone before entering a concert hall, theater, restaurant, or any other place where people gather to listen to each other or to enjoy paid entertainment. Believe it or not, humanity survived back in the days when folks called their baby-sitters from pay phones during intermission or between courses.

✔ Understand that walking down the street while engaged in a lively discussion — business or personal — looks ridiculous. If the communication is essential, be like Superman and duck into a nearby doorway or phone booth.

✔ Understand that it looks equally silly to be squeezing the cantaloupes in the supermarket while you gossip with a friend on your cellular phone.

✔ Remember that a ringing cell phone followed by a muttered conversation in the middle of a meeting is plain bad manners. (Beepers at meetings were bad enough!)

✔ Never initiate a cellular phone conversation while seated in a reasonably quiet restaurant. Do your communicating before cocktails or after coffee — and do it *outside* the restaurant. Many restaurants are taking a stand against patrons who insist on talking on cell phones at the table by having customers check their phones at the door.

Finally, keep this important point in mind: There are strange people out there who have listening devices that can tune in cellular phone calls. For the most part, they're just weirdoes who get their jollies by eavesdropping. But a few eavesdroppers record the conversations they overhear and make evil use of the material. The lesson? Keep your cell phone conversations innocent enough to withstand being overheard by an unknown third party!

Caller ID

Here's how Caller ID, a recent twist on technology, works: When someone calls, the Caller ID box displays the number and name of the person calling; it also records the date and time. Another feature that your telephone company may offer is callback, in which you dial a certain code after your phone rings and your phone calls back the last number that called you.

The main purpose of Caller ID is to stop harassing or obscene callers, as well as unsolicited sales calls. You may call back these unwanted callers and let them know that you will report them to the proper authorities if they continue to call. What Caller ID and some of the new phone features have changed is the person who is in charge. Now the person *being* called has the control, instead of the other way around.

One of the main etiquette challenges that Caller ID presents is people who check their Caller ID and then track down the poor souls who may have called their number by mistake and demand to know who they are and why they called. It may be time for some rules of fair play, so the following list answers some commonly asked etiquette questions about Caller ID:

✔ **Should I tell people that I have Caller ID?** Yes, the polite thing to do is to notify close friends and relatives that you have Caller ID. Tell them how it works and what the features are. Doing so will eliminate a lot of hurt feelings and embarrassment in the future.

✔ **If someone, even a friend, fails to leave a message, is it okay to call and see what he or she wants?** Yes, it's fine to call your friend back. Just let your friend know that you saw from your Caller ID unit that he or she called.

If you don't recognize the name or number, don't call the person back. The person may have dialed a wrong number and hung up upon hearing the voice-mail message.

✔ **If your Caller ID box tells you that, say, your neighbor is calling, is it okay to answer the phone "Hi, Scott" instead of the standard "Hello"?** Yes, that's fine. Again, announce to the caller that you have Caller ID, because people may be surprised that you know who's calling.

✔ **What's the polite response when someone tracks you down after you make an errant phone call or fail to leave a message?** Common sense and courtesy should prevail. Scolding someone for not leaving a message is rude. If someone calls you to ask why you called, just tell the truth: that another call came in, or you simply decided to call back later. If the person is being polite with you, be equally polite with them.

✔ **Should you even reveal that you have Caller ID?** The situation can get tricky if someone lies and tells you that he called you all day but you weren't home. You probably wouldn't want to let the person know that you have Caller ID at that point, unless the person is a very close friend or relative whom you can tease or joke with.

To save future embarrassment, you may want to say at this point that you have decided to purchase Caller ID and that you will have it installed in the very near future.

The Internet

There comes a time in many households when a member of the family discovers the Internet and begins to spend long periods of time online, tying up the telephone line. Unless you have a second telephone line or a system that alerts you to incoming calls while you're online, no calls can get through while the line is tied up, and no one can call out.

The solution is to have a family conference and establish firm rules about online time. If your household can afford it, you may want to get an additional line. If you can't or don't want to get a separate line for Internet use, set aside time to be online, perhaps later in the evening or early in the morning when incoming calls would be unlikely.

For much more on Internet etiquette (sometimes known as *Netiquette*), see Chapter 12.

Chapter 10

The Lost Art of Conversation

*P*eople seem to have lost the ability to converse with each other. If you need evidence, look around our culture. Popular after-work restaurants and cocktail lounges play loud music on the sound system. People flock to theater complexes showing 20 different movies. Cable TV systems offer 50 to 100 or more channels. Many people spend their days in front of computers and have lost at least some of their ability to use language to communicate with people.

Although times change, the basic human need to interact with other humans does not. Those people who have been able to cultivate the skill of conversation have a leg up on others who are stuck behind a computer or buried beneath a stack of paper. To become an interesting conversationalist, first keep in mind these three principles:

✔ You want to put the other person at ease and avoid saying anything that might cause discomfort.

✔ You want to show that you really care about what's on the other person's mind.

✔ You want to engage in a genuine exchange of information and opinions.

If your personality is sparkling and outgoing and if you have a genuine fondness for face-to-face conversations, you'll find the suggestions in this chapter easy to follow. On the other hand, if you're shy and you feel a bit uneasy about chatting with anyone outside your immediate family, you may need to work a little harder. The best way to do so is to force yourself to attend social functions more frequently and make an effort to circulate among acquaintances and new faces. In conversation, as with other skills, practice makes perfect.

Initiating a Conversation

Good conversation starters involve everyone in your group in a lively discussion. A talented conversationalist understands who is in the group and what is appropriate for the occasion. For example, it's not good to introduce the topic of baseball and then go on and on about statistics with the one other person in the circle who is a fan of the sport. The other people will feel distressed and left out. However, bringing up an interesting story that you heard earlier that day is a good way to involve the group in a lively conversation.

Some people are naturally at ease in social situations and never have trouble making conversation. Others are a little shy when it comes to small talk, especially with strangers. This section gives you some suggestions for surefire ways to get a conversation started. You'll be chatting away in no time!

Asking beats telling

A good way to break the ice is to ask a question. It all begins with a resolution on your part to say something when you find yourself making eye contact with another person. Here are a few ideas:

- **At a wedding reception:** "Hello. Are you a friend of the bride?"
- **At a company party:** "My name is Howard. Do you work in the headquarters building?"
- **At a dinner party:** "I heard our host introduce you as Captain Lawrence. My name is Judy Jones. Are you on active duty?"

As the other party, your duty is to respond with a reasonable answer. A simple yes or no turns off the whole conversation. Remember the power of question-and-answer and keep the ball rolling. Here are some sample responses:

- "Hi. I'm a fraternity brother of Jack's. We promised that we'd show up for each other's weddings. My name is Steve. What's yours?"
- "Yes, Howard, I work in the marketing department. You've probably seen my name on some memos — Betty Borden. Aren't you an accountant?"
- "I guess you could call it active duty. I'm with the police department. And if you call me Don, I'll call you Judy."

Some questions, however, are simply too corny to use as ice-breakers. No matter how strong the temptation, stay away from "What's your sign?", "Do you come here often?", and "What's a nice person like you doing in a place like this?" A little creativity goes a long way in the initial stage of a conversation. You're much more likely to get a good response if you take time to think of a good question to ask.

Complimenting someone

You're always on safe ground when you start the ball rolling with a genuine compliment. To be successful, a compliment should be sincere and specific. For example, say you notice someone's accessory — earrings, eyeglasses, a button — and admire it. Here are examples of three approaches:

- ✔ "Those are lovely earrings — and so unique! Do they have a story?"

- ✔ "I've never seen eyeglass frames like that. Where did you find them?"

- ✔ "That's an interesting button on your lapel. What does it mean?"

Here again, the power of a question starts a conversation or keeps it moving. If you're the recipient of the compliment, accept it graciously and help continue the conversation with a question of your own. For example:

- ✔ "Why, thank you! I picked up these earrings while I was on vacation in Thailand. Have you ever been to Thailand?"

- ✔ "It's so nice that you noticed. There's a new optical store at the mall. I thought the frames were great when I picked them out, but now I wonder if they're too big. What do you think?"

- ✔ "It's kind of you to ask. I got the button for 15 years of service with the county. Can you imagine working at the same job for 15 years?"

Finding Something to Talk About

There's a time and a place for every kind of conversation. If you're at a close friend's home casually having a drink, the two of you can share observations and experiences almost without limit. On the other hand, many situations call for a careful selection of topics and a reasonable use of the other person's time.

After the initial greetings and pleasantries, what do you say next? The etiquette of conversation is governed by your sensitivity. Topics that seem perfectly reasonable at a backyard barbecue may be totally out of place at a bar mitzvah. If you're at a funeral, discussing the latest news about the breakup of your favorite star's marriage will be seen as frivolous and disrespectful to the occasion, whereas at lunch with a couple of close friends, celebrity news may be completely acceptable as a light topic of conversation. Make sure to give yourself a second or two of time to think about the situation before opening your mouth.

In addition to an appropriate subject, timing is also of the essence. At a cocktail party, a five- or ten-minute conversation may be the maximum in order to allow everyone to circulate. Pity the poor person who gets stuck in a corner, hemmed into a 30-minute conversation about bad news in the local economy! At a dinner party, however, you may be expected to keep up a conversation with the people to either side of you for the duration of the meal, which may last two hours or more.

The following sections give you more tips on appropriate — and inappropriate — subjects.

Staying away from sex, politics, money, and religion

The most explosive conversational subjects are sex, politics, money, and religion. People tend to have strong emotions and can be highly opinionated about this group of troublesome topics. You'll avoid a whole lot of trouble if you keep these simple cautions in mind:

- ✔ There are moral, legal, and personal hazards inherent in any conversation about sex. Even in this supposedly enlightened era, many people consider sex to be a forbidden topic. They may take offense at sexual jokes or comments on the alleged sexual activities of others. What's worse, if you bring up a sexual situation in your conversation, you may unwittingly implicate a third party known to your conversation partner. Or, in the worst-case scenario, you may wind up defending yourself if that person takes your sexual stories or comments as sexual harassment.

- ✔ The give-and-take of political conversations is a basic component of democracy, and you may feel perfectly justified in expressing a strong opinion. But the conversation can take an ugly turn when the parties are on opposite sides of an issue. Stay alert for any sign that you're triggering an emotional reaction, and drop the subject with a comment such as, "I can see that we disagree. Let's talk about something a bit less divisive." Even if your mission is to win a convert to your point of view, you won't accomplish anything by making an enemy.

- ✔ In some ways, money is a greater taboo in American culture than sex. People become very uncomfortable when money is discussed in a group setting. You should never ask someone how much something costs or how much someone earns. Make any discussion about money in very general terms. For example, an inappropriate comment is

  "I heard that Richard Jones bought a house on Columbus Drive for $150,000 — doesn't that seem like a lot for that area? But the only reason he could afford it was that his parents gave him $10,000 for a down payment."

A more appropriate comment is

"Columbus Drive is getting to be a really nice neighborhood. I've heard that property values have appreciated considerably in the past year. In fact, Richard Jones just bought a house there."

✔ Religion means different things to different people. Some people quietly keep their religious beliefs to themselves. Other folks feel that they should be able to express their religious beliefs, and they may even make an attempt to convince others to join them. If you have strongly held religious beliefs, proper etiquette is to bring them up only when you're asked about them and to elaborate only upon further questioning. If somebody asks you to discuss some detail of your faith, by all means go ahead and explain. But be very careful about forcing religious beliefs on someone who may be unwilling to hear them.

Keeping your personal life personal

Good friends can discuss almost anything, but people you meet at social gatherings are not entitled to deeply personal details of your life. Moreover, there's a chance that something you think is interesting may bore another person. For example, if you just went through an illness and your friend asks you at a dinner party, "How are you feeling now?", give a simple answer. Something like "I've been back at work this week and really am on the mend, thank you" should suffice. There's no need for a detailed explanation of the virus that struck you or the havoc that it wreaked on your digestive system.

Likewise, if you're at coffee hour after church on Sunday morning and an acquaintance asks about your children, briefly state the news: "Brad is in Phoenix working at a law firm, and Terry is starting a new job at a public relations firm in Boston after getting back from a tour of Europe. They're both doing well, thank you." Details about boyfriends or girlfriends who have come and gone or raises or grades that your children have received are more information than most pleasant conversations require.

The question "How are you?" is particularly tricky for some people. It's a formal artifact of our society and is not meant to elicit a detailed response. Although you may be tempted to launch into an in-depth discussion of your failing health or your recent breakup, the only appropriate response to this question in a casual social meeting is "Just fine, thanks. How are you?" Try to visualize a chance meeting at a reception and this response: "I'm a little better tonight. My psychiatrist changed my anti-depression medicine, and I feel less like slitting my wrists." Or this horrible example: "I've never been worse. My ex-wife's attorney just slapped a lien on my condo, my car was repossessed, and I'm waiting to hear how my EKG came out."

Good manners start to overlap into self-defense when strangers start probing into your personal affairs. You certainly don't have to answer questions about your finances, your marital history, or anything else that you'd rather not discuss. Deal with a Nosy Nellie courteously but directly by looking her straight in the eye and asking, "Why do you ask?" or stating "I'd rather not talk about that." Doing so usually stops the current course of the conversation and allows you to introduce a new topic.

Finding successful conversation topics

Successful conversationalists know how to introduce topics that interest just about everyone. If you need a few suggestions, here are some ideas for topics that usually spark a lively conversation:

- ✔ **Current events:** It's a good idea to scan a news magazine, a news-related Web site, or the daily newspaper before heading off to a social event to find upbeat, interesting, or unusual news.

- ✔ **Congratulations:** Offering congratulations to someone on an accomplishment, such as a graduation, promotion, or new baby, can get the conversation rolling on a pleasant note.

- ✔ **Good news:** Providing happy news about mutual friends is an upbeat topic that puts people in a good mood.

- ✔ **Cultural events:** Talking about the latest play, musical performance, or art show interests almost everyone.

- ✔ **Sports:** If a sporting event is of national interest, such as the Olympics or the Super Bowl, everyone should be able to participate.

Listening: More Than Not Talking

Listening well is an act of generosity. To truly listen to someone is an unselfish act that you perform for the other person's benefit. How do you learn to listen? Ask a question of someone, and then let that person answer. Really concentrate on what the person is saying. Don't interrupt or interject comments that shift the attention to you. All these signals show the depth of your attention. Beyond that, there are some special ways to be a good listener.

Staying eyeball to eyeball

Eye contact is the glue of a conversation. When you look directly at a person and pay attention to the conversation (rather than letting your eyes roam around the room in search of other social opportunities), you give a signal that, for the moment at least, the person you're talking to is the most interesting person imaginable. Looking away, especially at your shoes or the ceiling, indicates your wish to be far away.

Utilizing the well-placed "Hmmm"

Keep your conversation partner going with little prompts. A well-placed "hmmm" here and there indicates your understanding of whatever is being said and shows that you're following along. A gentle nod of your head now and then offers further encouragement. Failing to respond and keeping your face in neutral have the opposite effect — they may even bring the conversation to a dead halt.

A soft chorus of affirmations is another trick. Little phrases like "Of course" and "Well, I should say" and even "Oh, no!" act as prods to keep you in the game and show that you're listening closely. "Tell me more" often spurns additional embellishment on the subject at hand.

Maintaining a sense of curiosity

The best way to learn is to listen — not to talk. If you maintain a lively curiosity about life, people, why things happen the way they do, how things work, and what people do in their jobs, for example, you'll always be at the center of good conversations. People are flattered when you ask questions about their life and work. Be curious. The more you learn, the more interesting you become.

Cheating with a notepad

If you're listening to someone during a telephone conversation, one way to remember the course of the conversation is to jot down a word or two on a notepad. Many people do this in business situations, but it also works in personal or social situations. Particularly if you're in a distracting environment or you have a lot on your mind, noting a word or two on a piece of paper can help you be an even better listener. When the other person mentions a fact, write it down so that you can repeat it or bring it up again when you speak the next time.

Overcoming Language and Other Barriers

Being caught without conversational resources when you're talking with someone who speaks a different language is inexcusable. Every bookstore carries small phrase books containing ordinary survival phrases. In the time it takes to fly to some foreign destination, you can easily learn how to say "Please," "Thank you," "Hello," "Goodbye," and "Where's the bathroom?" So don't be shy. Get out your phrase book and do your best.

At a gathering in your own country, assume that a foreign visitor is similarly prepared. Go ahead and introduce yourself. Speak your name clearly. Offer refreshments in pantomime by holding out a drink or a dish of canapés. The chances are overwhelming that your foreign visitor will have studied English in school and has a pretty good command of the language. Otherwise, the guest will probably be accompanied by an interpreter. If you know a few words of the other language, by all means give it a try. (See Chapter 21 for more on international interactions.)

A foreign language is not the only communications barrier that you can expect to encounter at some time in your social life. People who are deaf, blind, or afflicted with a neuromuscular difficulty are just as eager to socialize as you are. Those who can't talk can listen. Those who can't hear can read your lips or rely on the help of an interpreter. Those who can't see are often superb conversationalists and need only a minimum of assistance. (See Chapter 22 for more on disabilities and etiquette.)

You're a master of etiquette when you succeed in putting others at ease, making them comfortable, and accommodating their needs.

Ending a Conversation

Say you've been conversing with a person at a cocktail party for 15 minutes. This person won't get off the subject of his job, his health, or his children — three of the topics that are most likely to bore other people. No rule says that you have to remain trapped in a conversation you'd rather end. How you extricate yourself is just one more measure of your mastery of good manners. Here are some polite exit lines:

- ✔ "I didn't know that quantum electrodynamics was such a fascinating subject. Perhaps you can tell me more after I've finished saying hello to my cousin, who just arrived."

- ✔ "You know, that cat of yours sounds like a real character. I'll be thinking about her while I powder my nose."

- ✔ "Oh, for goodness sake! The time passed so quickly that I forgot to call my baby-sitter. Please excuse me."

A polite person is never cruel to another — no matter how bored you are. Smile, shake hands, and part graciously.

Chapter 11

Corresponding in the New Age

The telephone is close at hand. You can pick it up and dial the number of just about anyone in the world, and in a matter of seconds you're in voice contact. You can send documents via fax. You can e-mail anything from an informal note to a long text. There are so many communications options these days that the old-fashioned *letter* seems almost, well, quaint. Call me old-fashioned, but I still believe that nothing is as thrilling as receiving a nice, long letter full of news, intimacies, and real emotion — the kind of letter that you can read and reread. A telephone call may be welcome, but it doesn't allow you to replay the conversation. You can't hold an e-mail in your hand, admiring the ink and penmanship. And a fax . . . well, it's nice for a cheery greeting, but when it appears on the machine, there's nothing intimate about it.

This chapter gives you some helpful comments on the art of writing letters. (See Chapter 9 for information about telephone etiquette and Chapter 12 for information about e-mail etiquette.) The many details of letter writing communicate a whole lot more than just the words on the page. Follow along here and you'll pick up some insights that may have escaped you in the past. You'll also gain a better feeling for what to write and what *not* to write.

The Hardware of Letter Writing: Pen, Ink, Paper, and Brain

To write a "real" letter (that is, one that does not involve a computer), you need paper, an envelope, a pen (and ink if you use a fountain pen), a postage stamp, and, probably, a wastebasket.

✔ Personal letters should be composed on something a bit more dressy than those dead-white 8½-x-11-inch sheets that you feed into your printer. Investing in stationery is a good idea. I explain the types that you can choose from and their functions later.

✔ Do you have a fountain pen? Real ink looks wonderful on high-quality paper. You can find disposable fountain pens preloaded with ink for just a few dollars. Those inexpensive pens work a lot better than you might think, and if you get to the point where you really like writing with pen and ink, you can spend anywhere from $30 to more than $1,000 for a fancy pen.

✔ Ink, too, says something about you. Writing ink comes in many colors. However, dark blue and black are the most formal and correct. The standard dark blue ink conveys a neutral message; your reader won't even notice the color. Black ink looks very assertive. Green, purple, and brown inks are unusual enough to identify the writer as a creative individual. Red ink may appeal to you, but it is difficult to read under certain lighting conditions and on certain tinted paper stocks.

✔ While you're out shopping, stop at the post office and get some stamps that are more interesting than the "official" first-class stamps that they sell in rolls. Your stamp says something about you. You may wish to select a commemorative design that features a special interest or cause.

Your desk is an important part of success in letter writing. You need a large enough surface to provide a resting place for your forearm and elbow. Otherwise, your writing may have a messy, wobbly look.

Selecting stationery

If you've decided that your days of scribbling on a legal pad and stuffing the sheet into the nearest envelope are over, congratulations! Now that you want to stock up on real, adult stationery, what on earth do you need? And what purpose does each type of stationery serve? This section tells you what you need to know.

Half sheets

You should use this paper for most personal social correspondence. It's about 7¼ inches x 10½ in size, and sometimes women's-sized paper is smaller. While women can use any color of their choice, from tan to cream to pastels, men traditionally have used only white, cream, or gray. Engraving is usually done in a darker complementary color — dark gray on gray or dark brown on tan, for example.

Your stationery should have your name and address or your monogram at the top. The return address should be on the upper left-hand portion of the front of the envelope.

Because you should not write on the back of the first sheet, make sure that you also purchase second-page sheets, which are plain, with no engraving.

Insert the paper into the envelope by folding it in half with the bottom edge brought up to the top edge and placing it in the envelope with the back flap facing you. Once in the envelope, the fold of the paper should be on the bottom and the two edges held together at the top.

Foldover notes (informals)

These cards are used for writing notes and informal invitations. They are usually white, cream, or gray and are about 3¾ inches x 5¼ inches in size. You can have them engraved, embossed, or printed with your name or monogram in the center of the card. You may want to choose a colored border to match the letter and lined envelopes.

Pens and precautions

Your storehouse of information about etiquette and good manners should include a few notes and tips about fountain pens, ballpoint pens, and inks:

✔ Fountain pens are highly personal possessions. As the owner uses a fountain pen, the business end is gradually worn down by friction against paper. In time, the point (officially called the *nib*) will write perfectly only when held at a characteristic angle by the habitual user. Why should you know this? Because fountain pen owners are hesitant to allow anyone else to use their pens, and you should not ask to borrow another's precious writing instrument.

✔ Your daily activities should influence your choice of fountain-pen ink. If you work with others, use an ink that can be washed away if it happens to get on an item of clothing. At home, you can use indelible ink if you wish.

✔ Ballpoint pens are usually reliable writing instruments. But some of them have a habit of leaking a small amount of ink at the tip. The stray ink can get on fingers, clothing, official papers, and so on. Ballpoint pen ink is stubborn stuff that's extremely difficult to wash away. Check your ballpoint pens and those placed for others to use and make sure that they are clean.

✔ If you find a stray pen, give it to the lost-and-found department or post a note on the company bulletin board. Some pens are extremely expensive and, regardless of their value, may be highly treasured by their owners.

✔ Check your own pocket or purse when setting off for a day of business. Having a writing instrument available when you need to sign something or make a note is an indication of competence.

You can write on the bottom half of the inside of the card. Any monogramming makes it impossible to write on the top inside part because of the indentation. You can also write on the back side of the bottom half of the card. If the card is printed and not embossed or engraved, you can begin your note on the top side. Insert the card into its envelope right side up, with your monogram toward you as it is inserted in the envelope. The card's fold should be at the top.

As a single person, you should use the first initial of your given, middle, and family surname to create a monogram. "Lisa Beth Johnson" would be LBJ. A woman may make her surname the middle initial (it is usually slightly oversized), flanked by the initials of her given and middle names — in other words, LJB. A married woman drops her middle name and adds her husband's surname. If Lisa Beth Johnson marries Conrad Smith, for example, her new monogram would be LSJ or LJS.

Letter paper for everyday use

It's nice to have some lesser-quality paper with your name and address printed on it to use for writing about personal business. For example, you might write to request information about the stock of a public company or to ask about the status of an order or a bill.

Letters Last Forever

I always write a first draft of a letter on plain paper before I transfer the letter to my stationery. Doing so allows me to take a moment to contemplate what I am about to write. (It also saves on good stationery by allowing me to make mistakes on scratch paper first!) Letters can last forever, and your comments, relating of gossip, or scathing remarks about others may come back to haunt you. Choose your words carefully!

You don't expect your letters to be seen by anyone but the person you're writing to, but playing a game of pretend won't hurt. Try to imagine your letter reprinted on the front page of the newspaper — you may change your mind about referring to a third party as a jerk. That same caution may keep you from writing to your sweetie that the two of you will get married as soon as you break up with Stella.

The basics: Form and function

Informal and personal letters need not follow a rigid format, but you should follow the basics of form:

- ✔ **The address:** If your address is not printed at the top of the page, write it in the upper-right corner. If the recipient knows very well where you live, you can omit the address and simply use a dateline (see below).

- ✔ **The date or dateline:** Indicate under the address the date and place you wrote the letter. The dateline can be as simple as "Chicago, May 20, 2000." Dating letters — and even postcards — helps the reader when he or she rediscovers the note a long time after you sent it.

- ✔ **The salutation:** Place the salutation flush left. Personal letters are appropriately led off with a simple "Dear Eloise," with a comma at the end — "Dear Dad," "Dear Cousin Marlene," "Dear Professor Rubin," "Dear Dr. Jones," or "Dear Bobby and Nancy," and so on.

- ✔ **The main body:** Leave a space after the salutation and indent. Leave good margins at both sides of the sheet, write as legibly as you can, and, when mentioning important details such as airline schedules or a vacation address, make sure that the item is easy to read. Print if your handwriting is a bit eccentric or is difficult to read.

The content of the body very much depends on your reason for writing, of course, but the main purpose of the letter is to convey some news while reflecting your personality and expressing your thoughts in a clear, simple, and touching manner. Your purpose for writing should be stated fairly early on in the body.

You might start with "You will be glad to hear that . . ." or "What a wonderful surprise it was to see you on Thursday . . . ." A description of where you're writing and what you've been doing that day are also wonderful additions to the beginning of the letter. As you progress in the body of the letter, you want to convey news about what has been happening to you and to those you know.

Purely social and informal letters are intended to maintain contact with family and friends. Within reasonable limits, you can write whatever you would normally say in a face-to-face conversation. But do try to avoid some pitfalls in composing social letters.

News of good fortune is always welcome, but bragging is not. By all means, tell your former neighbor that your little Jennifer is doing well at school, but leave it at that. You may be proud that Jenny's teacher said she is the brightest 9-year-old in history and is reading at the college level, but your former neighbor may resent it, particularly if her own child happens to be having a difficult time in reading class — and you don't know it. In a similar vein, your mother in Spokane will be interested to know that you attended to your dental needs, but she doesn't need to read about the agonies of a root canal job and your struggle to find the money to pay for the procedure.

- ✔ **Headings:** If your letter is long and contains several unrelated subjects, you can help your reader by inserting headings where appropriate. There are no hard-and-fast rules for headings within a social letter, so you can invent your own. Two or three words, perhaps underlined, can separate unconnected reports and topics. Consider the following examples:

- <u>My job is fine</u>

  The area manager tells me that I'm in line for a promotion before the year is out, and I'm looking forward to . . .

- <u>Leroy is growing like a weed</u>

  We took him to the pediatrician a few days ago, and the doctor says that he is developing nicely. And he's talking like crazy! His vocabulary now includes . . .

- <u>The flower bed looks wonderful</u>

  Now that the weather is getting warmer, the tulips are in full bloom and the sunflowers are shooting up. We put some topsoil on . . .

✔ **The closing phrase:** The closing goes to the right, between the last line of your text and your signature. The single word "Love," "Fondly," or "Affectionately," or a phrase such as "Miss you," "Write soon," or "More later," works with family and close friends. "Warm regards," is a fine closing when writing to someone you don't know very well. "With every good wish for a speedy recovery," or "All best wishes for happiness in your new home," may suit the situation. Capitalize the first word and keep the remainder of the phrase in lowercase.

✔ **Your signature:** Sign the letter with your name — for example, Dad or Ronald. If you're less familiar with the recipient of your letter, or if you're unsure whether the person will immediately know you by your first name, sign your first and last names.

For example, in a note to your grade-school teacher who is retiring, sign your full name. The same goes for a thank-you note to someone you met recently who invited you to a large cocktail party (and may have included two other Daves in the group).

Do not use titles in personal letters. In other words, if you happen to be a physician, stay with Maxwell Farnsworth rather than Dr. Farnsworth.

When a title is required

If your social letter straddles the line between social and business use, such as a note from a professor to a student, use stationery that has a personalized letterhead with your official name and title. If the stationery says "William Smeeds, Ph.D." at the top and has a second line identifying you as "Chairman, Physics Department," you may safely omit a title and simply sign the letter "Bill Smeeds."

Keep these points in mind when addressing an envelope for a personal letter:

- ✔ **Include your complete return address.** Print your name and return address legibly in the upper-left corner of the envelope. It's also acceptable to write the return address on the envelope flap, although the U.S. Postal Service prefers to have it on the front. A complete address comes in handy if your recipient wishes to post a reply.

  Keep the lines aligned on the left. Write your street address and apartment number (if any) on one line. Start a new line for the city, state, and zip code. Use numerals instead of writing out numbers, and make sure that you use the postal code abbreviation for your state — that is, NY for New York, IL for Illinois, AZ for Arizona, and so on.

- ✔ **List the recipient's formal title and address.** Regardless of the informality of the letter itself, the address on the envelope should be complete, including the necessary honorific in the person's title. Even when writing to your sister, address the envelope to Dr. Denise Kaufmann.

  When writing to a couple, the man's name goes first. For example, if a married woman has retained her maiden name, an appropriate address might be Mr. Charles Delavan and Ms. Susan Birkholtz. Or suppose that Charles Delavan is an ambassador and his wife does not use his last name. In that case, the address should be written as The Honorable Charles Delavan and Ms. Susan Birkholtz. If the woman only uses her maiden name professionally, write the address as Mr. and Mrs. Charles Delavan or The Honorable and Mrs. Charles Delavan.

  If Charles is deceased, do not address Susan as Mrs. Susan Birkholtz, because that name indicates that she is divorced. Widows keep their husband's first and last names — Mrs. Charles Delavan. If Susan is divorced, address it to Mrs. Susan Delavan unless she has taken her maiden name again. In that case, you would write Ms. Susan Birkholtz.

  Some lawyers prefer to be addressed as Esq. If this is the case, do not use a prefix: Joseph Fox, Esq. When writing to a lawyer and a spouse, do not use Esq. They should be addressed as Mr. and Mrs. Joseph Fox.

  For doctors, the envelope should be addressed to Dr. Bill Smith and Dr. Elaine Smith. If only the wife is a doctor, you use Dr. Elaine Smith and Mr. Bill Smith. If Elaine goes by her maiden name, you use Dr. Elaine Cox and Mr. Bill Smith.

  If a couple is living together but is not married, place each name on a separate line, flush left, alphabetically. Do not link them with "and."

  Unmarried girls should be addressed as Miss until they are 21, when they can choose to be addressed as Ms. Officially, boys should be addressed as Master until age 8, when that title is dropped and the boy is simply called by his given name, such as David McDonald. At age 18, a boy becomes Mr.

✔ **Use the proper postage.** Affix a stamp with the correct postage to the upper-right corner of the envelope. When in doubt as to the amount, stand in line at the post office and get an expert opinion. Nothing is tackier than a letter that arrives with a notation of postage due.

✔ **Neatness counts.** If you mess up somewhere along the line, start over on a fresh envelope and do it right. Strikeovers, ink blots, messy erasures, and the like are signals that you don't really care, and of course you *do* care.

Sending Invitations

Invitations come in many forms, from a spur-of-the-moment telephone call for a get-together to a formal invitation for a dinner dance issued weeks beforehand. In this section, I cover the more formal, written invitations. For ideas on extending informal invitations, see Chapter 4.

A formal invitation should be mailed three weeks ahead of time if the event is a luncheon, cocktail party, or informal dinner, and four weeks before an important dinner party.

Other lands, other customs

A letter you send to someone in a faraway country may be treated quite differently than it would be in the usual domestic mail. Keep these points in mind:

✔ **Ask the local post office about delivery.** There are many kinds of postal service. If you want the letter to get there right away, be sure to use the service you need. Otherwise, it can take weeks for a letter to arrive.

✔ **Consider the political situation.** In some countries, certain letters are opened and read by security personnel. Do not put the other party in a fix by discussing sensitive political or national security issues.

✔ **Consider the interpreter.** If your letter must go through the hands of an interpreter, express yourself carefully. Unintended eyes may see, and share with others, what you write.

✔ **Remember the reply coupon.** This coupon can be important if you're corresponding with a person of limited means. Your local postal service can sell you a coupon good for postage on a return letter. Include it in your envelope, and you may save the other party the equivalent of two or three hard-earned dollars.

✔ **Use decorative stamps.** The recipient may be a stamp collector who will treasure a new item for his or her album.

Parts of a formal invitation include the following:

- ✔ Who (names of the hosts)
- ✔ Inviting phrase
- ✔ What (type of event)
- ✔ Why (purpose of event)
- ✔ When (date and time)
- ✔ Where (place)
- ✔ Reply instructions

For example:

> *The Reverend Malcolm McCloud and Mrs. McCloud*
> *request the pleasure of your company*
> *at dinner*
> *to celebrate their 50th wedding anniversary*
> *Friday, April first*
> *from seven to ten o'clock*
> *1520 North Shorewood Boulevard*
> *Oakland, California*
>
> *RSVP*
> *000-0000*   *Black Tie*

Or somewhat less formally:

> *Mr. and Mrs. John Henry*
> *cordially invite you to a dinner*
> *in honor of Allison Blair Pay*
> *Monday, June fifteenth*
> *from six to nine o'clock*
> *1500 North Lake Shore Drive*
> *Chicago, Illinois 00000*
> *RSVP 000-0000*

A formal invitation should be printed or engraved. However, plenty of less-formal options are available, including fill-in invitations with certain words printed — you write in the details. You can also design your own invitations at many paper stores, or you can write notes on your good personal stationery.

Responding Graciously to Invitations

No matter what type of invitation you receive, the most important rule is to respond promptly. There's nothing worse for a host than to have to wait until the last minute to find out who will be attending the function.

The easiest invitations to handle are those with enclosed reply cards, along with addressed and stamped envelopes. Formal response cards serve a definite purpose: They alert the caterer and other people responsible for the arrangements to the number of guests who must be accommodated. Your obligation is to *fill out the card and mail it back at your earliest convenience* (preferably within 48 hours). Imagine yourself as the host of an event that will cost you $75 for each person in attendance and being forced to pay for no-shows.

Mail the card. Just check the appropriate space — "X will attend," for example — and send it off. If you have any change to the invitation, or if a reply card is not included, you must reply on your own stationery. For example, if the invitation is addressed to "Mr. and Mrs. Howard Stamos" but Howard can't make it, Mary should reply with her own stationery: "Mrs. Howard Stamos accepts with pleasure the kind invitation of Mr. and Mrs. James Goldberg for Thursday, the second of May at 1 o'clock. Mr. Howard Stamos regrets that he will be unable to accept due to a previous business commitment."

If the invitation is an informal one, a telephone number will be indicated, and the host's preference is that you call to RSVP. Call immediately. If no telephone number is given, compose a brief reply in writing. Keep it short because the host is busy with preparations and really just needs to know your intentions. Here are a couple of examples:

Dear Mary,

Of course Jacob and I will be there to celebrate your daughter's first birthday. Thanks so much for inviting us, and we look forward to seeing you a week from Saturday. If there is anything I can do to help, don't hesitate to call me.

Love,

Wendy

Dear Mary,

I'm so sorry to tell you that Jacob and I will be in Acapulco next week and will miss Misty's birthday party. Please give our greetings to the others and assure everyone that we would have been thrilled to join you if we could have.

Love,

Wendy

Many people wonder how to politely decline an invitation in a situation that is not as cut-and-dried. A simple reply stating, "I sincerely regret that because of a previous engagement, I will be unable to accept your kind invitation," is the most graceful way to decline.

Bringing an extra guest

Some of the most unintended bruised feelings can arise from questions about uninvited persons. Questions arise when an invitation is addressed to only one of a married couple, when you have an unexpected out-of-town visitor you don't want to leave behind, when your kids are not mentioned on an invitation, and so on.

Formal invitations with response cards are carefully premeditated. If the invitation fails to mention another party, consider the omission to be on purpose. Accept or decline on your own, but don't quarrel with the host's intentions.

There are just a very few exceptions:

- If you were recently married and that fact is not known to your host, telephone the host, explain the situation, and wait for a response. A gracious host will insist on the presence of your new mate.

- Similarly, if the invitation mentions two persons but you no longer have an affiliation with the other person, tell your host. She may wish to rearrange the seating assignments.

When good manners prevail, flexibility always rules the day. For example, you and your spouse may be invited to a dinner party when your father is visiting from out of town. If you explain the situation to the host and explain that you may not be able to attend because of your father, the host may well invite you to bring your father along. (But don't be insulted if the host does not extend the invitation to your father; there may be space limitations or other reasons.)

Less-formal invitations may be a bit more flexible, but your duty as a paragon of good manners is to make it easy for the host to come up with an answer. You might phone and ask, "Is the affair suitable for children the ages of Tommy and Kenny?" Any hesitation on the host's part is a clear signal for you to arrange for a baby-sitter. Children should never be forced onto a party of adults.

Chapter 12

Politely Navigating Cyberspace: The Rules of Netiquette

In This Chapter

▶ Minding your manners on the Internet

▶ E-mailing and posting messages courteously

▶ Remembering the unspoken rules of cyberspace

*N**etiquette* is a clever word used by people who use the Internet frequently. Simply stated, netiquette is the rules of etiquette for the Internet. The Internet has developed its own unique rules for how to behave properly. Although the Internet may seem to offer up a perplexing array of new etiquette situations, the old rules still apply — basic courtesy always means considering others' needs first. It requires you to make others feel comfortable, and that forms the basis of netiquette.

Many netiquette transgressions are caused by the fact that the Internet allows people to be anonymous. Unfortunately, some people believe that they can use the Internet to get away with behavior that they wouldn't dare attempt in real life. Although the Internet has provided open social access (a good thing, I believe), it has a downside, too: A very small minority of people try to take advantage of that unusually open social access to behave poorly. That includes lying about who they are, trying to become too intimate too quickly, or boring or harassing people without fear of social ostracization. Offenses against common courtesy now exist that Emily Post herself never dreamed possible! But in truth, we all know what we should — and shouldn't — do. We all know that we can hurt others if we use e-mail thoughtlessly or attack an individual in a chat room discussion. But does this knowledge stop people from behaving inconsiderately? Unfortunately, not often enough.

Because the character of the Internet keeps changing and the lingo is awfully confusing, the rules of common courtesy may be hard to grasp the first few times you surf the Net. Add to this the fact that millions of people have access to the Internet, and that your etiquette faux pas has the potential to reach millions of people, and you may be a bit nervous about how to act on the Internet.

If you are just beginning to venture onto the Internet, pausing to familiarize yourself with its particular culture will make you feel immediately more comfortable. It's better to learn about the Internet culture now than do it the hard way by having others correct you! On the other hand, if you've been plugged into cyberspace for a number of years, you may understand the rules of netiquette instinctively. Although the information in this chapter may not be totally new to you, it's always nice to know the rationale behind it. Either way, it's important that you know how to distinguish yourself as a considerate person to your friends on the Net.

Understanding the Etiquette Rules of the Internet

Remember what it's like to experience a different culture for the first time? Whether that culture was a new school, a new town, or a foreign country, you may recall moments of being misunderstood by people in your new surroundings — perhaps because you said the wrong thing or dressed differently. Or you may remember taking offense at something that was said or done to you, only to realize later that the behavior was completely acceptable in that culture, and that no offense was intended.

You may have a similar experience when logging on to the Internet for the first time. People may offend you by what they write, and you may offend others without meaning to. Being a mannerly person, of course you would rather make friends than enemies. If you follow a few basic principles, you're less likely to make the kinds of mistakes that prevent you from making friends.

Know that behind every message is a human being

One of the main principles of Internet etiquette to remember is that you are interacting with real people. Even though all you see are words on a screen, a flesh-and-blood person is behind them. This live human being deserves the same respect that you would offer him or her face-to-face.

Just because you may never meet your correspondent in person, and just because you're protected by the shield of your computer, doesn't mean that you can allow yourself to be a Dr. Jekyll in real life and a Mr. Hyde on the Internet. Rudeness isn't acceptable anywhere.

Don't assume that you can be anonymous on the Internet. You can use a nickname, attempt to hide your e-mail address, and adopt other tactics to hide your true identity and location, but somebody out there knows how to trace your message back to you. A law-abiding, courteous Internet user has little to fear from this fact of life, but you need to certainly think about it if you're tempted to misbehave.

Make yourself perfectly clear

As a rule, Internet users do not appreciate subtlety. Your wisecrack or innocent comment may be intended as humorous, but words have a way of taking on innuendoes and double meanings when they travel across the Internet. Unless you're sure of your audience, think twice before you send anything that could be misinterpreted.

When posting a message or writing an e-mail, make yourself perfectly clear. The Internet is a unique medium of communication because you don't get any of the clues — facial expressions, hand gestures, and vocal intonations — that you get when you're speaking to someone in person or on the telephone.

If you insert a small joke in a sentence, mark it with a comment or a symbol. The combination of a colon with a right-end parenthesis, known as a *smiley*, is universally used to indicate attempts at humor. Similarly, a semicolon followed by a right-end parenthesis indicates a wink. These symbols can help someone understand that you're being lighthearted.

When all you have are words, you'd better be sure to use them carefully. If you're concerned that something you've written could possibly offend someone, you're probably right. Rephrase or delete it.

Whether you're exchanging e-mails or posting a response in a discussion group, reread what you've written before hitting the Send button — and then reread it one more time to be absolutely sure. That way, you're less likely to send a message that the recipient could take the wrong way. Make sure to proofread for typos and grammar, too.

Don't participate in the junk-mail and chain-letter problem

Don't become part of the problem of junk e-mail. The Net was not created for exchanging silly jokes, chain letters, or messages attacking other people. If you receive any of these annoying pieces of e-mail, my best advice is to simply ignore them. Hit the Delete key and move on to your next, hopefully more meaningful, piece of e-mail.

If a friend constantly passes along the annoying jokes and messages, a brief e-mail stating that you love a good joke now and again — but told *in person* — should do the trick. If it's a more serious matter (such as a personal attack) on an electronic bulletin board, use private e-mail to address the issue one-on-one with the author or the system administrator.

Write only what you would say in person

As a mannerly person, you avoid hostile confrontations with people in public. The same should go for the Internet. Arguments on the Internet sometimes escalate into ugly exchanges. You should avoid direct confrontations unless you're prepared for an endless exchange of increasingly hostile messages.

Even in a friendly situation in which you routinely exchange messages with someone, beware of assuming a false sense of intimacy or immunity from the rules of etiquette when you're online. Before you post a message or send an e-mail, ask yourself if you would say the same thing to the person's face. If the answer is no, take a few steps back. Reread your message. Edit it so that you would feel just as comfortable saying it to the person.

Many a hot-and-heavy Internet romance has fizzled when the partners come face-to-face. Why? One reason is that the Internet can give you a false sense of intimacy, maybe well before you would feel that comfort level with someone in person. Use restraint in your Internet relationships. Take things easy, one step at a time — just as you would in the real world.

Use lowercase letters

Don't use all-uppercase letters unless you're genuinely angry and want the recipient to know it. THIS LOOKS AS IF YOU ARE SHOUTING to an otherwise calm Internet user. When you send an e-mail message or post a message to a newsgroup, use uppercase and lowercase letters, just as you would when you type a social letter.

Know some key vocabulary

The Internet has developed its own special language. For example, *flaming* has nothing to do with being on fire. (Well, in a way it does, but only in the loosest sense!) On the Internet, flaming someone means that you are insulting them. And when you send a message to a huge number of people, you are *spamming*, even though you haven't eaten any meat out of a can. For the lowdown on Net vocabulary, check out *Internet E-Mail For Dummies* (also published by IDG Books Worldwide, Inc.).

Learn how to flame appropriately

Flaming is what people do when they express a strongly held opinion without holding back any emotion. It's not just an insult — it's an in-your-face statement. Although I am usually against such display of aggressiveness in dealing with others, I understand that it is common among some electronic bulletin board groups.

Netiquette allows flaming, which is a long-standing Internet tradition (well, as long-standing as anything can be on this relatively new invention). When made and taken in the right spirit (which is to say, not mean-hearted), flames can be lots of fun, both to write and to read. Sometimes, I hasten to add, the recipients even deserve the flack they get. However, flame wars (flaming that goes back and forth, ad nauseum) are not accepted netiquette. It may be amusing for everyone to read a brief exchange of flames, but sooner or later, they inevitably become mean-spirited and frankly, start to bore everyone else. Remember, you're in a group for the camaraderie. See to it that you don't spoil it by flaming.

Remember that what you write may be stored forever

E-mail may be electronic, but it's still mail. That means that your written word may be saved for posterity. And yes, those words may be held against you — whether it's by your spouse, a friend, or a court of law. Of course, I'd like to assume that no reader of this book would be in that kind of legal trouble, but even law-abiding citizens need to keep the potential repercussions of e-mails in mind. Even if you diligently delete all incriminating notes from your in-box, they may still be preserved by someone backing up a mainframe computer in your office where all messages are stored.

Just because you're not involved in criminal activity doesn't mean that you shouldn't be careful. Even if no one delves into your e-mail files, you aren't necessarily safe. Any message you send could be saved or forwarded by its recipient. You have no control over where it goes!

When it comes to posting messages on public boards, your words are there for posterity as well. Let me mention one word: archives. These are accessible to anyone at any time.

Take care to send messages properly

Write e-mails with care. Thanks to that little Forward command, your messages can travel far and wide. I have a friend who wrote a witty piece about why it's great to be a woman and shared it with other women in the small Midwestern advertising agency where she worked. A year and a half later, I received the same essay from a friend living in London. It had made its way around the world and back to its point of origin in 18 months! Once you send a message, you can never be sure where it's going to end up.

Always include a subject, even if a preceding e-mail had none. Use a greeting and a salutation. Jumping right in with a message is like calling someone and starting to state your business without saying hello first. Finally, try to respond to an e-mail within a day, even if it's just to acknowledge receipt of the message and to let the sender know that you'll be responding soon.

Understand that netiquette may vary

Before plunging into a discussion group, take time to read the messages and follow the flow of the discussion. Look back into the archives. You'll see that people "speak" differently to each other in different domains. In a stock-tip area, for example, you may note a lot of rumor and gossip, which may be completely acceptable in that area. However, if you move to a group discussing a book review at one of the Internet's well-known magazines, such as www.slate.com or www.salon.com, gossip and rumor do not fly very well. Remember where you are at all times!

If you spend time getting to know a group before saying something, your postings will be more relevant, and people will welcome you into the community more readily. People hate to have their time wasted by irrelevant postings that are not arcane to the subject or culture of the group. Your responsibility is to ensure that the time they spend reading your posting isn't wasted.

Respect other people's time

Although you may be intensely interested in the answers to a question you posted, or you may feel that the e-mail you just sent an editor about a book idea is incredibly important, you must remember that you are not the center of cyberspace. Try not to expect instant answers to all your questions, even though the Internet is a nearly instantaneous communications medium. And don't expect all members of a discussion group to be riveted by your arguments.

You should also respect the time it takes for people to open and read your messages. Face it: Some Internet connections are faster than others. For some people, just opening a posted note or article can take a while. No one is happy to wait ages for a message to download and then find out that it's a silly joke, a photo, or anything else not worth the trouble.

Don't abuse the Cc: button

Copying practically everyone on your e-mail is far too easy, and as often as not, people do. Doing so is very poor manners. Why? It shows a lack of consideration for other people's time.

You may think it an overly repeated cliché that people have less time today. Well, it's true, and do you know why? People have less time than ever before because they have so much information to absorb. Before you copy people on your messages, ask yourself whether they really need to know the information. If the answer is no, don't waste their time. If the answer is maybe, think twice before you hit the Send button.

Remember that grammar and language count

On the Internet, the only measure that people have to gauge who you are is how you represent yourself. So don't use offensive language, and double-check your grammar and punctuation. Complete sentences are appreciated, even on the Net! In fact, in some groups, people may become impatient with too many grammar and spelling errors. (Other groups, however, are more interested in companionship and are more forgiving of poor grammar.) Sloppiness in writing does not make a good impression.

Correct mistakes, but don't get self-righteous

Everyone makes mistakes, and next time, it might be you. (Knowing how the world works, once you correct someone's error, you will be the next to make one!) How often have you seen a message from someone correcting another's spelling mistake — and that message itself contains a spelling error? Believe me, the experience is humbling.

Just because you may know more than others in certain areas does not give you the right to gloat, taunt, or lord it over them. When someone makes a mistake — whether it's a spelling or grammar error, a stupid question, or an unnecessarily long answer — be kind about it. Think twice about correcting someone. If someone writes "compleat" instead of "complete," is it really necessary to say anything? Probably not. A well-mannered person realizes that having good manners (or knowledge of spelling or grammar) is not a license to go around correcting everyone else. In fact, doing so can be downright annoying and rude in and of itself!

If you decide the error is grave enough that it must be corrected, be kind. If it's possible, inform the person of the error politely, preferably by private e-mail rather than on a public electronic bulletin board. Give people the benefit of the doubt; assume that they are intelligent but just don't know this subject quite as well as they could. And never be arrogant or self-righteous in your message.

Don't get too informal in work e-mail

Just because you're sending an e-mail instead of a memo or telephone call doesn't mean you should let your professional standards relax. Although a touch of humor in the tone of an e-mail can be fine, make sure to preserve your professionalism. Although smileys may be helpful in social e-mails, try to avoid them in business.

Stay on the subject

If you're on an electronic bulletin board, stay close to the topic at hand. For example, if you're in a Cocker Spaniel grooming conference, don't post a question on German Shepherds and Great Danes. If you can't resist the urge to stray or to write a personal reply to someone's posting, label the message "private" and send it only to that person. Even though you may be excluding others, you are being considerate of their time, which is much more important!

An important corollary to staying on the subject is to know what you're talking about and to make sense. This may seem obvious, but you would be surprised at the amount of babble on the Internet. Please, pay attention to the content of your writing. Don't pass on speculation or hearsay; bad information propagates like wildfire on the Net. In addition, make sure that your messages are clear and logical. It's perfectly possible to write a paragraph that contains no errors in grammar or spelling but that still makes no sense whatsoever.

Share your knowledge

The Internet was founded and grew because scientists wanted to share information. It's especially polite to share the results of your questions with others on an electronic bulletin board. When you anticipate that you'll get a lot of answers to a question, or when you post a question to a discussion group that you don't visit often, it's customary to request replies to your personal e-mail address instead of to the group. After you get all those responses, write up a summary and post it to the discussion group. That way, everyone benefits from the experts who took the time to write to you. Sharing your knowledge is fun, and people will appreciate your thoughtfulness.

Part IV
Entertaining (And Being Entertained)

The 5th Wave   By Rich Tennant

"The lost art of conversation isn't lost at all. It's been kidnapped and held hostage by your sister-in-law."

In this part . . .

*E*ntertainment may seem like just the opposite if you spend the whole time worrying whether you're behaving appropriately — or if you find out later that you weren't. This part guides you through both sides of entertaining: being a host and being a guest. It talks about the gift-giving that so often accompanies special events. And because being a guest or being the recipient of a gift requires you to express your thanks, this part also covers the proper ways to thank people.

Chapter 13

Hosting a Well-Mannered Event

. . . .

. . . .

There's no getting around it: If you want to be invited to social events, you must reciprocate by acting as host to your friends, family, and business associates. There's no need for excessive formality or a lavish party-to-end-all-parties, but as the host, you want to put your own personal touch on the event and make the experience as pleasant and memorable as possible.

Entertaining can run the gamut from something as simple as a midday luncheon to something as complicated as a formal dinner party for 50. In either case, just as a chef blends compatible ingredients to turn out a memorable meal, you blend the party's elements — guests, food, and entertainment — to create a memorable event.

You may be an experienced host who needs only a word or two of encouragement and perhaps a checklist to make sure that you haven't overlooked anything. Or you may be new to entertaining and require a step-by-step guide. Either way, you can use this chapter as your plan for hosting a perfect event. Along with practical and clever ways to stay organized and save time, I provide a few suggestions for unique ways to entertain without breaking the bank.

One chapter can go only so far. For even more information about entertaining, see Suzanne Williamson's *Entertaining For Dummies* (also published by IDG Books Worldwide, Inc.).

Planning the Perfect Event

The key to any successful event is planning. As a host, your motto should be "Be prepared" (thank you, Boy Scouts!). Planning well in advance is the best way to ensure that you'll handle the inevitable unexpected glitches with grace.

The first step in the planning process is to decide on the type of event you want to host. There are as many different kinds of parties as there are hosts. From an intimate formal dinner party for four to an outdoor barbecue and pool party for the neighborhood to hors d'oeuvres and Champagne before opening night at the opera, the opportunities for a creative host are unlimited.

For most people, the only limits are time, energy, and budget. If your bank account won't support an elegant catered affair, don't fret! With some creativity, menu manipulation, and other tricks of the trade (all of which you can find in this chapter), you can replicate a catered affair for a fraction of the cost.

 To decide which type of party you want to host, consider the reason for the party or event. Is it to celebrate a family member's birthday, a colleague's promotion, someone moving to another city, or a 30th wedding anniversary? Is your goal to raise funds for a good cause? Maybe you just love to cook exotic meals for your friends and you want them to share in your authentic Indian curry or your grandmother's pot roast recipe. After you take time to reflect on the purpose for the event, you can decide how best to celebrate it. The visit of an out-of-town dignitary may be best marked by a dinner party with other luminaries in attendance. Your colleague's promotion may be best celebrated with cocktails at a restaurant near your office so that everyone can attend after work.

After you determine the occasion for your party, make a party checklist. If you need a role model for planning a wonderful event, consider Santa Claus: Like Santa, you too need to make a list and check it twice — even if you're hosting a simple impromptu dinner for four. In planning any event, attention to detail makes the difference. If you start by making a list, you'll remember all the details and stay organized. Things become hectic as party-time approaches, and you don't want to forget anything at the last minute.

Here's a checklist that you can use to keep your party on track:

Three to four weeks before the event:

❑ Select a theme.

❑ Determine the guest list.

❑ Mail the invitations, including the location, attire, date, and time. (Phone invites if you're hosting a casual get-together.)

❑ Plan the menu. (Consider the season when planning your menu so that you can use the freshest foods available.)

❑ Prepare your grocery shopping list.

❑ Select a caterer (if hiring a caterer is within your budget).

❑ Book the entertainment (if hiring entertainers is within your budget).

❑ Purchase decorations and party supplies.

❑ Arrange to rent tables and chairs (if necessary).

❑ Check your supply of linens and tablecloths, and purchase new ones if necessary.

❑ Make a bar shopping list if you're serving cocktails.

One week before the event:

❑ Call any guests who have not responded to the invitation.

❑ Buy groceries and beverages.

❑ Check your dishes and glasses for chips and cracks.

❑ Polish your silverware and silver serving pieces.

❑ Select trays and platters, noting which food you will serve on each.

❑ Plan your table decor, including the centerpiece, placecards, and candles or votives.

❑ Choose your favorite music to play at the party.

One or two days before the event:

❑ Wash your dishes, glasses, and flatware.

❑ Clean your house and yard.

❑ Organize your serving dishes.

❑ Prepare food items that can be made in advance and refrigerate them.

❑ Purchase fresh flowers and arrange them in vases.

❑ Coordinate last-minute arrangements with the caterer (if you've hired one).

❑ Set up the bar, and have plenty of ice on hand.

❑ Make sure that your closet has extra hangers, or provide a coat rack if the season requires.

❑ Unplug or remove your television (unless you're hosting a party for a special televised sporting event).

❑ Put away valuable and breakable items that you cherish.

The day before the event:

❑ Thaw frozen foods.

❑ Plan your outfit.

❑ Check your list twice, making sure that you've done everything you need to do.

❑ Mentally walk through your entire event.

Following such a schedule and party checklist helps lessen the emotional stress and makes planning your event a much smoother process. When you bring together good food and good friends, you want to be able to enjoy yourself, too!

Remember to have enough help. If you can't afford a catering staff, consider hiring teenagers, whether they're neighbors or children of friends, to help you serve and clean up. If you have teenaged children of your own, put them to work! They may enjoy helping and having a role in the event. Or ask a friend to share the duties of hosting the party.

Assembling the Right Crowd

The success of most events is measured by the mix of guests. (You thought the most important ingredient was the food? Well, that's a close second!) As you assemble your guest list, you want to consider inviting friends whose company you enjoy, guests whom you know mix well together, and those friends and family to whom you owe an invitation. All guests should feel special and know that they were invited because they have something special to contribute to the event.

Only you know for sure what will work and what won't regarding your guest list. For example, if Ken and Barbara had a perfectly amicable divorce and are now happily remarried to wonderful new mates, they may have no problem attending the same party. On the other hand, Ellen and Mike may be a different story. Ellen may have been left with no money, no car, three kids, and $10,000 in credit card debt, and she may have sworn to kill Mike if she ever sees him again. Take these essential pieces of information into account when you make up your guest list.

For some reason, people like to invite folks they *know* don't get along with each other "just to see what happens." Please resist this temptation. If you have any doubt about certain guests getting along with one another, *consult before you invite.* Call your friend and ask her how she feels about attending a dinner that will include her ex, Bob. If she says yes, make sure to check with Bob, too.

Extending a Cordial Invitation

An invitation should be so welcoming, so inviting, and so wonderful that it is impossible to resist. As the first announcement of your intention to host a social event, your invitation sets the tone and style for the affair.

Inviting your guests in writing

Printed invitations range from the classic and formal (think of a traditional wedding invitation) to the creative and unusual (I once received an invitation to a Chinese-themed dinner in a Chinese food takeout container). If your party has a theme, use it in your invitation — for example, if you're hosting a wine-tasting event, you can design your invitation to look like a wine label. Whatever you do, don't forget the basics:

- When the party starts
- When it will end
- What kind of attire is appropriate
- Where it will be held
- How to RSVP

Always let the guests know what the occasion is and, if you've designated a guest of honor, who he or she is. If you're hosting, say, a casual barbecue and you expect guests to contribute a dish or beverages, let them know in the invitation.

Inviting your guests orally

If you plan an informal gathering of friends or family, you can issue your invitations orally, either in person or by telephone. Make sure that you're clear about the time and date of the affair. Say something like this:

> "I'd love to have you join us for an informal brunch with a few other friends at my house a week from Sunday. We plan to get together at eleven, have a nice brunch, and play cards for a couple of hours."

Note that this invitation contains a lot of information. Your guests know how they need to dress and that others have been invited to the brunch. They know that the meal will consist of more than chips and dip, and they know that you expect them to leave after a couple of hours. Your guests will find all this information useful and will be grateful to you for providing it.

Considering significant others and children

Always mention exactly whom you're inviting when you issue invitations. For a married couple, mention both names. For a single adult whom you expect to bring a date, word the invitation as "you and your escort," "you and your date," or, if you know the name of the person's significant other, "you and Ian."

When you make up your guest list, be sure to include the people your guests won't leave home without. For example, it's not fair to expect your friend Jason to show up for dinner unless you also invite the new love of his life, Cynthia.

Some people take their children everywhere, but unless you specifically mention them on the invitation, your guests should understand that children are not invited. The only reasonable antidote is to be very specific in the way you address your invitation — make it read "Edward and Dorothy Smith" instead of "The Smith Family." If you want to include the little ones, state on the invitation, "You, Marvin, and the children . . . ," or write, "Children welcome."

If you have a feeling that one (or more) of your invited guests will want to bring along their children no matter how you word your invitation, telephone that person and say something along these lines: "We really hope you'll be able to attend our dinner. Did we pick a date when you can get a baby-sitter for the children?"

Requesting RSVPs

If you're having an informal party, you can request telephoned responses to your invitations. Include on the invitations your phone number and a note to leave word on your answering machine or voice mail if you're not home.

If you're hosting a more formal party, you may want to include separate RSVP cards in your invitations. RSVP cards are note-sized cards that the invitees fill in, telling whether or not they can attend the event, and mail back to you. (Although the traditional rules of etiquette call for the invitee to respond to an invitation with a written letter accepting or declining the invitation, many people neglect this courtesy in today's busy world.) Always include with your RSVP cards an envelope addressed to your attention and affixed with the correct postage.

The meaning of RSVP

RSVP stands for the French words that mean "respond, if you please." Why French? Because in early American history, the manners of the French were considered the world standard of graciousness.

Here is a sample format for an RSVP card:

Please respond on or before May 20, 2000

M_____

_____ *will attend*

_____ *will not attend*

If you have not received an RSVP from a guest, it's perfectly acceptable to call and ask whether he or she plans to attend. Just as a host has responsibilities, a guest also has "responsibilities" — and this is one of the most common mistakes that guests make. Guests are required to respond within a day or two of receiving an invitation.

Designating guest attire

Your formal invitation should include a freestanding line that specifies how you expect your guests to dress. If you want to see the gentlemen in tuxedos, your safest line is *Formal* or *Black Tie.* For suits and ties and cocktail dresses, use the phrase *Semi-Formal.* For slacks, sport coats, and bright, coordinated outfits, use *Business Casual.*

Terms such as *semi-formal* and *casual* mean many things to many people. If you're hosting a semi-formal gathering, you may want to verbally explain what dress is recommended to guests when they call to RSVP. You don't have to be shy about calling the shots for your own party. But no matter what your guests show up wearing, always make them feel at ease.

One extremely gracious host I know always wears a cocktail dress for her own formal parties, even though she tells her guests to dress in formal wear — which means long gowns for women. When asked why she was wearing a cocktail dress at one of her formal occasions, she stated, "At least one of my guests always seems to show up in a short dress, so I just want her to feel comfortable." Now that's good etiquette!

Giving directions

Don't expect your guests to fumble their way through an unfamiliar suburb or area of town. In the invitation, enclose a separate sheet of paper giving accurate directions to the location of your party. If necessary, make copies of a local road map and point out landmarks and distances.

Many Internet sites offer mapping capabilities. One example is `www.maps.excite.com`, which produces a map after you type in your address and the address of your destination. The result is a detailed map and written directions that guide you there street by street.

Providing parking

One of your responsibilities as the host of a large affair is to provide parking. Try to make provisions in advance. You can hire a valet parking company (most cities have them) or find a responsible college student with a valid driver's license.

If you're hosting an event at your home, alert your neighbors to possible parking on the street. If the parking situation is difficult and your street or home can't handle a large number of vehicles, you may want to look into hiring a shuttle or limousines for your guests. Doing so can solve the parking problem at a minimal cost.

If the event is to take place at an establishment with valet parking, arrange beforehand to handle the fees and gratuities for your guests. Otherwise, your guests might assume that they should pay their own way.

Decorating with Panache

Everyone loves a theme party. Today, creative hosts are coming up with unique ideas. Here are two I think are particularly clever:

✔ A host of a garden party used flowers and vegetables everywhere, for everything. Even the placemats were made from fresh string beans.

> ✔ At a very formal dinner party hosted by a movie producer, the host decorated everything white, including the china, linens, white orchids on each table, white candles, and white tulips everywhere. At the last minute, the caterer instructed one of her staff members to run out and buy 40 roles of film. The caterer removed the film from the canisters and wrapped one roll around each white linen napkin as a napkin ring. The film and napkin was placed on the main plate and the film flowed down over the table. It looked so elegant and was the talk of the evening!

After you select a theme, the decorations should follow naturally — all you need is a bit of creative thinking.

If you have trouble coming up with a theme, consider the time of year. This not only provides the freshest bounty, but it also can give you access to wonderful decorating items, such as gorgeous grape vines to add to your table or floral arrangements. You can decorate a winter or holiday buffet with brightly colored pomegranates and persimmons, with figs and nuts for an inventive centerpiece. In the fall, a walk into the countryside can produce shafts of wheat or small branches that you can spray-paint gold and make into a lovely mantle or table decoration.

Interesting plants, ivy, and exotic herbs make for inexpensive ways to decorate. You can find them in small produce markets and floral shops. Your friends and neighbors may even have beautiful and interesting flowers and herbs growing in their gardens.

If you have a nonsmoking household or do not have a place for smokers to go outside, let them know in advance that the event is a nonsmoking one. Otherwise, do try to make accommodations for smokers so that they feel welcome but don't bother nonsmoking guests. Design a creative sign stating where smoking is permitted — a room designated for smoking could have open windows or a balcony, for example. Provide ashtrays and a fan; scented candles and fragrant flowers add a nice touch.

For the comfort of your guests, do what you can to keep the air fresh. For example, you can run the exhaust fan in your kitchen, open the windows (if the weather allows), and run an overhead fan at low speed.

Menus: A Matter of Taste

Your menu can be as simple or as elaborate as you'd like it to be, and as your budget and culinary talents allow. You may want to stick to simpler dishes for casual events and save the gourmet treats for more formal affairs. But remember that elegant and exotic don't always translate to difficult; these menus can be simple and easy to arrange. The following sections provide tips for menu-planning for each type of event, plus information about setting a beautiful table.

Hints and tips for casual occasions

✔ Be considerate of your guests' schedules and lifestyles when choosing a date for entertaining. For example, if it's a weeknight, make sure that the party doesn't run late for those with early work schedules.

✔ You don't have to make the menu too elaborate.

✔ If you'd like friends to bring something, or if they offer to, request specific items so that there's no duplication.

✔ If you think that organizing the event is more than you can handle, ask a friend to share the duties of hosting the party — doing so adds to the pleasure without adding additional stress.

✔ You can never have too much food at a party. Remember to have plenty of hot coffee, tea, and snacks on hand, too, for events that go late into the evening.

Casual buffets

If you're having a casual get-together, you want a menu that you can prepare and serve with a minimum of fuss. That way, if you must serve as host, cook, and server, you can handle the job with just some advance planning — and you'll have time to socialize with your guests.

When deciding on a menu, don't bother looking for a dictionary definition of *casual*. Casual can mean whatever you want it to mean — just make sure that your prospective guests are in agreement with you. Among very close friends, casual may mean pizza ordered in and a couple of six-packs in a bucket of ice. Casual can also mean a three-course luncheon served at a nicely set table.

A buffet is an excellent way to serve a group of guests without having to traipse back and forth to the kitchen. Utilizing a buffet enables you to arrange everything on a side table, stack up the plates and silverware, and let your guests help themselves. The buffet concept can work beautifully if you keep a few rules in mind:

✔ Make sure that you plan the timing. After about one hour of cocktails and perhaps some hors d'oeuvres, it will take another 45 minutes for your guests to make their way through the buffet and consume a meal.

✔ Unless you're planning a formal sit-down buffet with properly set tables, think of how your guests are going to manage to eat while holding plates on their laps. Avoid pieces of meat that you have to cut, as well as long, unwieldy strands of pasta.

✔ If you're hosting a cocktail buffet at an open house, choose foods that taste good at room temperature (unless you have the use of chafing dishes or servers standing by to refill hot dishes). A cocktail buffet should also include bite-sized foods, with small bowls of snacks and nuts placed around the room. The buffet might include the following foods: a cold pasta dish with chicken, a salad, a large basket of assorted breads and rolls, a platter of various cheeses, crudités with dip, fresh fruit salad, and a rich dessert (chocolate is always popular).

✔ If you're intent on offering a more elaborate buffet menu for a large group, you must keep hot foods hot and cold foods cold. As foods approach room temperature — from either direction — the growth of bacteria is greatly accelerated. Instead of pleasing your guests, you may be at risk of poisoning them. To keep cold foods cold, arrange them in metal serving containers and then rest the containers on top of lots of ice in an even larger container. To keep hot foods hot, use electric warming platters or alcohol burners.

✔ Arrange the food in the following order: entrees, side dishes, salads, bread, butter, and condiments.

✔ Prepare extra portions (make enough for 16 if you're expecting 12, for example). Not only do you not want to run out of food, but some people may take larger portions than they can finish.

✔ Consider those guests who can't easily serve themselves in a buffet line. Serve these guests first, or invite them to the buffet table just a moment before you issue a general invitation to dine.

Set the buffet up on a dining room table or sideboard. Also provide an open bar, plus sodas, bottled water, and fruit juice. Make sure to set the bar up a fair distance from the food to avoid traffic jams. At one end of the buffet, make a stack of large plates, utensils (a fork, a spoon perhaps, and, only if absolutely necessary, a knife). It's thoughtful to place utensils in large napkins to create neat, easy-to-grab packages. Be creative! You can tie these with a ribbon or cord, tuck in a flower, and place them in a basket for a decorative touch. You should also provide enough extra dishes and silverware so that people who go back for seconds can enjoy their new selections on clean dishes.

Do make provisions for bones, fruit pits, peelings, and other inedible pieces of food, such as additional dishes set out for used food picks, shells, and shrimp peels, by placing a waste bin nearby. Otherwise, you may find unusual items in your potted plants!

Sophisticated menus

For a more formal event, your menu may vary, depending on the time of day and the degree of formality you want to achieve:

- A typical luncheon menu might begin with an appetizer or salad, followed by a main course (a cold dish such as cold poached salmon in summer, or a hot dish such as pasta in wintertime), and ending with dessert and coffee or tea. You can serve wine, but don't be surprised if your guests avoid alcohol during the day.

- For a small, casual, seated dinner, you can serve a substantial main course (including meat, vegetable, potato or rice, salad, and bread), plus dessert, with a choice of red or white wine.

- A more formal dinner would include a first course such as baked clams, oysters, or soup, followed by a main course and then dessert, with red or white wine at each course.

- If you want to pull out all the stops, a very formal dinner would include a light soup, a light fish course, a main course of meat or fowl, two accompanying vegetables (one vegetable and potatoes), a salad and cheese course, a light dessert, a choice of red or white wine, and Champagne with dessert.

Hints and tips for planning a perfect menu

Great cooks seem to have a knack for planning perfect menus, as artists create masterpieces. Considerations in menu planning are usually practical rather than artistic, but the secret lies with both. Not too often is a perfect menu an accident. Here are some guidelines that can help you create a menu that would please even the most discriminating guest:

- **Texture:** Include in your menu a variety of firm, chewy, smooth, crunchy, soft, and flaky foods.

- **Color:** Colors can stimulate the appetite as well as be pleasing to the eye. Use foods of bright, vivid colors for contrast and harmony.

- **Harmony:** Consider including a variety of compatible flavors and temperatures, using raw and cooked foods.

- **Safe dishes:** If you don't know your guests well or you're hosting a business meal, use simple ingredients for the main course for the less-than- adventuresome. Appetizers provide you the opportunity to try something unusual.

- **Time:** Estimate the time it will take to prepare each course, and select a menu with dishes that you can make ahead of time.

Special occasions call for special meals. I hope that the following two menus help to get your creative juices flowing.

Brunch on the Beach

Bucket of Crudités and Dip

Crispy French Bread

Assorted Shellfish on Ice

Grilled Herbed Salmon

Seafood Seviche

Mixed Greens with Avocado and Papaya

Sand Dollar Cookies

Blanc de Noir Sparkling Wine

Pinot Blanc

Formal Dinner

Caviar Pouches

Roast Duckling with Orange Sauce and Wild Mushroom Rice

Sauté of Zucchini

Endive and Watercress Salad

Raspberry-Chocolate Torte

Champagne

Cabernet Sauvignon

Sparkling Muscat

The rules of the tools

The easiest thing to do is to plan to eat at your dining table and invite only as many guests as you can seat around the table. (Guests appreciate having a bit of elbow room, so keep that in mind when deciding how many people can *comfortably* fit.) If the group becomes too large, conversation becomes difficult. Besides, putting everyone at one table enables you to avoid dealing with the politics of who sits at which table when more than one table is involved.

If the group absolutely must be larger than your dining table can accommodate, consider renting tables and chairs and setting them up in a separate room. Then you can use your dining room table for a buffet.

How you set your table depends on the formality of the event (not to mention the extent of your dinnerware, silverware, and glassware supplies!). A basic table setting consists of the following items:

- ✔ A dinner plate
- ✔ A salad plate
- ✔ A salad fork, dinner fork, and dessert fork

    For a restaurant touch, chill your salad plates and salad forks in the freezer and remove them just before serving the salad.

- ✔ A dinner or luncheon knife and a fish knife (if you're serving fish)
- ✔ A soup spoon and dessert spoon and/or teaspoon
- ✔ A folded cloth napkin

- ✔ A water glass

    Fill the water glasses before your guests sit down at the table.

- ✔ A coffee cup and saucer (if you're serving breakfast or brunch)
- ✔ A wine or iced tea glass (if you're serving either beverage)

Here's how you arrange these items on the table:

1. **Place the dinner plate at the center of the place setting.**

2. **Place the forks to the left of the dinner plate, with the tines pointing upward.**

    The salad fork (the smaller one) lies farthest from the plate, with the dinner fork in the center and the dessert fork closest to the plate.

    At a fancier affair, you place the dessert fork and spoon at the top of the plate, fork tines pointing to the right.

3. **Place the folded napkin to the left of the forks.**

4. **Place the knife and soup spoon to the right of the dinner plate, with the knife blade facing inward and the spoon on the other side of the knife.**

5. **Place the water glass and any other beverage glasses above the plate, to the right.**

When setting a table, remember the rule: Solids (such as a bread plate, if you use one) to the left and liquids (beverage glasses) to the right. You place the salad plate on top of the dinner plate and then remove it after your guests finish the salad course.

You serve guests from the left and remove dishes from the right, unless the arrangement of the tables and chairs does not allow you to do so. Remember to serve the most senior guest(s) first.

Coffee cups or teacups and saucers are not brought to the table until dessert is served. However, if you're serving a brunch or breakfast, you may place them on the table to the upper right of the plate, with the water glass or goblet to the right of the cup and saucer.

Silverware manufacturers have come up with utensils for every imaginable menu item. There are special forks for eating oysters, cute little picks for eating lobster, gorgeous knives and forks for eating fish, special knives and forks for fresh fruits, different spoons for coffee and tea, and so on. (Chapter 16 shows you some of these special utensils.) Although you may own some of these exotic utensils and yearn to use them, a casual luncheon isn't the place to get that fancy. For a formal meal, though, you can pull out all the stops. See Chapter 16 if you need advice on which utensils go where.

Welcoming Your Guests

As your guests arrive, do your best to greet them at the door. If you have someone else doing the greeting, make sure that you are close by and that the person welcoming your guests knows where you are at all times.

I once attended a formal dinner in someone's home where a member of the catering staff greeted the guests. A few of the guests who had not met the host previously thought that the staff member greeting them was the host. Unfortunately, one guest after another shook the catering staff person's hand and said, "Thank you for inviting me to your home." Each time, the poor staff person had to explain who the host was — an awkward and embarrassing situation for everyone.

If you're hosting a fairly large event, consider providing a guest book and inviting your guests to sign in as they arrive. Not only is this a nice touch, but you'll also have a list of the guests who attended. If you need to send thank-you cards to the guests who brought gifts, you'll have their addresses handy, too. You can even make a notation later in the guest book of the gift that each guest brought.

If you're hosting an event in which most of the guests are meeting for the first time, consider using name cards. Doing so gives you the opportunity to have some fun and be creative.

Offering drinks

Normally, as your guests arrive, you should offer a drink or show them to the bar. In addition to a selection of alcoholic beverages, always have nonalcoholic beverages available during the cocktail hour. Keep cocktail napkins close at hand or offer them with the drinks.

If you plan to serve cocktails before a meal, anywhere from 30 minutes to an hour is acceptable. If the cocktail hour runs much longer than an hour, make sure to provide plenty of appetizers and snacks.

Serving a Champagne punch is a great alternative if you don't want to be busy opening bottles or pouring drinks during your party. Guests may help themselves! And mixing the sparkling wine with fruit juice or soda is easier on your budget.

Keeping an eye on the party for any sign of accidental overindulgence is a host's duty. Before-dinner cocktails, wine with dinner, and cordials afterward may sneak up on guests and impair their ability to make a safe trip home. Make sure to monitor your guests' conditions and, if you're serving mixed drinks, make adjustments to the strength of follow-up servings if necessary. Offer more nonalcoholic drinks as the evening progresses, too. If you have a guest who is not fit to drive home, you can enlist the transportation assistance of another guest, call a taxi, or as a last resort, provide a guestroom for an overnight stay.

Be considerate of those guests who choose not to indulge in alcohol. Serve plenty of juices, soft drinks, and the like, and don't push anyone to have "just one drink." Think about the foods that you serve as well. If you plan to serve anything with an alcoholic content, such as the sauce on a dessert, make that fact known to your guests and have a nonalcoholic alternative available.

Seating your guests

Each guest needs a place to sit, preferably with a table surface for a plate (a coffee table or end table is fine). People will juggle dishes on their laps if they have to, but you may be asking for a carpet-cleaning job the following week if you require them to do so. Try arranging the furniture to accommodate small seating groups, with end tables close by on which guests can place drinks and empty plates. For very informal occasions, you can put cushions on the floor, which makes for a perfectly good seating arrangement.

Seating arrangements at a buffet meal should enable all the guests to dine in the same room. If everyone won't fit, announce before the buffet is served that seating is available in an adjacent room, point the way, and try to have one of the hosts sit in that room. Limit your guest list to a number that you can accommodate gracefully.

After everyone begins eating the main course, go back to the kitchen and start the coffeemaker and the water for tea.

Ending the Party

One of the toughest challenges for a gracious host is the delicate process of getting the guests to go home. Moving your guests homeward is really a two-sided issue, because guests are expected to exhibit their own good manners by knowing when it's time to leave.

The invitation is the first and best opportunity to let your guests know the proper time to leave. Say, or write, the times of the event on the invitation. Make it look (or sound) like this: "Jerry and I would love to have you join us between noon and 3 p.m. for a buffet luncheon at our home."

In the absence of a stated quitting time, don't rely on hints and subtleties. If circumstances dictate, make a matter-of-fact announcement that you need your guests to leave. You can use a statement like the following:

> "You all know where the refrigerator is, and I hope you'll make yourselves at home, but I have to leave at 5 a.m. for our trip to State College, and if I don't get a few hours of sleep, I'm likely to run off the road. Good-night, all of you, and thanks so much for coming."

Otherwise, start cleaning up, turn off the music, and say something like, "What a great evening it's been! How did it get so late?"

Absolutely *perfect* manners require you to remain cheerfully hospitable until your guests leave without prompting. Absolutely *perfect* manners also require your guests to leave shortly after the final offer of after-dinner refreshments and a noticeable slowdown in conversation. Etiquette necessitates obligations on both sides.

Hosting a Semi-Formal or Formal Occasion

After you successfully host a few buffet luncheons on your patio and sit-down suppers for your close friends, you may feel ready to spread your wings and soar into the world of semi-formal and formal entertaining. Say you have a 40th anniversary or a graduation coming up. These are perfect occasions to launch your entry into more formal entertaining.

If you feel an obligation to host a fancy social affair and you can't imagine handling all the details yourself, you can always reserve a private room at a nice restaurant or hotel and let the staff handle everything. Or you can hire a caterer to come into your home and arrange everything from the seating to the flowers to a gourmet meal. However, there's no reason why you can't pull off a truly impressive affair on your own. So what if you overlook some small detail? What counts is your determination to be gracious and to provide others a good time.

The following steps can help you along as you plan your semi-formal or formal event:

1. **Set the date.**

   Plan your event far in advance to avoid conflicts with other popular events, and don't clash with religious or national holidays. Planning four months in advance gives you ample time to coordinate the rest of your event.

2. **Rent the room, hire the caterer, and so on.**

   Popular places and service organizations schedule their work far into the future. If you have to change the date of your party to accommodate the help you need, do so.

3. **Write out an agenda for your event, setting the time and place for every activity.**

   You'll go over this exercise several times, making little changes. Nothing helps the planning process more than a minute-by-minute schedule — you may find yourself remembering to get help with parking, assigning a friend to assist with greeting guests, conferring with the caterer about hors d'oeuvres, arranging for music or other entertainment, and so on.

4. **Compose your invitation and obtain nice cards and envelopes, or confer with a printer about a more formal invitation.**

5. **Determine your guest list, make a sketch of the seating, and work out the seating placements.**

6. **Review your guest list and see whether anyone has special dietary needs.**

   If so, alert the caterer or arrangements manager, or make a note to yourself.

7. **If the party will be at your home, you may want to invite your neighbors. If that's not possible, inform your neighbors of what's on your calendar and ask them to tolerate a bit of temporary disruption.**

   Sending a small gift along wouldn't hurt, either!

8. **Address the invitations and the envelopes for the RSVP cards in long-hand, and affix attractive postage stamps to both the inner and the outer envelopes.**

   Mail your invitations well in advance — five or six weeks is not unreasonable for a semi-formal or formal affair.

9. **Find a place to store the RSVP cards as your guests return them, and keep a checklist of the cards that you receive.**

   You'll need to give the caterer the total number of guests. You may have to telephone a few invitees to determine their intentions as the date draws closer. If you haven't heard yet from a guest, you may want to call and say something like this:

   "Hi, Bill, this is Joan calling. I'm in the process of confirming numbers with our caterer and am wondering whether you're planning on attending the costume party next Saturday night."

10. **Make a schedule for the big day and stick to it.**

    Remember to leave time to get yourself ready, as well as time to take care of quite a few last-minute distractions.

Choose the right equipment for the agenda

A semi-formal dinner party is a splendid opportunity to use your wedding silver and your china and crystal. If you don't have enough matching dinnerware and silverware for the group, your caterer can provide whatever you need.

Different courses of a meal require different eating utensils — soup spoons for soup, salad forks for salad, dinner knives and forks for the main course, dessert forks and/or spoons for dessert, and coffee spoons for coffee. (See the section called "The rules of the tools," earlier in this chapter, for the proper place to put all these utensils.)

You may also want placecard holders, napkin rings (unless you know how to do a nice folding job), water glasses, salt and pepper shakers at convenient intervals along the table, serving forks or spoons suitable for the relishes and other items, and, if you're employing a serving staff, a little bell that you can ring to summon one of the servers. If a cocktail hour will precede the call to dinner, you need glasses, ice, and a good supply of alcoholic and nonalcoholic beverages.

Welcoming your guests

Before your guests begin arriving, make one last trip through the kitchen to verify that the cook or caterer is on track and to inspect the public rooms for stray newspapers, magazines, and personal items. Then position yourself near the front door and take a deep breath.

As your guests arrive, greet them, show them where to put their wraps, steer them to the living room or cocktail area, and invite them to request a refreshment. You're on safer ground if you avoid drinks and hors d'oeuvres yourself — shaking hands and hugging while holding a dish is difficult. Likewise, leaving little moisture or a few grease spots on other people's clothing is definitely bad form.

In the event of a spill or other minor accident, summon a server or other worker to handle the problem, move away, and then put it out of your mind. If you don't have help, take a few minutes to attend to the guest yourself. If all else fails, you may be able to offer a piece of your own clothing. It is gracious, also, to offer to send the stained garment for cleaning.

Introduce newcomers all around the room until the number of guests gets too large. When that time arrives, introduce newcomers only to the people who are closest at hand. Keep an eye out for shy guests who plaster themselves to the wall. Engage them in conversation and introduce them to someone you hope can draw them out.

Making it through the meal

In all that happens at this event, you're the leader. When the time comes, select an honored guest as your escort and move toward the dining room — other guests will follow. Take your seat right away and place your napkin in your lap as a sign that others should do the same.

As soon as the wine is poured, offer a short toast. For example, you can say something like, "Here's to the great pleasure of dining with friends." If a special occasion has prompted the dinner, suit your toast to the event: "To an absolutely wonderful fundraising season for the Society to Protect Cobblestone Streets." Begin eating at once so that your guests may follow suit. As soon as you take the first bite, you can continue eating at your own pace.

As the host, you have the responsibility to pace the meal. Do not eat too quickly or too slowly; watch the balance and harmony of the table.

After dessert, when you rise from the table, everyone else will, too. Make sure that the slowest guest has finished eating before you stand. When you lead the way to the den, the patio, or some other room, others will follow. Try to engage every guest in at least a short period of personal conversation after the meal.

Saying good-bye

As guests begin to leave, station yourself at the door, accept their compliments, and wish them a good evening. Don't apologize for the roast being overdone or the gin running out — just say how pleased you were to have them at your party.

Accommodating an Uninvited Guest

As a host, you face one of life's little challenges when an uninvited guest arrives at your carefully planned party. Allow the way that you handle the situation to demonstrate your mastery of etiquette.

In some circumstances, your guests may be forced to bring along someone you didn't invite. Perhaps a relative arrived from out of town, and it seemed rude for your guest to leave her at home alone, or your adult son shows up with a girl he introduces as his fiancée. You even have the off chance that an old college roommate will ring your doorbell just as you're about to sit down to a catered dinner with 11 other guests. In such as situation, your college roommate may initially refuse your insistence on joining the party. As a gracious host, you need to ignore such protests. Assure the person, "There's a ton of food and some people you'll just love to get to know."

How you handle these types of situations is as good a test of your manners as anything else that can happen to you. Remember, the success of your party depends on lots of laughter, good friends, delicious food, and everyone feeling welcomed and comfortable — invited or not. This section provides some guidance.

Hugging while thinking

Greet an uninvited guest as if you were hoping for just such a visit. Say how wonderful it is that she can join your other friends for the evening. Begin making introductions immediately to make the extra guest feel at home.

Word your introductions to put everyone at ease. Use the following scripts for inspiration, modifying them as necessary:

✔ "Andrew and Gina, please say hello to my niece, Ruth, who just arrived from Fargo. Ruth is usually so busy participating in equestrian competitions that I seldom get to see her, so I'm thrilled that she's here. Ruth, Andrew is a veterinarian, so you two will probably have plenty to talk about."

✔ "Charlie and Sara, I'd like you to meet Winston McClure, who has wooed and won the heart of our dear Minnie. I hope you'll help me make him feel welcome as a member of the family."

Rearrange the seating and shoehorn an extra place setting onto the table. If you have to, move the centerpiece to a sideboard. The situation of a surprise guest can work if you make it work.

Stretching the food

Twelve steaks and 13 guests — your worst nightmare? Not at all. You can't find a menu for a family-sized group that can't be stretched to feed an extra mouth. Simply slice the steaks in the kitchen and arrange the pieces nicely on a tray. Push the dinner rolls, cook an extra potato in the microwave, open a can of soup and add it to your homemade stew, and carry on bravely. Your guests won't even notice if you carry yourself as though you have no worries.

If you host such events frequently, you can prepare yourself ahead of time for unexpected guests by having easy-to-prepare foods on hand. Salad greens, packaged turkey breast or ham that you can slice and serve, and ready-to-eat frozen foods that you can heat in the microwave can serve in a pinch. And fancy cookies and ice cream are all you need for a nice dessert.

Chapter 14

Being a Gracious Guest

In some ways, being a gracious guest is as challenging as being a good host. A good guest is a rare gem — a person who adds sparkle and zest to an event while helping the host in subtle ways that are undetectable to other guests. These are the people who always seem to have a full social calendar and who receive loads of fun invitations.

In this chapter, you can discover everything you need to know about being one of these gracious guests who always get invited back.

Note: Dressing appropriately is certainly a part of being a good guest, but because attire can get complicated, especially when you attend a formal or semi-formal event, I've devoted a separate chapter to it. For information about attire, see Chapter 7.

Responding to an Invitation

Step 1 of being a gracious guest is responding to invitations promptly. I recommend responding within a day or two of receiving an invitation. This is a reasonable amount of time to check with your spouse or partner, coordinate calendars, or make arrangements for a baby-sitter. Any longer and you may leave the host wondering.

If the invitation is telephoned and you aren't able to give the host an answer over the phone, say something like this: "What a lovely invitation! Thank you so much for thinking of us. I'll check with Tom and get back to you on Wednesday." Note that you should be specific about when you will be able to accept or decline.

If the invitation is written, either RSVP to the telephone number (if one is given), return the RSVP card, or write your own response. (To find out how to write a response, see Chapter 11.)

Arriving at an Event

Being prompt is a guest's most important responsibility. The host carefully chose a time for the event to begin, and you must respect that choice by showing up at that time. Keep the following points about time in mind:

- ✔ **Fashionably late is unfashionably rude.** When an invitation specifies a time, as most wedding and banquet invitations do, you're supposed to arrive at that time. If the affair is held in a hotel or other public place, getting out of the house a few minutes early won't hurt, just in case you get caught in traffic or have trouble finding a parking space.

- ✔ **You should not arrive later than 15 or 20 minutes after the scheduled start of an event.**

- ✔ **If the event is a dinner party and you're running late, phone ahead to request that the host start without you.** If you arrive late and the meal has already begun, do not disrupt the other guests or bother the host. Take your seat swiftly, and do not expect the other guests to stand and greet you.

- ✔ **Informal invitations that use words like** *sevenish* **imply a somewhat looser definition of arrival time.** At a private residence, when the host asks you to arrive around sevenish, plan to ring the bell between 7:15 and 7:30, and no later. Never, under any circumstances, arrive a minute before 7:00.

- ✔ **Arriving too early is as unacceptable as arriving too late.** Unless you're prepared to pitch in with the last-minute vacuuming or to open the Cabernet Sauvignon so that it can breathe, never ring a host's doorbell before the appointed hour. You're imposing another burden on a busy host who now has to entertain you as well as make the final preparations. If necessary, drive around the block a few times, stop at a local convenience store, or refuel your car to kill time.

- ✔ **Do not assume that additional company is welcome.** The host carefully plans for the number of guests who returned an RSVP, basing the amount of help, food, and beverages on that figure. Don't bring an uninvited guest with you! If you happen to have an unexpected houseguest show up on the day of the scheduled event, you can call the host and ask if it's possible for you to bring a friend. Present the question in a manner that does not put the host on the spot.

A word about the grand entrance

Really important people are expected to wait in another room until all the guests have arrived and then make a grand entrance punctuated by applause and gentle murmurs of admiration from the guests. These entrance-worthy people include presidents, kings, queens, princes, princesses, international leaders of religious organizations, and returning interplanetary explorers.

Follow this general rule: If you received an invitation, you're not quite qualified to make your own grand entrance. Save the grand entrances for those who deserve the honor, and arrive on time, mix with your fellow ordinary mortals, and try not to draw too much attention to yourself.

Before you attend an important event of an international nature, such as a party in someone's home honoring a guest from another country, take a moment to learn a few words of the guest's language and to learn some of the specific etiquette rules and customs of the country. You can find this information in most reliable country guidebooks. Doing so may take you a few minutes, but it gives you added confidence, which leads to a more relaxing and enjoyable experience for everyone.

Bringing a Gift

When you've been invited to someone's home, it's always a nice gesture to take the host a small gift, even if the invitation instructs you not to. Bringing a bottle of wine, a flowering plant, or candy is a considerate way to show your appreciation. If you want to give cut flowers, try to bring them already in a vase so that the host doesn't have to take the time to arrange them. Gifts of food and wine are acceptable, as long as you let the host know that it's not necessary to open or serve them. In fact, you should tell the host that you hope he or she will enjoy the gift later.

Gifts of special blends of coffee and tea are acceptable, too. If you know that the host loves to garden or cook, for example, consider a gift or memento for that special interest. The gift does not need to be wrapped or come with a card. And it's not necessary for the host to send a thank-you card.

Mingling

Knowing how to mingle with other guests is part of the responsibility of being a guest who's always invited back. You already know what *you* like, what *you* think, and what *you* need. It's just as important to really learn about other people — what *they* like, what *they* think, and what *they* need. That's the basis of talking with other people: communicating. And one of the ways you do that is to have a conversation. (For an extensive discussion of how to converse, see Chapter 4.)

What is a conversation? It's what happens when two or more people exchange ideas. There is give and take. You talk. The other person talks. The exchange moves back and forth. A conversation is not one person doing all the talking while the other person does all the listening! And most of the time, conversations don't "just happen." You invite other people to talk with you.

As a gracious guest, you need to be able to start a conversation as well as to participate in one. You need to learn how to listen and how to be patient and not interrupt. And you need to think about what someone is asking and respond appropriately, just as you need to think about what you want to say and say it clearly.

So let's look at some of the skills you need to have a conversation with someone. First of all, you need to think about other people and care about them. If you're shy or quiet, you need to learn how to open up to others and not always wait for them to draw you into a conversation. If you're an extrovert and extremely outgoing, you may need to learn how to reign in your enthusiasm and let other people have the floor.

Be pleasant, cheerful, and upbeat when mingling, no matter what your mood. If you've had a bad day, don't rain on anyone else's parade by talking about your negative experience — unless, of course, you want to be left standing alone. And when ending a conversation, say that you enjoyed talking with the person or that it was a pleasure meeting him or her.

Minding Your Manners

Here are a few situations that you may encounter as a guest at an event and the right ways to handle them:

✔ If you inadvertently spill water or wine on the guest seated next to you, promptly blot the table. However, do not blot the other person's clothing. Make your apology, assist in pulling back the chair to let the person escape to the bathroom, and hope that your dinner partner comes back to the table in a reasonable state of repair.

✔ Whether or not the event is a nonsmoking one, be considerate and go outside to smoke, away from the nonsmoking guests. Occasionally, accommodations for smokers are made, but always ask before lighting up. Cigars should not be smoked unless the host invites the guests to do so.

✔ Consume alcoholic beverages in moderation in all social and business situations. Nothing spoils a good party faster than forcing a host to cope with an inebriated guest who creates a scene that makes the other guests uncomfortable. A guest who overindulges rarely gets invited back. If you encounter an inebriated guest, don't antagonize the person or do or say anything to make matters worse.

Although it's not a guest's responsibility, asking if you can assist the host in smoothing things over is a kind gesture. You could call a cab, offer to drive the guest home, or help take the guest to a separate room. Doing so affords the host the opportunity to continue entertaining the other guests.

If you have embarrassed yourself by drinking too much, call the host the next day to apologize. If you can't muster up the courage to call, send a note of apology.

✔ Guests are expected to leave the bathroom or guest room as clean as they found it. Be as clean and thoughtful in your host's bathroom as you would in your own bathroom. Pick up after yourself! Don't splash water everywhere, don't throw anything on the floor, and don't forget to flush! If you make a mess around the sink, use a paper towel to clean up your spatters. Men should keep the seat down.

✔ If cloth guest towels are left out, leave the used towel unfolded so that no one else mistakes it for a clean towel. A good host will supply paper hand towels; make sure to toss them into the wastepaper basket. Remember that behaving properly involves being courteous to the other people who will use the same facilities.

✔ Dressing appropriately shows respect. A well-mannered host will let you know what the attire is for the event. However, if you're not certain of the appropriate dress, call ahead and ask. One rule to keep in mind is that it's better to be overdressed than to be dressed too casually.

Knowing When the Party's Over

Just as a good symphony ends on a beautiful chord, a party, too, should end on a nice note. You certainly don't want to catch your host yawning at three o'clock in the morning while you sip away at the Courvoisier.

You know it's past time to go home when . . .

- ✔ They close the bar.
- ✔ The orchestra plays "Goodnight, Ladies."
- ✔ The catering staff has packed up and left.
- ✔ The guests of honor have departed.
- ✔ The janitorial crew is waiting around with brooms in hand.

A well-mannered guest should stay at least an hour after dinner ends. If the majority of the guests stay and all are enjoying the evening, you certainly may stay longer. No matter when you leave, always thank the host for inviting you. Say something along the lines of, "Thank you for having us. We had a wonderful evening." Try not to engage the host in a long good-bye, which keeps the host from entertaining the other guests.

If you must leave an event early, try to be discreet and make your exit quietly. You don't want the other guests to think that the party's over.

Home Away from Home: Being a Well-Mannered Houseguest

When you're invited to someone's home for a weekend or longer, knowing what to do to maintain harmony is essential. There's nothing like sharing living quarters to bring out tensions between guests and hosts — and it's up to the guest to do his or her best to avoid tense situations.

Here are some tips that are sure to please your host:

- ✔ As a gesture of appreciation, bring a small gift for the host. A picture frame, candles, a flowering plant, or a nice bottle of wine or liquor is appropriate.

- ✔ During your stay, it's up to you to adapt to the host's lifestyle. Do not try to run the show — be open to the host's suggestions for meals and recreation. If the host sleeps late, be considerate; don't expect him or her to get up earlier to entertain you.

- ✔ When asked to spend the weekend with friends, never assume that bringing your pets, children, friend, or family member is acceptable if you're not directly told or invited to do so.

- ✔ Keep your voice down late in the evening or early morning, and if the guest room has a television, keep the volume low.

✔ Clean up after yourself, make sure not to leave your belongings strewn around the house, and make your bed.

✔ Know when it's time to go home; don't wear out your welcome. If you agreed to leave on Sunday afternoon, don't extend your stay until Monday morning. Remember the old saying, "Fish and houseguests begin to smell after three days."

Following Up with a Thank-You Note

Following up with a thank-you note, card, or letter of appreciation is a must. If you've attended a party or celebration, you're expected to send a thank-you note within a few days (the sooner the better!).

If you were a weekend guest in someone's home, send your thank-you note as soon as you return home. If you happen to be traveling, you can always drop a postcard in the mail when you arrive at your next destination.

A thank-you note should be handwritten on good-quality stationery. Do not send a note with smudges or words that are crossed out. Try writing your note on scratch paper and then rewriting it on the stationery. Be sincere, using warmth but not being overly expressive or sentimental. Always proofread it for spelling and grammar mistakes before you seal it in the envelope. A thank-you card is also acceptable, but make sure that you include a hand-written note inside. (See Chapter 11 for more on the ins and outs of correspondence.)

Here's an example of a thank-you note for a party:

> Dear Jean and Tom,
>
> What a fantastic dinner party! Jim and I had a wonderful time. It was so nice to meet Dr. Bastian while he was in town. And your pork loin dish is always a hit. Thanks so much for including us.
>
> Love,
>
> Betty and Jim

If you're a houseguest, here's a sample thank-you:

> *Dear Missy and Russ,*
>
> *Alex and I had such a wonderful weekend, and all thanks to you. I can't believe how much fun your jet ski is! We so enjoyed the barbecue on Saturday night, too. Thanks for all you did to make for a very relaxing weekend.*
>
> *Fondly,*
>
> *Lisa and Alex*

The rules of how to act with others and how to behave as guests in a polite and considerate manner are rules that have stood the test of time. Although some rules of etiquette have relaxed in this century, being rude or thoughtless will never be in style. Always remember that when you're a guest, you should treat the host as you would want to be treated if *you* were the host.

Chapter 15

Giving and Receiving Graciously

*O*ne of the great pleasures of life is giving to others. If you have a large family or a big circle of friends, it may seem that every month offers an occasion for giving. Between birthdays, weddings, graduations, anniversaries, holidays, moments of affection, and appeals from a good cause, there always seems to be a reason to give. The decisions you make regarding your selections of gifts and the way you present them are always a matter of personal choice, but you need to consider some important etiquette guidelines. I outline those guidelines in this chapter.

I believe that when you give, you receive even more. Sometimes, that comes true through reciprocated gifts! When it's your turn to get a gift, you also need to keep etiquette in mind. You have definite actions to take, and a few mistakes to avoid, as the recipient of a gift. There are even certain circumstances in which you should politely turn down a gift. This chapter provides you with advice about receiving gifts in a way that delights the giver and displays your good manners.

Looking at the Basic Responsibilities of the Giver and the Recipient

No discussion of good manners can divide the action of giving a gift from the action of receiving a gift; the two halves of the process are inseparable. Each party has obligations that are easy to understand.

A giver has these responsibilities:

✔ You must choose an appropriate gift for the recipient.

✔ You must ensure that the gift arrives on time.

✔ You must give the gift freely, with no strings or conditions attached.

A recipient bears equally an important burden:

✔ You must acknowledge the gift promptly with a thank-you note.

If you're receiving several gifts at once (on the occasion of a significant wedding anniversary, for example), writing down a description of each gift and the name of the gift-giver in a diary may come in handy at a later date. See the section "Expressing Your Thanks for a Gift," later in this chapter, for more information about receiving gifts.

Walking through the Gift-Giving Process

Giving a gift isn't a simple matter of spending as much as you can afford on an item and handing it over to the lucky recipient. (Well, it can be, but you risk creating an awkward situation if you do so.) You must decide whether to give a gift at all, select a gift that's appropriate for the occasion, and deliver the gift in the proper way. The following sections demystify this process and guide you through each step.

Determining whether a gift is in order

How do you know when a gift is in order? Begin by keeping a good year-round calendar and clearly noting the birthdays and anniversaries of close family members and friends. Review your calendar frequently to remind yourself of upcoming birthdays, anniversaries, and holidays that require gift-giving, such as Christmas, Mother's Day, and Father's Day. Invitations to weddings, graduations, religious milestones, and the like also alert you to ceremonial gift-giving occasions. When you receive an invitation, make a note of the event in your calendar and mark a date a week or two before the event to shop for a gift.

Some occasions may throw you a curveball. Is a gift required at your nephew's birthday party? Should you give your son's girlfriend a high school graduation present? The answer depends very much on your personal situation, but if you're wondering whether to give a gift, you probably should. In the case of a party, you might ask the host if other guests will be bringing gifts and then follow suit.

Here are some additional occasions that may require gifts:

- ✔ Meetings with business clients (see Chapter 3 for advice on giving business gifts)
- ✔ Baby showers and births (see Chapter 19)
- ✔ Thank-yous
- ✔ Illnesses
- ✔ Congratulations (such as for a job promotion)
- ✔ Housewarmings
- ✔ Retirements
- ✔ Moving away
- ✔ Welcoming of new neighbors

Some of the most memorable gifts are not for any special occasion at all. Surprising someone with an unexpected gift just to let that person know that you care can be more meaningful for both you and the recipient.

Selecting a gift

A gift is a free-will offering that expresses your affection and regard for another person. However, although the world may insist that it's the thought that counts, there *are* some rules to consider when it comes to selecting gifts. For example, you must give a gift that suits the recipient, not that you think *should* suit the recipient. You don't want to give your sister a copy of your favorite classical music CD when you know that she prefers country music.

A bit of research and thought can make the gift-selection process a whole lot easier. If you rush out at the last minute and grab the first thing you see, the gift will usually reflect that haphazardness. (Did that jar of lavender bath salts really suit your Uncle Bill? I think not!)

When selecting a gift, consider the person's hobbies and interests. A person who loves to read might enjoy an anthology of short stories, for example. Someone who likes music might like a new pair of headphones or tickets to a concert.

Here are some other tips for selecting a gift that the recipient will love:

- ✔ **When choosing gifts for children, gather information from their parents about what they like.** Your donation to a wildlife conservation fund on a child's behalf may not thrill him quite as much as a new baseball mitt would.

✔ **Be forewarned that clothing is a touchy area.** Unless you're absolutely sure of the person's tastes, purchase gift certificates in lieu of clothing. You may have perfectly good taste, but everyone's preferences differ, and a gift certificate to a favorite shop may save the recipient from having to return the gift.

✔ **Remember that some of the best gifts can't be purchased at any store.** Perhaps you have a skill or talent that you can use to create a painting, a handicraft item, or a piece of pottery that will have special meaning to the recipient. Remember, too, that you can often accomplish as much with a carefully selected greeting card and a handwritten message as you can with an expensive material item.

Staying within your means is an important point to remember when selecting a gift. Don't cross the line between a gift and a sacrifice. Your cousin Sue will probably be just as pleased to receive a book that discusses her special interest as she would be to get a more expensive gift. Make your selection according to your best judgment, wrap it nicely, and don't worry about how much you did or didn't spend.

Presenting your gift promptly

Always present your gifts no later than the day of the event. A late gift is better than no gift at all, but an on-time gift is far better.

If you see the person on the designated day, you can hand over your gift along with a handshake, hug, or kiss. If you live many miles from the recipient, make sure to send off the gift in plenty of time. (Mark the package with a *Do Not Open Until . . .* label if you want him or her to open the gift on the exact date of the special occasion.) Remember to wrap fragile objects carefully.

Note: Wedding gifts call for special etiquette. See Chapter 20, which is all about the etiquette of weddings, for more information.

Open now or wait until later?

You should open gifts when they are given, except for wedding gifts or gifts at a large party, where opening many gifts would be impossible. Part of the fun for the giver is to see the recipient's reaction.

When you're opening gifts at parties and celebrations, etiquette insists that you behave in a way that puts everyone at ease. Be sensitive to the situation and show equal excitement and enthusiasm while opening all gifts.

Expressing Your Thanks for a Gift

People give you gifts for all sorts of reasons — presents for your birthday, financial help when you're trying to pull together a down payment on a house, souvenirs from vacations, awards for professional work, and so on. Your success in communicating your gratitude helps you maintain your good relations with these generous individuals.

Always express your gratitude immediately upon receiving a gift. If the giver is there in person, say a sincere thank you when you receive the package. If you open the gift on the spot, say something specific about the gift, other than just "Thank you." You might try something like, "Oh, Paula, I just love this little lamp. The color is perfect for the little table in my bedroom. This is going to be great for reading at night." If you receive a gift delivered by mail or an express delivery service, pick up the phone and let the faraway giver know that the gift arrived in good shape and that you adore it.

Even if you thanked Aunt Helen when she handed you a gift at your birthday party, you need to mind your manners by writing a well-constructed thank-you letter (no, an e-mail is not acceptable!) as soon as possible. The letter should include as many of the following items as possible:

✔ A specific reference to the gift

✔ A sincere expression of gratitude

✔ Some indication of how you will use the gift

✔ An appropriate closing sentiment

Reviewing a few samples of proper thank-you notes may be useful. Here's one that you might write to a friend to thank her for a birthday gift:

Dear Paula,

I just rearranged my dresser top and found the perfect spot for the art deco lamp you gave me last week. Just as I expected, it's perfect for the room, and I love the way it lights up what used to be a dim corner.

Thanks so much for your thoughtful gift. I know that I'll think of your generosity every night.

Love,

Susan

Money can be tricky, but it's still best to describe how you plan to use it. Here's a note that does so quite succesfully:

Dear Aunt Jane,

You didn't have to send me money! I'm doing okay with my part-time job at the student union, and I've been able to stay within my budget. But because you were so generous, I was able to get a new set of tires for my car, and it felt much more steady on the road during last night's rainstorm.

Thanks again, and love,

Owen

Mothers always want to know what you do with the money they give you, and they definitely don't want to hear that you hosted a beer bash for your entire dorm. Tires are good, a new coat is okay, and putting her gift into your savings account is best of all.

The following note shows how you might thank someone for a larger monetary gift:

Dear Aunt Helen,

William and I are overwhelmed by your generous check. Thanks to your thoughtfulness, we now have enough money to furnish our living room.

We expect to be settled in another five weeks, and we look forward to welcoming you as one of our very first visitors.

With love and gratitude,

Sharon and William

Children can be encouraged to include some news about what's going on in their lives, especially when writing to close relatives who live far away. Here's a good example:

Dear Grandma,

I was so excited when I opened your package and found the beautiful pen and pencil set you sent me. I'm writing this note with the pen! It writes as beautifully as it looks.

I hope you can visit us this summer. I have a new pet gerbil and he's a friendly guy who will eat peanuts right out of your hand.

Thanks again,

Love,

Sammy

Finally, writing thank-you notes for wedding gifts can seem like an endless task. You can make your notes a bit shorter, but make sure to include the same types of information, as in the following note:

Dear Beatrice and Nathan,

We are so delighted with our new blender — and we can't wait to see it in action! You must come over for Scott's famous margaritas as soon as we're settled into our new home. Thank you for a splendid wedding gift.

All our love,

Sue and Scott

You may write your thank-you notes on your personal stationery — you don't have to use special thank-you cards. For more on how to select stationery and format a thank-you note, see Chapter 11.

Remember, too, that it's never too late to send a thank-you note. And if you're writing a belated thank you, it's not to give an excuse for being late. Apologize and thank the giver for the gift!

Exchanging, Returning, or Refusing Gifts

Society is governed by laws and organizational rules regarding gifts. No matter how generous someone has been, there are situations in which the recipient simply cannot accept a gift. In this section, you can find out how to gracefully refuse a gift that you can't accept, and also how to exchange or return a gift without hurting the giver's feelings.

Politely turning down a gift

Believe it or not, some gifts are unwanted. Maybe you've broken off a relationship — be it a friendship or romance — and then you receive a bouquet of flowers from that person that you don't want as a reminder. Perhaps a gift is horrifically tacky or outrageously expensive — so much so that it makes you uncomfortable. How do you handle these awkward situations?

When you receive an expensive gift, you're perfectly justified in saying, "What a lovely gift, but you really shouldn't have gone to such an expense." Although expensive gifts are embarrassing, there's little you can do. If you need to reciprocate, don't worry about matching the gift financially; just buy what you can afford.

As a woman, if you receive an expensive gift from a man other than your husband, fiancé, or boyfriend, first ask the giver, "And what did I do to deserve such a nice gift?" If the answer is that you just brought in a huge piece of business for your advertising agency and the boss is showing his appreciation, you might feel perfectly comfortable accepting it. However, if the man has romantic intentions that you don't reciprocate, you should not be afraid to refuse the gift. A simple explanation such as, "I'm sorry, but I simply can't accept this gift — we hardly know each other!" should suffice.

Some people, such as journalists and government employees, are not allowed to accept gifts. In business, people who influence purchase decisions or issue purchase orders are frequently prohibited from accepting any sort of gift from a vendor. The rules are often so strict that these people can't even pick up a lunch tab for a buyer or an employee of a company that buys their goods or services.

If someone sends you a gift that violates the letter or spirit of such a rule, return the gift promptly along with a note that explains the situation and expresses your gratitude for the gesture. Here's a good example:

Dear Tom,

It breaks my heart to return such a lovely bottle of wine, especially one that comes from such a fine vineyard, but my company specifically forbids me from accepting any sort of gift.

I appreciate the thought, and I hope that you will not, in any way, take my conformance to company rules as a comment on our excellent relationship.

Sincerely,

Mary Smith

Exchanging a gift

If you receive a gift and need to exchange it for any reason, be honest and tell the giver that you exchanged the item for something that you needed, that fit properly, or that was another color. Most people are understanding about exchanges if a gift that they gave is not quite right.

Wedding gifts are normally exchanged only in case of duplication. When buying wedding gifts, remember to include the receipt without a price on it so that the couple knows where they can exchange it, if necessary.

Giving a Fitting Gift for the Occasion

Different situations have unique "rules" when it comes to appropriate offerings. This section details how to give appropriately for common occasions.

Gifts within the family

The first place everyone learns about giving gifts is the family. Birthdays and holidays are often occasions for gift-giving — and, depending on the family, there may be a dozen other potential gift-giving occasions during the year.

If you belong to a large family, gift-giving can become a financial burden, especially around holidays. One way to keep everyone happy is to draw names. This way, each adult family member gives one gift. My family has been doing this for years, although my mother has a hard time abiding by this rule and sneaks in small gifts for all of us!

A photo album; a diary or journal; a cookbook; tickets to a sporting event, concert, or play; a how-to video or book for a new hobby; a gift certificate for a facial or a day at a spa; a book on tape; or a food gift basket all make wonderful family gifts.

The family setting is a good place to teach children the etiquette of giving and receiving gifts. For example, you can take very young children to a shopping center, give them a modest allowance, and encourage them to select birthday and other-occasion gifts for their siblings. The shopping process is educational in a number of ways, not the least of which is beginning to understand the value of money by understanding how much a gift costs and what a child can or can't afford on a certain budget.

Children should be discouraged from giving items of significant material value to their parents. In families that have two or more siblings, this practice can rapidly escalate into a contest between children to see who can come up with a better gift. As a parent, you might suggest that Dad needs a new shirt and golf club head covers (which have a similar financial cost) and let the two children decide who wants to give Dad which gift.

Tailor gifts to senior family members to the occasion. More than anything, most seniors appreciate the gift of your time. For example, tickets to a concert, plus an invitation to dinner beforehand in a nice restaurant, with you (the gift-giver) providing all the transportation, would be a nice gift.

Gifts at the office

You can probably think of a dozen reasons to give gifts at the office. Perhaps it's a coworker's birthday, or your boss just got elected to the board of directors. Maybe you're enjoying a vacation in a foreign country where little handicraft items are inexpensive; your heart is just full of generosity; and you want to give, give, give.

Even though your coworkers may appreciate your generosity, you need to consider the risks of giving gifts at the office. Will someone misinterpret your gift as an indication that you want (or are grateful for) a better parking place, or a little faster turnaround with those photocopies, or a computer with more memory? Will the boss think that you're trying to soften her up for a better performance review? Use the following simple guidelines to keep yourself out of trouble:

✔ Don't "gift up" with a gift of intrinsic value. You can send a birthday card or a note of congratulations to your boss, but giving cufflinks, candy, wine, or pen-and-pencil sets is inappropriate.

✔ When you "gift across," include everyone. If you send a birthday card to one coworker, be sure to send *every* coworker a card at the appropriate time. Equal treatment is so important that keeping a little gift diary is worth the effort. That way, you can ensure that you don't overlook anyone.

✔ When you feel like "gifting down" the chain of command, stop to consider the real length of the chain. Participating in the collections that go around the office from time to time may be better than buying for an entire workforce. Don't try to please the four people who report directly to you when, in reality, 200 people consider you the boss.

✔ Prospective and active romances are a private matter between two consenting adults, but company rules may try to keep Cupid out of the workplace. Receiving flowers from a spouse or significant other at the office is fine, but know the rules and be sensible. Save your romantic gifts for after-hours and weekends.

For more on corporate gift-giving, see Chapter 3.

Gifts to charities and other good causes

The world is full of good causes. Your own community has needs that only the gifts of generous donors can meet. Many law enforcement agencies conduct programs for disadvantaged children. Libraries are always seeking financial help from the community to expand collections, provide computer access, and improve their facilities. Just about every human illness has a research organization dedicated to seeking a cure or a support group to assist patients. The list of needy agencies and associations is endless, and these organizations widely publicize their appeals for assistance.

When you're faced with a gift-giving occasion for a person who has no need for material goods, a charitable gift in that person's honor is a fine alternative to yet another little household trinket. If you're aware of that person's favorite charity, send off a check to that organization, along with the name and address of the person you're honoring. Make sure to mention the occasion for the donation — the grateful organization will send a nice letter of acknowledgment to the honoree. If you don't know a person's preferred charity, select one of your own and make a contribution in your friend's name.

If you receive notice that a contribution has been made in your honor, a thank-you note is appropriate etiquette. The note's wording should follow this general guideline:

Dear Joan and Bill,

I just received notification from the Marine Mammal Rescue Center of your generous contribution in memory of Louis. Thank you so much for helping one of Louis's favorite organizations carry on with its good work. Every time an unfortunate animal is nursed back to health and released into the sea, I'm sure that Louis's spirit will soar.

Your thoughtfulness at this sad time is deeply appreciated.

Love,

Ellen

If you're a member of the congregation at a religious ceremony, such as a wedding, bar mitzvah, or confirmation, you usually find an envelope intended for offerings. If you insert a check or cash and indicate the honoree, your contribution will be mentioned in the next bulletin or newsletter. You can tailor this nice gesture to fit within your budget.

Here again, if someone makes a contribution in honor of you or a loved one, a simple note of appreciation is in order:

Dear Martin,

Thanks so much for your donation in honor of Christie's confirmation. Our congregation is always seeking funds for various good works, and all of us are grateful for your generosity.

Love,

Rhonda and Mike

Anytime you contribute to a good cause, try to think of someone deserving of your kind thoughts. Dedicating your contributions to friends and relatives brings unexpected moments of pleasure to the honorees.

The gift of your time

Giving a material gift is not the only way to give. The gift of your time for volunteer work or for helping out a friend or neighbor is also a form of giving — and one that might be appreciated more than a material item. Because many people think that they don't have enough time, a gift of time is one of the most valuable gifts you can give.

When I find it difficult to think of a useful gift for a friend or family member, I give that person a card stating, "This is good for one day of yard work." Imagine your elderly neighbor's delight if you offered to help her with yard work! Or, for no particular occasion, I'll make a date to take my mother to a nursery, let her select some plants, and then help her plant them.

Giving and Receiving Compliments

Giving and receiving isn't only about gifts and favors. It's also about graciously giving and accepting compliments — "Don't you look great?" "Well, thank you!" Here are a few tips to remember about compliments:

- ✔ Be sincere when complimenting someone; it's usually obvious if you're not.

- ✔ When you receive a compliment, always say "Thank you," and do not discount or dispute what the person said. For example, when someone compliments your outfit, don't respond with, "This old thing?" Simply say something like, "Thank you, yes, I love it, too!" or, "My mother bought this for me."

- ✔ Try giving more compliments; you'll be surprised at how good it makes you feel, especially if your compliments make people feel better by cheering them up.

Not accepting or giving compliments properly is usually a sign of low self-esteem or low self-confidence. It's okay to like yourself!

Part V
Dining with Delight

"I'm pretty sure the Popsicle stick goes to the left of the Goofy straw."

In this part . . .

*W*hen people think of etiquette, they often think of eating utensils and the seemingly confusing rules about which utensil to use for what. Because you spend so many hours of your life sitting around a dinner table, whether it's with your family or a group of business associates, dining manners are especially important. This part tells you everything you need to know: which utensils and glasses to use when, how to select and order wine, and how to conduct yourself at a business meal. *Bon appetit!*

Chapter 16

Manners Matter at the Table

• •

In This Chapter

▶ The when, what, where, and how of dining

▶ Looking at a formal table setting: China, crystal, and silver

▶ Understanding the two styles of dining: European versus American

▶ Eating each course of a meal

▶ Minding your "peas" and Qs when eating challenging foods

• •

*P*olite dining at the table, whether the meal is formal or informal, has developed as one of the behaviors that sets human beings apart from animals. Nowhere else is our difference from beasts more evident than in our eating manners and social behavior.

In Western civilization, there was a time when people didn't use forks and knives — or even plates, for that matter. Dogs roamed the dining rooms, and people threw scraps and unwanted portions on the floor for their dinners. And this was not so very long ago, historically speaking! Even after people started using utensils, they were often shared among several people at one table.

As a result of social development over the last 400 years, we have produced not only the technology to create and manufacture a complex set of utensils but also a system for using them. The code of manners about what is and is not polite to do at the table evolved from these innovations.

In the 19th century, dining utensils and dining etiquette in polite society were probably more elaborate than they have ever been at any other point in history. (A perfect example of this complex but wonderful style of dining is found in scenes from the film *The Age of Innocence*.) Although formal dining today still reflects this level of etiquette, most dining in the late 20th century has been simplified.

Polite behavior at the table, whether informal or not, has not disappeared or gone out of style. Table manners and etiquette are just a means to an end. Dining etiquette is important because it enables you to enjoy the finer things in life — good company, good food, and good conversation. (If you aren't convinced, think about how many people fall in love over dinner!)

Knowing about these refinements not only makes dining more enjoyable but also can give you a competitive edge in business. When you're confident of your manners, you're a more relaxed, savvy, and polished representative of your company. Most of my clients are corporate executives who understand that it's very important for their employees to learn these skills. Business deals are made over breakfast, and prospective employees are scrutinized over lunch. Why put yourself in the position of being in an interview not knowing which fork to use? If you're confident in knowing the rules, you can focus on more important things, such as getting the job.

Extending Pre-Dinner Courtesies

With dining, as with any social event, there is a beginning, a middle, and an end. Unless you arrive late (and frankly, there's nothing fashionable about arriving late to any meal), you need to contend with the awkwardness involved in getting the event underway. Remember that most people are a little nervous when eating with strangers. In such situations, dining etiquette can be a real help, providing form and guidelines to move everyone gracefully through the meal.

Perhaps you're beginning a lunch with a small, well-known group of business associates. Maybe you're meeting your girlfriend's parents for the first time in their home. Or maybe you're about to sit down to dinner with a table full of complete strangers who are also important business contacts. In these and all other dining situations, the basic rules remain the same.

Formal seating

Certain rules govern where guests sit during a formal meal:

- Almost every meal has a host — the person in whose home you're dining or who invited you out to a restaurant. The host sits at the end of the table. If a couple are hosting, the man sits at one end and the woman sits at the other.
- The male guest of honor sits on the hostess's right.
- The next most important man sits on the hostess's left.
- The female guest of honor sits to the host's right.
- The second most important woman sits to the host's left.

In many formal situations, you find yourselves at round tables, which facilitate group conversation and put everyone on an equal basis. Whatever the shape of the table, couples should be separated and men and women seated alternately.

Many hosts use placecards to indicate where each guest should sit. At a smaller event, you may need to look around the table to find your name on a placecard. At larger events, you may find a table at the entrance to the dining room on which every guest's placecard sits. In this situation, you find the placecard with your name on it, look to see which table you have been assigned to, and take your seat at that table. Each table should have a sign on it identifying the table number or name.

If placecards have been used, never move them or change your seat; your host probably put some creative logic into seating you there.

Coming to table

Whether you're having cocktails and conversation in a restaurant lounge or in your living room, at some point you must go to the table with your family or group. There are very specific ways to offer and take a seat:

- In formal situations, the men escort the women by the arm individually to their seats and assist them in being seated.
- In informal situations, the men allow the women to approach the table in a group and then assist them in taking their seats.

Here's how it's done, step by step: The woman approaches her chair and waits to be seated. The man stands behind the woman's chair and draws it back for her. The woman then begins to sit. When she is halfway down, the man pushes the chair gently beneath her. Once she is seated, she can move it closer or farther from the table as she wishes by holding the sides of the seat and scooting it forward or backward. The man then seats himself to the left of the woman he just seated.

If more women than men are being seated at the table, the men should seat the women on both sides of themselves and around the table, if necessary, before taking their own seats.

In a formal dining situation, no one sits down until the host(s) or guest of honor is seated.

Everyone Is Seated — Now What?

Once you're seated, wait for your host or guest of honor to pick up the napkin and place it on his or her lap. (The napkin will be placed either to the left of the forks, beneath the forks, or on the main plate. In a restaurant, the napkin may be folded in a fancy way and placed on the plate or in a glass.) After the host's or guest of honor's napkin is in place, gently put your own napkin in your lap.

What to do with your handbag

Women, be aware of where you place your handbag — never on the table or hanging on the back of your chair. If it can't sit in the back of your chair, set it on the floor slightly under you chair so that the waitstaff or others won't trip over it.

Note: In more upscale restaurants, your waiter places your napkin on your lap for you.

It's not necessary to fully open a large napkin; just fold it in half. However, you can completely open a smaller luncheon napkin. No matter what the occasion, you should not flap your napkin around like a flag before placing it in your lap, and men should not tuck their napkins into their shirts like a bib.

The purpose of your napkin is to dab the corners of your mouth. Never use it to wipe off lipstick or to blow your nose!

Ordering from the menu

When ordering from a restaurant menu, the man traditionally orders for himself and the woman. Today, however, it's perfectly fine for the woman to order for herself. In making your food selections, you may want to keep in mind that some foods are more difficult to eat than others (see the section called "Taming the Wild Spaghetti: Dealing with Difficult Foods" later in this chapter) and to steer clear of those foods, especially if you're on a date or you're meeting with a business client and you want the other person to come away with a good impression of you and your table manners.

If you're ordering a bottle of wine, you want to decide on your meals so that you can choose a wine that complements the food. (For more on wine and pairing wine with food, see Chapter 17.)

If you dine in restaurants that specialize in international cuisine and you don't speak the language, take the time to learn four or five food items ahead of time. That way, you won't order something you don't like by mistake. If you're still unsure when you get to the restaurant, though, it's certainly acceptable to request assistance from your server.

Minding your posture

You need to pay attention to your posture and body language. During the meal, keep both feet flat on the floor or cross your feet at the ankles. Don't cross your legs at the knees, and don't prop your feet on chair rungs or table legs or wrap them around anything handy under the table.

(CAUTION) Keep your shoes on! I've heard numerous stories about people who removed their shoes while dining. Their shoes were kicked around under the table, and when they got up to go the restroom, they had to search for their shoes. One woman told me that she had to almost crawl under the table to reach one of her shoes.

You can rest your hands up to your forearms on the table, but don't prop your elbows on the table. Keep your elbows close to your body so that you don't bump into others and so that you can generally control your arm movements better. Between courses, or anytime you want to rest, you can place both hands in your lap or place one hand in your lap and the other on the edge of the table at the wrist.

As you eat, sit up straight on the front three-quarters of your chair. This way, you shouldn't have to bend over your food; you can simply bring your utensils to your mouth. Don't rush when you lift your food from the table to your mouth. Don't bend closely over your plate or try to meet your utensils halfway.

Excusing yourself

If you must leave the table during a meal for any reason, do so with as little interruption to others as possible. Politely and quietly excuse yourself, lay your napkin on your chair, and leave without fanfare. While you're away, your server may replace your napkin with a new one and place it to the left of your plate.

If you have to cough or sneeze while dining, simply turn your head toward your shoulder and cover your mouth and nose with a tissue or your handkerchief (or in an emergency, your napkin). If you have a fit of sneezes or hiccups, or you must blow your nose with force, excuse yourself, go to the restroom, and take care of your business. Medication should be taken in the restroom as well.

When you've finished your entire meal and you're leaving the table, place your napkin to the left of your plate. You don't have to fold it again, but leave it sitting neatly, with no soiled areas showing. Do not put it back in the napkin ring!

Bring on the meal!

When should you start to eat? When your host begins to eat. If the first course is brought to the table in twos or threes and not everyone has his or her food yet, do not begin to eat. Wait until all the people around you have been served the first course, and then begin to eat together.

In this situation, the host may encourage you to go ahead and begin eating. If he or she does so, it's perfectly fine to begin eating. If you wish, though, you may continue to wait until everyone has his or her meal before you begin, chatting with the other guests in the meantime.

Looking at Table Settings

The first step to informed utensil use is to understand where the basic utensils and dishes go on a dining table and how to use them. That said, take a look at the basic tools of dining, shown in Figure 16-1.

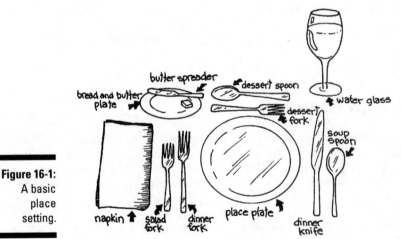

Figure 16-1:
A basic place setting.

As you can see in Figure 16-1, you have a plate, a bread-and-butter plate, a napkin, several utensils (commonly called flatware or silverware, even if they are not silver at all!) — usually consisting of a knife, a fork, and a soup spoon — and at least one glass. Sometimes you have a coffee or tea cup and saucer as well.

When you add a salad fork and a dessert spoon or fork, you've filled out the simple place setting that most people have come to recognize. Sometimes a salad plate rests on the table instead of being delivered with the salad, and sometimes the dessert utensils and dessert plate and coffee or tea cups and saucers (along with spoons) appear after the meal. But in general, these are the plates and utensils that you see on the table when you sit down at most meals.

This setting is, however, an abbreviated version of a full or formal place setting, which can have any number of other utensils, plates, and glasses. If you saw the movie *Titanic*, you may remember the scene in which Jack (played by Leonardo DiCaprio) asks, "Are all of these mine?" Molly Brown (played by Kathy Bates) whispers quietly in response, "Yes, start from the outside and work in." Better dining advice was never given! In fact, the two most important rules to learn in dining, whether casual or formal, are the following:

✔ Liquids are to the right and solids to the left.

✔ You start from the outside utensils and work inward with each course.

By examining a formal place setting, as in Figure 16-2, you can get a good idea of what each course will be. In this case, the salad is served after the entrée (or main course). The following sections provide some details about the various parts of a formal place setting and how to use them.

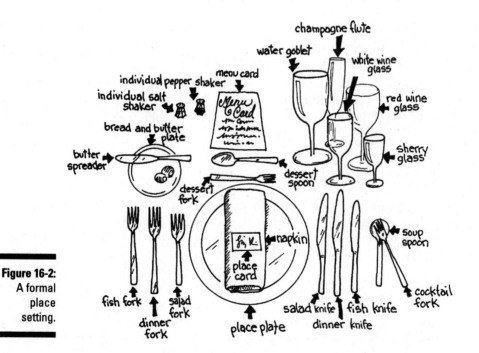

Figure 16-2:
A formal
place
setting.

CAUTION

Using salt and pepper judiciously

Although you find salt and pepper on nearly every table, good manners call for you to thoughtfully taste your food before you add any seasoning. The chef (whether your host or the chef at a restaurant or banquet facility) tried to achieve perfect seasoning, and when you reach for the salt and pepper, you indicate that perfection was not quite achieved.

If you're asked to pass the salt or the pepper, always pass them together. They should stay together on the table throughout the meal.

Plates and bowls

The *place plate,* or main dinner plate, is in the center in front of each chair setting. In formal dining, there is usually an underplate or charger as well. The bread plate is always to the left, slightly above the forks. It has a small knife across the top, which is called a butter spreader.

Note: Sometimes a small bowl and a small plate with a doily, a small fork, and a small spoon rest above the dinner plate. These dishes are the finger bowl and the dessert plate, respectively; I cover them later in this chapter.

If soup and salad courses are served, the soup bowl and salad plate are brought to the table and later removed. The soup bowl is placed on a service plate, which sits on the dinner plate. The salad plate is also placed on top of the dinner plate.

Utensils

Forks are placed to the left of the plate, and knives and spoons to the right (with the exception of the cocktail fork, which is placed on the soup spoon, as shown back in Figure 16-2, or to right of the soup spoon). The dessert fork and spoon are placed above the dinner plate.

Depending on the course, the salad fork, which is smaller than the dinner fork, is normally farthest to the left. (If fish is being served as the first course, a fish fork rests to the left of the salad fork.) Next is the dinner fork, which you use for the entree. Salad is sometimes served as the third or fourth course, in which case the salad fork is closest to the plate. The butter spreader is placed on the bread plate, on the left above the forks.

To the right of the plate, starting from the outermost utensil, are the cocktail fork, the soup spoon, the fish knife (if fish is being served), the dinner knife, and then the salad knife nearest the plate. The cutting edge of each knife is turned toward the plate.

Finally, the dessert fork or spoon is placed horizontally above the place plate, tines facing to the right or spoon bowl facing to the left.

Glassware

In a formal setting, you usually have five glasses at the table. They are always to the right, above the knives, because the majority of people are right-handed. If the glasses were to the left, you'd have to reach across your food to reach them, possibly soiling your sleeve.

To suit the beverage with which it is filled, each glass is slightly different in shape and size:

✔ The glass farthest to the right is a sherry or aperitif glass. This is the first glass you use, because sherry is poured during the soup course.

✔ Next is the white wine glass, which is used during the fish course or appetizer.

✔ Behind the white wine glass is the red wine glass. This glass is larger, with a fuller bowl that allows the red wine to "breathe."

✔ The largest glass is the water goblet, which usually sits just above the dinner knife.

✔ Behind and to the right of the water goblet is the Champagne flute. This glass is not used until dessert is served.

You hold most stem glasses by the bowl, except for a white wine glass or a Champagne flute. Because white wine and Champagne are served chilled, you don't want to warm them with your hand. Also, you don't want to shake hands with a chilly hand.

Other items in a formal place setting

Most table settings include salt and pepper shakers or grinders. At formal meals, you see very small, individual salt dishes with tiny spoons. These are called *salt cellars*.

At a formal dinner, you also have a menu card, which lists each course to be served, with the exception of the sorbet or intermezzo. Your host may also include the wines offered with each course. The date, location, and purpose of the dinner are on the card at the top — this is the only (or usually the main) keepsake for guests, so the information should be there to identify what, where, and why.

You may have a placecard as well, which helps you find your assigned seat. (The section called "Formal seating," earlier in this chapter, provides more information about placecards.)

Understanding European and American Eating Styles

There are two basic methods of handling and using silverware at a meal: the American style and the European, or Continental, style. You can use either version, but stick to one or the other.

Some experts believe that when knives and forks first became popular in Europe in the early 17th century, most people used the utensils in much the same way that Americans do now. Later, in the 19th Century, the upper classes in Europe began using what is now called the Continental style. The practice spread, but not to the United States.

Fortunately, though, one task is the same in both the European and the American style: You cut your food the same way, as shown in Figure 16-3. First, you hold the knife in your right hand. Place your index finger on the handle and a little of the blade if necessary. Hold the fork with your left hand, tines facing down (with the curve pushing up). Then cut your food, one or at most two bites at a time.

Figure 16-3:
Cutting
your food
properly.

The knife is held in your RIGHT hand. Your index finger should be on the handle and should overlap the blade no more than 1 inch. Hold fork, tines DOWN &, in your LEFT hand. Cut 1 piece at a time!

The rest of the process differs from style to style.

American style (The zigzag)

People in the United States and Canada are the only people in the world who use this method of eating, which is also known as the *zigzag*. In the American style, after you cut your food, you lay the knife on the plate near the top, cutting edge facing in, and switch the fork to your right hand. Holding the fork with your thumb over the end, your index finger underneath, and the tines up, you then pick up the food, either with the tines or by slipping the food onto the tines, and eat. (See Figure 16-4.)

Figure 16-4:
American-style knife-and-fork work.

Hold your fork like a pencil. Steady it between your middle and index fingers. (Turn your thumb up, not down, like you would a pencil.)

After you cut the meat, lay your knife on your plate. The cutting edge should always face the center of the plate. Switch the fork to your RIGHT hand before you raise it to your mouth.

After you finish a course, you place your knife and fork side by side in the 4:00 (sometimes called the 10:20 o'clock) position on the plate, the blade of the knife facing in, as shown in Figure 16-5. This way, your server knows that you have finished this course and that he or she can remove those dishes and utensils and bring the next course. If you wish to rest between courses, you use the same position but space the utensils farther apart and slightly higher on your plate, as shown in Figure 16-6.

all done!

Figure 16-5:
The finish position in American-style dining.

When you are finished with a course, place your knife and fork on your plate at the angle shown. This position means you are finished.
On a clock, it would look like the 10:20 position. Tips of knife and fork at the 10, and ends of handles at the 4.

Figure 16-6:
The rest
position in
American-
style dining.

The rest position. Use it if you are talking, drinking, using your napkin.

European or Continental style

In the European or Continental eating style, instead of switching the fork to your right hand and placing the knife on the plate to eat, you keep the fork in your left hand and use it to pierce the food and bring it to your mouth. Remember to raise the fork to your mouth with the tines down, but turning your forearm toward your mouth, as shown in Figure 16-7.

Figure 16-7:
European-
style dining
requires
that you
keep your
fork in your
left hand.

Raise fork, tines down, to your mouth. Twist the wrist and raise your forearm slightly. Keep the knife in your RIGHT hand. You may add a small amount of the other food to your meat on the tines of the fork.

The knife stays in your right hand, ready to be used again. If you must maneuver something onto the tines of your fork, gently nudge it with your knife. You may rest your wrist on the edge of the table while you hold your cutlery.

To rest your cutlery in the European or Continental style of eating, you cross the fork (tines down) across the knife, cutting edge in the 10:00-4:00/2:00-8:00 o'clock positions, as shown in Figure 16-8. Place your utensils in this position if you must leave the table, take a drink, or use your napkin. The finished position is the same as in the American style; however, you place the fork with the tines down.

A Continental caution

American table manners allow for considerable latitude in the use of fingers while dining. European etiquette, however, is much more rigid. In France, particularly, touching any food item except for bread with your hands is considered unmannerly. When you dine overseas, be especially watchful for the behavior of your local companions. When in doubt, use a knife and fork.

Whichever method you use, remember not to wave your utensils around while you're talking. You're not conducting an orchestra! And at no time should you hold your utensils in any other fashion. It doesn't matter whether you're left-handed. Never saw at your food; simply request a steak or meat knife. Never cut your meat into bites all at once. And don't place your utensils by their tips on the edge of the plate, letting them hang onto the table. After you pick up your utensils, they should never touch the table again.

Figure 16-8:
The rest-position in European-style dining.

Eating Each Course of a Meal

When you first sit down to dine in a formal situation, remember to touch nothing on the table until the host or guest of honor begins — not even a sip of water. The following sections walk you through a typical meal course by course, giving you suggestions for what to do and not to do.

Bread

Bread is placed on the table or passed around the table. If a bread basket or bread plate is sitting in front of you, it's your responsibility to begin passing the bread. If the table is round, offer the bread to the person on your right, and do not help yourself until the bread comes back around to you. If the table is rectangular and you can see that the bread may not come back your way, help yourself and then pass to your right.

When bread is served half-sliced in a basket with a napkin, you take a portion of the napkin in your left hand and hold a section of the bread, *without touching the bread,* and you use your right hand to tear off one piece. The napkin is in the basket to cover and protect the remaining bread.

If you'd like some butter for your bread, take it from the serving dish and place it on your bread-and-butter plate, not directly on the bread. Never use the knife with the butter dish to butter your bread. If no knife rests on the butter dish, you may use your own butter spreader.

Do not butter an entire slice or roll at once. And don't butter your bread in the air above your plate! Break off one piece, butter it over the plate, and then eat it. If it's a crunchy hard roll, keep it as close to your bread plate as possible. And you can relax; it's not the end of the world if a few bread crumbs get on the table. The waitstaff will sweep them away later in the meal.

Dipping, dunking, or wiping sauces with your bread is not polite, except in the most informal gatherings or with certain dishes that are designed to do just that — such as fondues, certain au jus dishes, and olive oil. If you're dipping your bread into a communal sauce, never double-dip!

Soup

Soup can be served in a variety of bowls and cups, hot or cold. A clear soup is served with a large oval soup spoon (known as a *bouillon spoon*). A cream soup is served with a small, round soup spoon.

You eat all soups the same way: by holding your soup spoon or bouillon spoon the way you would hold a pencil, between your index and middle fingers with your thumb up. Spoon the soup away from you toward the center or top of the bowl, and then sip the soup from the side — not the point — of the spoon. Rest the spoon in the soup bowl while you pause. After you've finished, place the spoon on the saucer or plate beneath the cup or bowl; do not leave the spoon in the bowl or cup.

Blowing on your soup to cool it down is not polite. If you're worried that your soup is too hot, gently stir it, or spoon soup from the edge of the bowl first.

At a formal meal, a sherry or aperitif may be served with the soup course.

Salad

Salad may be served before or after the main course; the placement of the fork will tip you off. In a basic table setting, you usually have only one knife. For this reason, some Americans seem to think that this knife is for the main course and that they cannot use it for the salad. Not true! A fine restaurant or a considerate host always serves salad with the lettuce in bite-sized pieces. However, if you're served large pieces, cut one bite at a time by using the knife provided. Using your knife to cut lettuce is perfectly fine — just request a clean knife when the main course arrives.

If a salad is the main course, such as at a luncheon, use the entree fork. If a salad is served prior to or after the main course, use the smaller salad fork. When a salad is served during a formal meal, you always have a salad knife. It is usually smaller than the dinner knife. (Refer to Figure 16-2.)

After you finish your salad (or any course, for that matter), never push your plate or bowl away from you. The placement of your cutlery informs the wait-staff that you have finished.

Sorbet or intermezzo

A sorbet or intermezzo may be served between the appetizer and entree to cleanse the palate. You need to have only a small taste; it's not necessary to finish the entire dish.

Entree

The main course is normally beef, chicken, duck, or lamb, and you eat these foods with a knife and fork. Finger foods, such as fried chicken, are usually served at informal occasions and not in formal dining situations.

If you're served a large steak, you may cut it into two or three sections, but not into many small pieces. (You may be given a special steak knife to help you cut the meat without sawing.) Otherwise, continue to cut one or at most two bites at a time.

TIP

> ## Serving food
>
> At banquets or in banquet-style serving, platters of food are served to you on the left. A serving spoon and a serving fork are usually on the serving platter, spoon with bowl up and fork with tines down. Take the fork in your left hand, tines remaining down, and use it to steady the food. Using the spoon in your right hand, lift the food and steady it with the fork while bringing it to your plate.
>
> Serve the food in individual portions, as it is presented on the platter. Don't take more than one portion. If the food is presented as a whole — mashed, grouped, or in gels — take an individual portion with the spoon, using the spoon sideways to cut, if necessary. Then remember to return the spoon and fork to the serving plate as they came to you: spoon bowl up on the right, fork tines down on the left.

Red wine is served with most entrees. These days, the rule of white wine with fish and chicken does not always apply — it depends on how the dish was prepared. For example, sea bass can be served with a rich veal reduction sauce, so either red or white would complement the meal. (See Chapter 17 for more on pairing wine with food.)

Finger bowl

A finger bowl is presented after the main course and before dessert arrives. Your server places it in front of you on a plate, usually with a doily under the bowl. The bowl contains warm water with a slice of lemon and occasionally a small flower. A small dessert fork and spoon are also on the plate; you bring these utensils down and place them to the left and right, respectively, of where the dessert plate will go.

Dip just your fingertips in the water and dry them on your napkin. Remove the doily and bowl and place them to the left. A waiter then removes them.

Dessert

Dessert is normally served to you, along with a dessert wine or Champagne. If you're served ice cream, use your spoon; if you're served cake with a sauce, use both the spoon and the fork. In a Continental-style setting, you hold your spoon in your right hand and your fork in your left, tines down.

Fresh fruit and cheese are sometimes served as dessert. You eat these foods with a knife and fork.

Taming the Wild Spaghetti: Dealing with Difficult Foods

Most etiquette guides assume that you eat from civilized menus that offer foods such as pot roast, mashed potatoes, broccoli, and blueberry pie. The standard etiquette rules work well with these types of foods. But real life is full of surprises, and today's multiethnic society encourages the serving of foods that fall far outside the conventional grasp of good manners. This section offers a few words of advice on various dining challenges.

Artichokes

Artichokes are delicious vegetables, but they represent the ultimate challenge to dinner guests. Regardless of your mastery of etiquette, artichokes are sure to test your table manners.

The fanciest way to serve artichokes requires the server to place a whole, steamed artichoke on a special dish that includes a small well to hold the vegetable upright. This special dish is accompanied by a separate, small dish of warm hollandaise sauce, mayonnaise with lemon, or melted butter.

To eat an artichoke served in this fashion, follow these steps:

1. **Use your fingers to break off an outer leaf (which practically falls away from a well-cooked artichoke).**

2. **Dip the thick base of the leaf in the butter or sauce, put the leaf — meaty side down — about halfway into your mouth, and then withdraw it through almost-closed front lower teeth, scraping the tender flesh away from the long strings of the leaf.**

   The end result is a very small taste of artichoke.

3. **Repeat this ritual with the other leaves until you come to the center of the vegetable.**

4. **Use your knife and fork to excavate the tender and delicious bottom portion of the artichoke. Cut the heart into sections by using a fork and knife, pierce a section with your fork, and dip it into the sauce to eat.**

Asparagus

In a more casual setting, eating asparagus as a finger food is acceptable. But at a formal dinner, it's best to use a fork and knife, cutting one bite at a time.

If you're serving yourself from a platter that's passed around the table and the asparagus has a butter sauce, hold the vegetable over the serving platter and allow it to drain before placing it on your plate.

Bacon

When bacon is cooked crisp, you can consider it a finger food. When it's soft, however, use your fork and knife to cut one bite of bacon at a time.

Fish with bones

You can remove small fish bones with your fork or your forefinger and thumb — as always, try to be discreet. The food goes out of your mouth the way it went in.

Foods that you eat with chopsticks

Westerners use various utensils to raise food to their mouths, chew, and swallow. But in many Asian countries, such as Japan, chopsticks are used at every meal as spoon, fork, and knife, making eating simple and practical. There's a technique to using chopsticks; however, it's easy to master with just a little practice.

Here are a few pointers for eating with chopsticks:

- ✔ You hold chopsticks between your index finger and thumb.
- ✔ Your lower chopstick should rest in the web of your hand and remain still.
- ✔ You hold the top chopstick as you would hold a pencil; it does most of the moving. Use your two middle fingers to maneuver it.
- ✔ Do not hold chopsticks too tightly; mobility is easier if you hold them loosely.
- ✔ Do not hold chopsticks too close to the tip, because doing so makes you lose leverage, which makes it difficult to pick up food.
- ✔ If a piece of food is too big, you may cut it with your chopsticks or hold it with your chopsticks while you take a couple of bites.
- ✔ As with Western eating tools, never point, gesture, or talk with your chopsticks.
- ✔ Between bites, you place your chopsticks on the rest provided, or you may lay them across the lower dish or plate. Do not leave your chopsticks pointed upright in your rice or soup bowl.
- ✔ Never take food from another person's chopsticks.

If you're not ready to try using chopsticks, it's perfectly fine to request a fork and knife.

Peas

Depending on which style of eating you're using — American or Continental — peas can present a challenge. But there are a number of ways to get peas onto your fork. Either move them against the meat and scoop them onto your fork, or use a crust of bread to help push the peas onto the fork. If you're eating Continental style, you can use your knife or other food on your plate, such as mashed potatoes, and push or smash them onto the backs of the fork tines.

Olives and other pitted foods

Olives and other pitted foods are finger foods once they're on your plate, so you may pick them up with your fingers. Large stuffed olives are best eaten in two bites. Discreetly remove the pits with your forefinger and thumb.

Poultry

When you order turkey, it comes to you in nice, manageable slices. Chicken isn't too difficult, either, because you've probably learned to eat it from a young age. But what about game hen, duck, or quail? These foods show up on dinner plates every now and then. If you're lucky, the kitchen crew or the server will debone or cut them into manageable pieces that you can then handle with your knife and fork. Otherwise, try these approaches (listed in order of mannerly preference):

- Ask your waiter for help in disjointing the bird.
- Ask for a sharp knife if you don't have one.
- Do your best to separate the bird at its major joints.
- Pick up tiny legs and wings by a protruding bone and then eat the meat as finger food.

Place all bones to one side on your dinner plate.

Shellfish and mollusks

Lobster and crab: Lobster and crab are almost always served in informal situations. The host provides bibs, and the host and guests generally accept that a lot of finger work is proper behavior. When in doubt about the correct method, ask your host for guidance. If you're unfamiliar with the procedure for eating a whole lobster and you find yourself confronted by one, the other guests are likely to have plenty of good advice.

Mussels: Steamed mussels may be eaten with a fork and spoon or a cocktail fork. Spear the mussel, dip it into the sauce provided, and eat it whole.

Oysters: Oysters on the half shell are usually served on ice or rock salt with a small dish of cocktail sauce or vinegar. They remain attached to the bottom shell by a slender little membrane. To free the meat from the shell, slip your oyster fork underneath the meat and wiggle it back and forth a time or two. Use your cocktail fork to spear the oyster and dip it into the sauce. Eat the oyster in one bite. At an informal setting, it's acceptable to pick up the shell with your fingers and suck the oyster right off the shell.

Shrimp: Shrimp can present special challenges. If it's served ready-to-eat in a cocktail appetizer, pierce the shrimp on a cocktail fork and bite off a succession of manageable pieces. If the shrimp are large, place them on your plate and cut them with the fork provided before dipping them into the sauce. Steamed shrimp served in their shells, however, are definitely a finger food. Before you tackle a serving of shrimp in their shells, make sure that you have a large fabric napkin on hand. Ask for a bib if you fear for the safety of your shirt or blouse. Usually, a large bowl is provided for the empty shells. If you don't receive a bowl, just accumulate the shells in a neat little heap on your plate.

Snails (Escargot): Pick up one escargot at a time, using the escargot tong that's provided to secure the snail. Remove it with a cocktail fork prior to dipping the meat into butter sauce. Many restaurants serve escargot already removed from the shell and placed in special dishes with sauce — a nice convenience.

Spaghetti

Eating spaghetti may look difficult, but really it's easy. You normally twirl spaghetti on the edge of your plate with your fork. However, you may use your fork and a place spoon as well. The place spoon serves as a base of operation. Place a forkful of spaghetti strands (not too many!) into the bowl of the place spoon and then twirl it around until the strands are firmly wrapped around the fork in a bite-sized portion.

It's also acceptable to use your fork to cut the spaghetti into bite-sized portions, although you rarely see this method used in Italy.

Sushi and sashimi

Japanese and Westerners alike love sushi. Originally, sushi was created as a way of preserving fish — normally carp. From this practice evolved a large, varied assortment of sushi or *nigiri-zushi,* meaning hand-shaped sushi.

Sushi, which is usually fresh raw fish and vinegared rice, is served in hand-shaped, bite-sized pieces so that you can easily eat it with chopsticks. You can use chopsticks or a fork, but many aficionados prefer to use their fingers. No matter how you choose to eat sushi, you should eat it in one or two bites. Sushi is served with soy sauce and various condiments for dipping, with ginger provided as a refresher for the palate between courses.

Distressing Mealtime Moments and Common Blunders

Eating in any social setting may result in mishaps. Use the following tips to steer yourself out of common mishaps that can occur:

✔ **You drop a utensil onto the floor.** Never lean over and pick up the utensil (unless, of course, you're at your mother's dinner table and no waiters or servants are present, in which case you may use your napkin to retrieve the wandering fork, walk it out to the kitchen, and get yourself both a clean napkin and a clean fork). In any situation where servers are present, beckon a server and explain what happened. The server will pick up the utensil and bring you a clean one.

✔ **You're served a piece of food that is not cooked properly.** This situation can be especially dangerous with meat. If you encounter such a situation, call over a server and quietly explain the situation. Trust the waitstaff to reappear with a different plate of food for you.

✔ **You find a foreign object in your food.** Again, find your server and tell him or her about the problem in a very discreet manner. Rest assured that your meal will be replaced quickly, and may even be complimentary.

✔ **You dislike the food that is being served, or you are allergic to it.** The polite thing to do is try a little of everything; however, if you're allergic to a food, just smile and say "No, thank you." It's not necessary to say anything critical.

✔ **You have bone, gristle, or some other unwanted food item in your mouth.** Discreetly remove the food onto the tine of your fork and place it on your plate. If possible, hide it under a garnish or other food on your plate so that the people around you can't see it. Never spit anything into your napkin!

The Zen of Dining

I understand that this may sound like a lot of rules, but even if you forget an occasional rule here or there, keep in mind that you should always eat with respect for others — those with whom you're dining and those who prepared and served the meal.

The most important common-sense advice I can give is this: Don't present other diners with an open mouth full of food. This is the biggest mistake I see. And as you eat, make sure that you aren't wolfing your food down; pace yourself and watch the others at the table. Try not to eat too fast or too slowly, and chew your food well. Doing so not only makes the meal more pleasant but is better for your digestive system as well!

Meals are meant to be eaten mindfully, in an environment of calmness, harmony, and balance. I call it the Zen of dining. Remember that people make character judgments based on the way you handle yourself in dining and social situations. *Bon appetit!*

The top ten dining mistakes

10. Speaking too loudly

9. Playing with your hair or earrings, or touching your face and head

8. Pushing away the plate or bowl when finished

7. Eating too fast or too slowly

6. Using cell phones and pagers while dining

5. Poor posture

4. Leaving your purse, keys, sunglasses, or eyeglasses on the table

3. Elbows on the table

2. Picking your teeth

1. Talking with food in your mouth and chewing with your mouth open

Chapter 17

The Wonders of Wine

*A*mericans have always had a complicated relationship with alcoholic beverages. As recently as 1919, alcohol was prohibited completely. Traditionally, Americans drank mostly whiskey and other hard liquor, but today, wine and beer are much in fashion.

Wine in particular can pose etiquette challenges. A glass of wine is a pleasant accompaniment to a meal that adds a note of flavor and enhances the food that is served, but at the same time, the drinking of wine involves many rituals, including ordering, tasting, and enjoying. If you don't understand the rituals, you might find it somewhat stressful to select and order a wine.

If you're unfamiliar with the ins and outs of what makes a good wine and how it pairs with food, you may be tempted to avoid it altogether, especially in public. But there are times when you may have to deal with it, such as when you're the host of a business dinner. Relax; once you know a few guidelines, you can make your way through the process of selecting, ordering, and drinking wine. This chapter explains those guidelines.

This book can only touch on the complex topic of wine. You can find out much more about wine in Mary Ewing-Mulligan and Ed McCarthy's *Wine For Dummies,* 2nd Edition (also published by IDG Books Worldwide, Inc.).

The history of wine in the U.S.

The popularity of wine in the U.S. is a relatively new phenomenon. Historically, wine was always very expensive, because most wine was imported and subject to tariff duties. Wine appeared regularly only on the tables of the wealthy.

Especially in the 1870s, when the temperance movement was in full swing, the drinking of wine was condemned, even though little was drunk. The efforts of these groups eventually led to national prohibition in 1919.

California had made wines before the Gold Rush, but when Prohibition took effect, manufacturing alcoholic beverages became illegal in this country. Thirteen years of Prohibition virtually ruined the wine industry, and only about 100 wineries survived in California, New York, New Jersey, Ohio, and Missouri by legally making sacramental and medicinal wines, salted cooking wines, and grape juice.

Today, American winemakers produce wonderful wines, and the popularity of wine is steadily increasing.

Selecting Wine

You and your guest have been seated, and you've been presented with a wine list. Now what? This section can help you choose a wine that both pleases your guests and complements your meal.

Remember that the purpose of wine is to enhance the meal and make your guest feel special. Select carefully, and you'll make a good impression.

Who selects?

Whether for business or for pleasure, navigating the wine list and ordering wine, as a rule, is done by the official host — the person paying the bill. As a host, you may pass the wine list around the table for others to inspect or offer to have one of the guests select. If you regularly conduct business at a favorite restaurant, you might consider calling ahead and having them plan a menu and select a wine, or arrive early to discuss the menu, wine choices, and prices.

How much should you spend?

The first rule is to have a price range in mind before you order. A sensible guideline is to spend about as much on a bottle of wine as you spend on one complete dinner. Fine wines can vary in price from a few dollars to many tens of dollars to even hundreds of dollars, so make sure that you know what you're doing if you select an expensive wine. (Because many wine drinkers have become more savvy about wine selection and prices, most restaurateurs now price their wines by doubling the retail price and adding ten dollars.)

The most expensive wine on the wine list isn't always the most impressive. When you're looking for value, don't follow the trends; select lesser-known or local wines, which are normally priced lower because of lack of recognition.

If you are a beginning wine drinker, you may want to enlist the help of your waiter in making a selection. Better establishments have a wine steward, or *sommelier,* on hand to assist you. If you enlist this person's help, tip him or her 10 to 15 percent of the cost of the wine (in addition to the normal tip).

Be enthusiastic about your wine selection! Don't be afraid to ask your server or the wine steward for assistance, and remember to mention how impressive the wine list is. Taste, learn, and drink what you enjoy. Personal preference should be the final deciding factor.

Which wine complements your meal?

Wine and food go together. The key to choosing a wine is to find one that won't overpower the food or be overpowered by it. The following are examples of wines that generally match certain foods:

- ✔ Light meat dishes (such as pork), poultry, or full-flavored fish (such as salmon) go well with a red wine such as Pinot Noir or French Burgundy.

- ✔ Lighter fish and shellfish dishes are fine with a light-bodied white wine, such as Chenin Blanc, Sancerre, Pinot Grigio, or German Riesling.

- ✔ Lobster or richer fish dishes are complemented by a full-bodied Chardonnay, Semillion, or Viognier.

- ✔ Chicken and pasta can go with either red or white wine, depending on the sauce. A heavy meat sauce is better complemented by a medium-bodied red wine, such as Merlot or Cabernet Franc, while a light vegetable or cream sauce goes well with a white or sparkling wine.

- ✔ Stews, roasts, game, duck, and other full-flavored dishes go best with full-bodied red wines, such as Cabernet Sauvignon, Petite Syrah, or Zinfandel.

Some international foods were not designed to go with wine, so be creative and experiment with different varieties. Chefs across the country pour Champagne with everything from Asian-influenced main courses to Indian curries. The effervescence of Champagne can refresh the palate so that the spices do not overwhelm the wine. The right sparkling wine can make a meal memorable and create a festive mood.

Pairing wines with zesty foods

If you're enjoying a spicier, ethnic meal, try these food-and-wine combinations:

- **Cajun:** Alsatian white wines, Champagne

- **Mexican and Indian:** Chardonnay, beer

- **Sushi:** Sauvignon Blanc

- **Chinese:** White Zinfandel

Red wines are normally served at room temperature, and white wines are chilled so that the flavor and aroma are at their peak. If the day is a very warm one, a slightly chilled red wine may be more desirable.

What do your guests prefer?

When selecting wine, also ask your guests if they have any preferences. It's fine to offer or suggest an aperitif, Champagne, or white wine to be served with the first course.

Inquire as to what your guests' meal choices are. If everyone at the table decides to have a rich meat entrée, then a red wine is appropriate. If guests are having lighter chicken or seafood dishes, suggest a lighter-bodied white wine. Occasionally, one guest does not drink red wine; if the majority of guests are having red wine, you may suggest that the guest order an individual glass of white wine.

One bottle of wine serves approximately four glasses. Make sure to request an adequate number of bottles for the number of guests. If more than four guests are present, choose a white wine and a red wine.

Note: If you are a guest, you have every right to avoid wine for whatever reason. Some people, for example, are allergic to sulfites, which are found in most wines. If you do not wish to partake of wine, just call over your server and say, "I will not be having any wine this evening." The server will remove your wine glass and then ask you for an alternate beverage order. Never turn your wine glass upside down!

Can those old rules be thrown out?

Normally, you order red wines with red meats and other robust dishes and white wines with fish and other delicate entrees. Yet some of these old rules are changing. Even wine experts don't always adhere to the basic guide-lines — they drink what they like.

Oftentimes, there are particular reasons to break the rules. And some dishes just don't fall neatly within the guidelines. Consider these situations, for example:

- What if you order oven-roasted sea bass served with a veal reduction sauce — do you order a white wine to complement the fish or a red wine to complement the rich veal sauce? If a dish has a wine base, say a Pinot Noir, a buttery Chardonnay is an excellent choice — or try to choose an appropriate Pinot Noir to match the sauce. You'll find it a sure hit. If you're not certain, ask your waiter to make a suggestion.

- Suppose an unexpected guest drops by and stays for dinner, you're serv-ing leg of lamb, and you have only white wine on hand. You don't need to omit wine just because you don't have the proper or recommended red wine. Just serve what you have and enjoy it.

The guidelines are there to allow you to get the most pleasure possible out of your wine and the food that you're having with it. Use them if you want to, but don't consider them to be ironclad rules that you can't break under any circumstances.

Examining the Wine

After you order a bottle of wine, your server brings it to the table and pre-sents it to you. This is the time when you examine the label, making sure that you received the wine and vintage that you ordered.

If you do have the correct wine, the next step is for the server to remove the seal, take out the cork, and place it on the table next to you. Your job is to visually examine the cork. (It's not necessary to sniff the cork to see if the cork is in good condition; in most cases, inspection of the cork is ceremo-nial.) Unless the cork bears a different name than the label or the cork looks dry and crumbly, you have nothing to worry about.

Occasionally, you may find a cork that is moldy. This does not necessarily mean that the wine has been *corked* (spoiled), but you should alert your server to the situation.

You may also want to feel the bottle with your hand to determine whether the wine seems to be at the correct temperature.

Tasting the Wine

The person who ordered the wine is normally the one who does the tasting, although the host may request that one of the guests do so.

After you verify that you received the correct wine, your server pours a small amount of wine into your glass. Because color can tell you much about the age of the wine, look carefully before you taste. Red wines lose their color when aged, and white wines become deeper yellow or gold.

Gently swirl the wine in the glass by holding the stem firmly while the glass remains on the table. Swirling wine provides oxygen, which assists in releasing the aroma — or *nose*. Now sniff the wine. Most everything to know about wine can be determined by the smell. If you'd like, take a small sip. It's not necessary to swish the wine through your mouth as you'd do in an official wine tasting, but hold the wine in your mouth for a moment before swallowing.

Now is the time to determine your overall impression of the wine and to check that the wine hasn't spoiled. Wine is a foodstuff, and as such, it can spoil just like any other food. Even though it may be uncomfortable, if the wine tastes "off" to you, this is the time to say so. The usual remedy for spoiled wine is for the server to bring another bottle of the same wine. If that particular vintage is not available, the wine steward will suggest or bring a similar wine.

Serving precious red wine

Serving white wine is pretty simple: The host or server usually places it in a bucket of ice to cool a bit before pouring. But serving red wine — especially an older, more precious red wine — is a bit more complicated.

In finer restaurants, the wine steward or sommelier usually serves a fine red wine. The bottle itself is placed in a cradle so that it tips at about a 45-degree angle, simulating its position in the wine cellar. This position moves the settled material, known as sediment, into a lower "corner" of the bottle. The wine steward then brings the wine from the cellar with great care so as not to disturb the sediment.

The steward also brings to the table a crystal decanter. After opening the bottle, he or she pours the wine into the decanter, taking care not to disturb the sediment. The steward then holds a candle beneath the neck of the bottle so that he or she can see the approach of sediment as the bottle empties into the decanter. A perfect performance results in a decanter that contains totally clear wine, with only a small amount of wine and sediment left in the original bottle. The wine is now ready to drink.

Better restaurants will always offer to replace wine without hesitation. However, returning a bottle of wine if you only dislike the taste is impolite. If the wine hasn't spoiled, make a comment such as "Excellent. Please serve it."

Holding the Glass: Stem or Bowl?

Wine is usually served in a clear glass, which shows off the vivid colors of the wine. The wine glass that is used has a particular shape for logical reasons as well.

Finer restaurants preset tables with at least two wine goblets — a long-stemmed glass for white wines and a conventional, tulip-shaped glass for ordinary red wines. (In some establishments, you also see a very wide-mouthed goblet with a deep bowl for older and more expensive red wines.) When you order wine, the server leaves the appropriate goblet on the table and removes the other(s).

Here is some additional information about glassware:

- Rhine and white wine glasses have long, slender stems so that you can hold the stem and thus keep the heat of your hand from warming the wine. The bowl of the glass is smaller than that of a red wine glass, with a more fragile look to complement the delicate flavor and clear color of the wine.

- A red wine glass has a shorter stem with a larger bowl to allow the robust wine to breathe. You hold the glass closer to the bowl because the heat from your hand releases the wine's flavor.

- Sherry and port glasses are small and open because these wines are more potent in aroma, flavor, and alcoholic content.

- Champagne glasses are tall and narrow and are designed to display the effervescence and flavor of sparkling wine.

During the meal, an attentive waiter will watch your wine glass and refill it when it's close to empty. If you don't want a refill, leave a noticeable portion of wine in your glass.

An attentive host will keep an eye on the wine supply and order an additional bottle if the situation warrants. As a gracious guest, make sure to compliment your host on his or her wine selection.

Dessert wines, sherry, and vermouth

Dessert wines often go unnoticed or neglected. These sweet, rich-flavored wines go well with desserts of cheese, nuts, and fruit and are served best at room temperature (with the exception of a sweet Champagne). Particularly outstanding are sweet Marsala, Angelica, Tokay, Malaga, cream sherry, port, Madeira, and muscatel.

Dry sherry usually has a nutty flavor that goes well with appetizers, soups, and bisque. Sherry may be chilled or not, depending on your taste. Sweet and dry vermouth, normally herb-flavored, is excellent with before-meal appetizers. Vermouth may be served on the rocks, chilled, or at room temperature with a twist of lemon zest.

Drinking Alcoholic Beverages Sensibly

Whether you're the host or a guest, take care not to overindulge in wine or other alcoholic beverages. Nothing is less mannerly than losing control after drinking too much — and nothing can ruin an evening more quickly for everyone else. Make sure that you eat while drinking, and pace yourself by alternating alcoholic beverages with nonalcoholic ones.

Keep in mind that drinking any alcoholic beverages causes dehydration, so be sure to drink enough water!

Enjoying Champagne

Champagne is normally served before a meal or with dessert. This sparkling, bubbly beverage adds a festive air to any occasion, but you don't have to save the Champagne for a special day; it goes well with many casual foods — even Mexican!

Everyone loves hearing the "Pop!" upon opening a bottle of Champagne, but you need to open the bottle with a minimum of fanfare to protect your guests from a flying cork. Holding the bottle at a 45-degree angle from your body, making sure not to point it toward anyone, follow these steps:

1. **With your thumb over the cork, remove the foil and wire cage from around the cork.**

2. **With one hand about two-thirds of the way down the bottle and the other over the cork, twist the bottle while pushing down on the cork.**

3. **As the cork emerges, continue putting pressure on the cork so that it makes only a quiet hiss as it's released from the bottle.**

Technically speaking, Champagne is the official name for sparkling wines made in the Champagne region of France. Sparkling wines made outside that region are not officially allowed to use the name Champagne. Whatever you call them, Champagne and other sparkling wines come in a range of dry-nesses: Brut is dry, and Sec is sweet. (You can find everything from Extra Brut, the driest, to Demi-Sec, the sweetest.) Generally speaking, you want to pair dry sparkling wines with savory foods and sweet sparkling wines with sweet foods.

Toasting

The term *toast* comes from the old English custom of placing a piece of toasted bread in the bottom of the glass to enhance the flavor of beer or wine. After the toast was saturated with the liquor, the person would eat the toast. Who knows where that tradition disappeared to! Today, you can make a toast with Champagne, wine, or any other beverage (omitting the actual piece of toast, of course). Children, young adults, and those who don't drink can toast with water or whatever beverage they're drinking; doing so is not bad taste or bad luck.

For a long time, the rule has been that you do not drink a toast to yourself, although some people feel that it's okay to raise your glass but not drink. Follow your preference in this matter, but to be perfectly correct, simply smile and nod to everyone if you're toasted to.

Who makes toasts and when? Toasting was once a man's job, and only men drank the toast, while women nodded and smiled. But now, it is perfectly appropriate for anyone to make or respond to a toast, regardless of gender. The host can and should propose the first toast to begin the meal — a wel-come toast. If a guest of honor is present, the host also proposes a toast to that person over dessert.

Rising and sitting during a toast depend on the formality of the occasion. If the guest of honor is a dignitary, a very important person, or a distinguished elder, everyone should rise with the toast as a sign of respect. At large events where you want to command the attention of a room or more than one table, rising for the toast is traditional. Simply ask for everyone's attention, or rise and ask for everyone's attention in a larger gathering. Once you have the floor, be respectful, take a minute or less to make the toast, and then be seated. At smaller occasions, if fewer than ten people are at the table, rising is unnecessary.

Don't clink silverware or crystal to gain everyone's attention. Clinking of glasses is gauche, and it can also break fine crystal. The custom of clinking glasses began in the Middle Ages for the purpose of spilling a little of the drink into the other person's glass to assure that they were not being poisoned — not a real danger today. Some believe that clinking also was thought to drive away evil spirits.

The guest of honor responds to the toast by toasting and thanking the host. In fact, whether or not you are the guest of honor, you should always respond with a toast after you are toasted.

Chapter 18

Making Deals While Breaking Bread

*B*usiness meals can be high-stress situations, even if you've been through the exercise many times and you know what's expected of you. The pressures of wanting to look right, eat right, behave right, and advance your own interests, all at the same time, can be stressful! Your mastery of good manners comes in handy in business situations like these because you can conduct yourself properly without having to think too much about your behavior.

This chapter tells you what you need to know about doing business over a meal, whether you're the host or a guest, and whether you're on your home turf or in a foreign country where you have to cope with different customs, unfamiliar regional names for foods, and possibly even a language that you can't understand. I also give businesswomen some special advice, because they face a few challenges that men seldom encounter in the business world.

Understanding the Whys and Wherefores of Wining and Dining for Business

It's amazing to consider how much business is done over meals. From staff breakfasts to working lunches to cocktail receptions for clients, being in your best business form at any meal really pays off. Not only do you need to be knowledgeable in your field, but you also need the style and grace to get yourself through these events so that you emerge with your professional image intact — and even enhanced.

Heeding the rules and regulations

Rules and regulations govern much more of today's business environment than was the case just a few years ago. Your company probably has rigidly enforced rules about expense account charges and the giving and receiving of gifts. Your organization, like many organizations, may regard enjoying a fancy meal at the expense of somebody else as a gift.

Government agencies in particular usually forbid employees from accepting any gift from a vendor. Government agencies may also require you to pay your share of the tab no matter where or with whom a meeting over a meal takes place. This rule is commonplace even in private industry. Check with your supervisor or the human resources department for your company's official policy.

Both your company and the IRS may require you to keep a diary of business meals, especially when you are the host. Include the name and location of the meeting, a list of the attendees and their affiliations, and a description of the business that you conducted. Always include a copy of the receipt in your records as well.

How you handle yourself at business meals can establish your credibility as a businessperson. If your etiquette is lacking, you may make people wonder how in the world you got to be where you are!

Everyone likes to work with a person whose polished manners and thoughtfulness make business dining situations thoroughly enjoyable. If you take the time to hone your skills, you'll find yourself being sought after as a valuable representative of your company — and as a great dinner companion.

Your conduct during business entertainment functions that take place during the course of personnel recruiting, company mergers, and other high-level negotiations can have a significant effect on the outcome. The behavior of luncheon and dinner meeting participants influences many important organizational issues. As you read through this chapter, try to envision yourself in all the different roles. Today, you may be just another attendee at a departmental breakfast; but tomorrow, you may need to host a dinner to ease the way for a multimillion-dollar merger.

Doing Your Homework: A Little Knowledge Is a Big Advantage

Whether your mission is to buy, sell, merge, or recruit, research is your secret weapon. Doing a little homework before a meeting can help you appear on top of things and possibly avoid an unwitting offense.

First, make sure that you know something about the other party's company. Check the Internet or the library for a profile. Get to know the company's location(s), the various divisions, the names of the top executives, the annual sales figures, and so on. Make a few notes on a small card and study them before you set off for the restaurant.

Also, memorize the names of the guests beforehand. Speak with your sales representatives, read contact reports, study resumes, and so on to collect some background information. The correct use of a person's name in a business situation is essential to good manners.

If you're entertaining guests from another city, a minute or two on the Internet can provide you with information about the hometown of your colleagues. Think how pleasant it will be to start off the evening by saying something like "I bet the blossoms are spectacular in your city's famous rose garden" or "I hope the drought isn't causing too much damage to your landscape."

In the absence of advance knowledge — for example, if an unexpected guest shows up at your business dinner — try a question that leaves a lot of room for a reply:

- "I've never been to Duluth, but I understand that the fishing around there is spectacular. Do you like to fish?"
- "Are the subways in Tokyo really as crowded as our news reports show them to be?"
- "How would you compare Italian restaurants in America to the food back home?"

Any efforts that you make to draw out another person will be appreciated. Don't forget to include the quiet guest who seems to appear in every group. If awkward moments arise, don't panic or make useless small talk; wait a moment so that others can add to the conversation. Remember, silence can be golden.

Taking a Business Meal Step-by-Step

As do most other rituals, business meals have a beginning, a middle, and an end. This section takes you through the etiquette of a business meal, from making the arrangements to settling up after the meal.

Making arrangements ahead of time

When you coordinate a business meeting that involves a meal, make arrangements with the restaurant at least a week ahead of time. Alert the restaurant manager or maitre d' that you are hosting an important meeting, notify the restaurant that you will be paying for the meal, and give them your credit card number. Let the restaurant manager or maitre d' know whether any VIPs require special attention. Also specify any special needs for tables, rooms, seating, special meals, parking, and audio/visual aids such as flip charts and overheads. Arrange to pay the gratuity or guest parking fees beforehand as well.

Make sure to arrange for an appropriate measure of privacy as well. Widely spaced tables in a large dining room may give you enough privacy, or you may decide that you need a private dining room. You don't want unknown people in the same establishment to overhear your business.

As the host, you should arrive early to make sure that the table or room is what you had previously arranged and decide on appropriate seating. Arrange the seating by rank and position. The guest or most important person should be seated in the best chair, which is normally the one with the best view and location. The maitre d' offers that seat first. As the host, try to situate yourself so that you can see each person and converse easily with everyone.

Finally, if the meal involves a large group, place name cards at the table ahead of time to ensure that people sit where you want them to.

Getting together

Greet your guests at the restaurant entrance or directly inside the door. Never be seated or waiting at the table when your guests arrive. Always greet your guests with a firm handshake. Have your business card handy so that you don't have to dig through your pockets or search through your purse or briefcase. Present your card in a relaxed manner — don't rush.

When the guests arrive, get off to a good start by making formal introductions. Have everyone stand up for introductions and exchange handshakes (and business cards, if the parties are being introduced for the first time at the meeting). As the host of the meeting, make remarks similar to these:

> "Good evening. I'm so glad you could join us. I'm John Robbins, vice president of marketing for XYZ Corporation, and this is Ann Murphy, our sales manager. Ann, I'd like you to meet Robert Smith, operations manager of ABC Industries, and his production manager, Charlie Wilson."

As the introductions are made, each person should repeat the names of the others and offer a handshake and a brief pleasantry, such as, "How do you do, Charlie."

Presenting business cards properly

Business cards can be used as gift enclosures, clipped to documents, or presented in person as a means of introduction. When you're handing out your card at a business meal, keep the following tips in mind:

✔ Always carry business cards. Keeping them in a neat little leather business card case looks professional.

✔ Make sure that your cards are in good condition. If a card is ripped, bent ,or dirty, it will do nothing for your professional image, and you shouldn't hand it out. Wait and have new cards made.

✔ Present your card face up and turned so that the person receiving the card can read it.

✔ Don't dole out cards as if you were playing Gin Rummy. Be selective in giving out business cards. At a business meal, wait to hand your card to a senior executive until you are asked. This way, you don't appear overeager.

✔ Exchange cards only before or after a meal — not while people are dining.

As the host, you also need to mention the purpose of the gathering. Try saying something like this: "I know that we're here to discuss my company's capability to meet your delivery requirements, and I look forward to reaching an outcome that pleases all of us. But first, let's enjoy what promises to be a delicious meal."

Making small talk

After the introductions, and once your party settles down at the table, engage your guests in informal conversation. For example, you can say that you've briefly visited Dubuque (or wherever the other party's office is located) and ask about the community, or you can mention a widely publicized sporting event in the news and ask for an opinion. If some of the participants had to travel a significant distance, you can inquire about their trip. Listen carefully to their responses and indicate your interest by asking follow-up questions.

Avoid discussing your personal life, sex, politics, or religion — you want cordial conversation, not controversy. (See Chapter 10 for more conversation do's and don'ts.)

Useful discussions often take time to develop. When important business is on the agenda, be prepared to spend as much time as is necessary at the meal. Don't book an appointment too close to the time that you think the meal should end, because you don't want to be rushed or to appear preoccupied to your guests.

Exercising moderation

You can have a drink or two before dinner as an icebreaker; for some people, doing so may be a normal way of life. If you intend to conduct business, however, protect your mental clarity by drinking in moderation, if at all. There's no disgrace in ordering mineral water or some other nonalcoholic beverage, regardless of the choices that others make. Moderation is the rule, and everyone at the table will appreciate your consideration.

When you are the host, it's best to follow the lead of your guests. If your guests do not order cocktails before the meal, you should forgo cocktails as well. If you're a nondrinking host, you should certainly suggest to your guests that they have a cocktail, and offer to order wine during the meal.

Selecting your meal

When it comes time to order, again, follow your guests' lead. Let the highest-ranking person order first; the other guests should follow this person's lead and order similar dishes at similar prices. If the VIP orders appetizers, you should order one, too, so that your guests don't have to eat alone. If you know the restaurant menu well, your guests may appreciate your recommendations of favorite dishes.

During a business meal, your mind is on business. Don't overburden it by ordering foods that challenge your table manners and your wardrobe. As you survey the menu, be alert to the following hazards:

- Foods with deeply colored sauces or gravies

- Hard-to-manage foods, such as spaghetti

- Foods that require a great deal of on-the-plate management, such as a whole lobster, crab, and spare ribs

- Food that you eat with your hands or fingers, such as hamburgers and french fries

- Unfamiliar foods that may challenge your digestion, your allergies, or your personal preferences

It's always good etiquette to avoid selecting the most expensive item on the menu. If a client or your employer is paying for the meal, it's best to order from the mid-priced offerings.

If you have special dietary needs or prohibitions and you know in advance where you'll be dining, call ahead and discuss your needs with the restaurant personnel. Otherwise, there's no need to be shy about requesting a reasonable accommodation to your diet. In most cases, menus include a wide enough variety of selections to provide you with acceptable choices.

Minding your manners during the meal

You can expect conversation to continue during the meal, so be prepared to participate. Take small bites that you can swallow easily, and take small sips of water or wine. Don't get caught chewing a large hunk of steak when the company president asks you how your children are doing in school. Follow the host's lead when it comes to starting the business-related discussion. Many people believe that no business should be discussed until the plates have been cleared and everyone is relaxing with a cup of coffee or an after-dinner drink.

Use your best table manners (see Chapter 16 for a thorough discussion of table manners) and mind your posture — doing so makes an enormous impression. If the food or the wine is especially good, mention it to your host, but keep your complaints to yourself. If you must leave the table for any reason, rise from your seat, put your napkin on your chair and say a simple "Excuse me" as you depart. When you return, resume your seat without comment.

Silence your cell phone, pager, and other gadgets that may disrupt the meal. If, for some reason, you're contacted because of an outside emergency, briefly explain the situation to the others before excusing yourself: "I regret the interruption, but my wife has been involved in a traffic accident and I must go to her aid immediately. I will be back in contact with you all as soon as I take care of this emergency."

If there's a problem with the service or the food, handle it discreetly. Either excuse yourself to handle the situation with the manager or maitre d' in private, or wait until the guests have left. Never make a scene in front of your guests, which has the potential to embarrass everyone.

Getting down to business

After everyone has finished eating, the host introduces the business at hand by saying something like this:

> "Now that we've had a chance to restore our energies, let's see if we can set your minds at ease regarding our company's ability to deliver the equipment you need. Larry, please start us off by outlining your company's needs . . . ."

As the business conversation takes place, listen carefully. If remembering details is important, take a small notepad from your pocket and make pertinent notes.

If you want more coffee or some other beverage during the discussion, signal a waiter. Try not to interrupt any speaker when you do so.

Paying the tab

The person who invited the others to the meal should pick up the tab. A gracious host prearranges for the server to present him or her the tab or, better yet, for the establishment to send the bill to his or her company address. Try to make arrangements with the restaurant ahead of time: Either call ahead or arrive early and give them your credit card.

Business meals almost always have a designated host; therefore, guests don't need to make a ceremonial attempt to pick up the tab. However, if company rules absolutely forbid you from accepting hospitality, say so, make a quick mental calculation of your share of the bill, and give the money to your host. Most hosts will object to situations like these, but your insistence that company rules obligate you to pay will carry the moment. In such a situation, make your declaration to your host before the meal begins and ask that the server keep your expenses separate and present them to you afterward.

Leave with your guests, thanking them for their time. Although not essential, it's a nice gesture to follow up with the guests via phone or e-mail the next day.

A Final Word on Business Dining

Your table manners can make the difference between getting that promotion or not, and between closing that business deal or not. Fortunately, old habits *can* be changed, if you want to change them — and all it takes is a little effort. For a thorough discussion of proper dining etiquette, see Chapter 16.

Special considerations for women in business

Business affairs were the province of men for so many centuries that the world is still catching up to the rapidly increasing numbers of women in executive and managerial positions. Every etiquette reference to the male gender applies equally to women, of course, but a few special considerations may make dining situations a bit smoother for today's female businessperson.

As the female host of a business meal or other function, call ahead to the restaurant or club and alert them to your position as host. Your statement can be as simple as "This is Gloria Wilson from XYZ Widgets. I'll be hosting a dinner meeting at your establishment at 7 p.m., and I want to make sure that the waiter presents the tab to me. I will identify myself to the maitre d' when I arrive at the restaurant." (The same goes for a man hosting a meal.)

At any dining establishment, ask your waiter for the wine list as soon as you're seated. This simple action serves to identify you as the host.

Part VI

Conducting Yourself in Special Situations

The 5th Wave   By Rich Tennant

"Psst — Philip! I'm not sure what the etiquette is here, but I think you should take your hat off."

In this part . . .

This part covers those situations that you encounter less frequently, but that often require you to remember a different set of etiquette rules. Special occasions such as weddings and funerals can put your manners to the test. Travel, whether it's within your own country or it brings you in contact with an entirely new culture, poses challenges as well. And interacting with people who have disabilities may take you into a new realm of etiquette in which you're unsure of the proper behavior. Look to this part of the book for help in these and other similar circumstances.

Chapter 19

Marking Life's Major Events

● ●

In This Chapter

▶ Welcoming a new baby into the world

▶ Celebrating rites of passage

▶ Dealing with death in a dignified way

● ●

The human family forms a circle without end. Babies are born; children grow up, get married, and have children of their own; and eventually, life comes to an end. Every culture celebrates, honors, and mourns these milestones in its own ways, and many groups within a larger society have their own variants on those traditions. What draws all of us together is a common understanding and appreciation for the importance of these events and a willingness to share in some of the most meaningful events of our lives.

Life's major events are often a challenge: They call on you to stop what you're doing, take pause, and give of yourself to others — whether it's taking a weekend to travel to a high school graduation or spending time with your sister at home after the birth of her baby. What counts most is that you're there for your friends and family and that you care. This chapter gives you the information you need to make it through life's big events with grace and style — and your composure intact.

Note: Because weddings necessitate an in-depth discussion of etiquette, I cover that rite of passage in its own, separate chapter. See Chapter 20 for more information.

What a Beautiful Baby!

Fortunately for the mother, giving birth to a baby isn't a social occasion to which you invite guests. However, as new parents, or as friends and family supporting the new parents, you should do a few thoughtful things before and after a little one comes into the world.

Holding a baby shower

Traditionally, a woman only has a shower with her first child. But times are changing, and I (and everyone else I know) don't see why Mom can't have a shower for every child who joins her family. This is especially true if the new baby is a different gender, or if multiples are expected. If Mom already has everything she needs for the baby and you just want to do something nice, a little get-together in her honor is a lovely idea. For example, you can host an afternoon tea and ask each guest to bring a small item related to tea for the mom-to-be.

Notices/Announcements/Invitations

When inviting guests to a baby shower, include these components on the invitation:

- ✔ Guest of honor's name
- ✔ Shower date and time
- ✔ Host's name and phone number
- ✔ Address of shower
- ✔ Map of shower location (optional)
- ✔ RSVP date and phone number
- ✔ Shower theme information (if applicable)
- ✔ Sex of the baby (if known)

Mail the invitation to out-of-town guests about six weeks prior to the shower, and about four weeks prior for local guests. A good guideline for the RSVP deadline is two weeks before the shower.

The shower is usually held two to three months before the baby's due date. This gives the mother time to evaluate what she's received at the shower and decide what she needs to purchase or borrow herself. It also provides some excitement in the last weeks of pregnancy (as if an expectant mother doesn't have enough excitement in her life!).

Be very wary of holding a shower within a month of the due date. You may find yourself with a new guest at the shower (baby, that is) if you cut it too close and the baby decides to arrive early!

Showers are usually held before the birth, but in certain circumstances (such as a difficult pregnancy), it may be wise to wait until after the baby is born. This allows everyone to meet the new arrival and ensures that the occasion will be a joyous one.

The shower is usually hosted by a good friend of the mom-to-be. In the past, it was considered inappropriate for a family member to give a shower, but today, it's common for the mom-to-be's family to help plan a shower.

Adopted children should be welcomed as warmly as any other child, and a shower is great way to do so. If the adopted child is older, consider having a welcoming party, which is similar to a birthday party. When planning a shower for the adoption of an infant, make sure that the adoption is final before selecting a date for the shower. For this reason, many people wait until after the child is adopted to give a shower. If the shower is after the adoption, you may want to allow at least several weeks before hosting the shower for the new family to get adjusted.

Who attends/Who's invited

Traditionally, only women attend showers; however, many showers today include men as well. If you're going the traditional route, immediate female family members of both the mother and father-to-be's families should be invited, as well as close friends of the mother-to-be. It's best to consult with the parents-to-be when making up the invitation list. If the shower is to be a surprise, make sure to check with the parents-to-be's families when making up your guest list.

Showers usually have between 6 and 25 guests. If the number of guests seems too large, consider having two showers — one for family and relatives and one for friends. Usually, a shower is held in the host's home, but it can also be held in a restaurant, a tearoom, a community room, or a church social hall. The shower should last about two hours.

Infertility and miscarriages can be emotionally painful issues. If you're inviting a guest who is having a difficult time conceiving or recently had a miscarriage, you may wish to call her before sending an invitation. She may prefer not to attend, but it's best to let her know that you'd like her there and let her make the decision.

Dress

Dress at a traditional baby shower held on a weekend afternoon is relaxed, but nice. A pantsuit, dress, or long skirt and sweater are all good choices. If the shower is themed, it may call for special dress. When in doubt, ask the host for advice.

Flowers/Gifts/Donations

As the host, you are responsible for guiding the guests to presents that are needed and will be appreciated. If possible, the host should sit with the mom-to-be and make a list together. Things to discuss include whether or not she knows the gender of the baby, the style of the nursery, whether she plans to breast-feed, whether she'll be using cloth or disposable diapers, and whether she wants a breast pump. If she hasn't already done so, suggest that she register at one or two baby stores. You can then advise individual guests about her wish list. Occasionally, people host theme showers, such as nursery items (bedding, changing table, and so on), "for the outdoor baby" (mosquito netting for carrier, baby backpack), or "what little boys are made of" (boy clothes and toys).

As the host of a baby shower, you may want to present the guests with party favors. Favor ideas include small pots with flowering plants, decorative soaps, sample-size bath salts, nice chocolates, and sachets.

As a mom-to-be, if you are concerned about the health of your baby and would rather wait until after the birth, it is absolutely fine to throw yourself a welcome-home party after the birth.

Announcing the baby's birth

The first announcement of a baby's birth is usually a joyous phone call made by the new father or proud grandparents. The next step is for the parents to visit a stationer and select an announcement card to send to relatives and friends. You can design your own card or do something as simple as having the child's name and date of birth and the parents' names and address printed on a card and attaching a pink or blue ribbon.

It's perfectly appropriate to ask family members or close friends for help in preparing and mailing the birth announcements. When you're caring for a new baby, you have many pressing issues (other than stuffing envelopes!) to deal with.

You can tell the whole world about your new baby if you wish, but remember to address envelopes to out-of-town grandparents, aunts, and uncles first, followed by in-town grandparents, aunts and uncles, and then other relatives and close friends.

When you receive a birth announcement, you should send a note of congratulations back to the parents. If you wish, you may send a gift to the parents at home or deliver it when you visit in person. If you're close to the new mother, it's nice to send something along for her, too. Any bath or beauty product for Mom is a thoughtful addition to a baby gift.

Selecting a name

People will ask for your baby's name as soon as he or she is born — and even before the big day arrives — so you need to prepare your selections. You can find a good selection of baby name books at bookstores, and relatives and close friends are sure to provide plenty of suggestions. The choice is yours, of course, but here are some customs that you may wish to consider:

✔ **Pass down a name.** Some families give one child in each generation the same name. (This is much more common for boys than it is for girls.) For example, you may have John Williams, the grandfather; followed by John Williams, Jr., the father; and then John Williams III, the son. What happened to John Williams II? That name is reserved for another boy in the family who isn't in the direct line of father-son-son. Usually, the name is given to the firstborn child of that gender — in this case, the firstborn son.

✔ **Perpetuate the mother's family name.** This gesture is especially nice when the mother is the only remaining representative of her birth family — for example, if the mother was an only child or had only sisters and no brother to carry on the family name. Many families use the mother's maiden name as a middle name. For example, if the mother's maiden name is Blair and the father's last name is Pay, the child would be named Allison Blair Pay.

✔ **Honor a much-loved, departed relative.** Many families honor a deceased relative by naming a child in his or her honor. You want to explain this to your immediate family before formally announcing the name. Saying that Aunt Joan meant the world to you and left wonderful, warm memories of her many kindnesses, and that you are naming your child in her honor, is an appropriate way to announce the news.

Visiting the brand-new bundle of joy

Unless you're the baby's grandparent or another member of the immediate family, check with the mother before you visit the hospital. Today, the mother and child's stay at the hospital is very brief. In addition, getting used to motherhood is complicated business — sometimes further complicated by the mother's recovery from a long labor. Many new mothers would rather that you waited to visit until they are settled in at home.

Once they're settled in, most new parents welcome visitors, because new parents love to show off their little ones. Before you visit, telephone and ask for the best day and time to drop in. Bring a little gift for the baby if you want to, admire the child, be lavish with your compliments, and leave before you wear out your welcome. Don't expect to be served a meal — especially not during those very early days.

If the new baby has come into a family that includes other children, especially young children, you may want to bring a little gift for each sibling, too. You needn't spend a considerable sum on these gifts, but suddenly being overshadowed by a baby is hard for children to understand, and they'll appreciate the extra attention.

Giving and receiving baby gifts

If you wish to send a gift for the baby after the birth, by all means do so. However, a note of congratulations is all that is required. If you're a new parent, make sure to send a handwritten thank-you to everyone who sends a gift. It should be signed with the parents' name — not the baby's! Thank-you notes that come signed by Baby Emma are a bit too cute, and besides, everyone knows that Baby Emma can't write. To find out more about appropriate cards or writing paper when sending and receiving gifts and advice on wording thank-you notes, see Chapter 15.

Because so many aspects of etiquette involve the exchange of gifts, it bears repeating that no gift needs to exceed your means or your comfort level. Other people may be able to afford to give a prepaid college education or a large certificate of deposit (well, that may be extreme, but you get the point!), but if your budget limits you to the purchase of a small stuffed animal or a colorful rattle, do what you can and present your gift with love. Your thoughtfulness and prompt response are all that are necessary.

Dealing with challenging situations

In this day and age, you see more and more nontraditional families and births. Children are born to single mothers, and babies are adopted by single dads and gay couples. Whatever the situation, remember that the welcoming of a new baby is an occasion for joy, no matter how it happens, and your role as a friend or family member is to do your best to offer your warm congratulations and share the parent (or parents') happiness. The following sections address a few of the more common situations that you may encounter.

Adoptions

Couples who adopt newborns are parents in exactly the same sense as those who give birth to their own, and they should be treated as such. The new families send announcements, receive gifts and notes of congratulation, entertain visitors, and observe all the other rituals of new parenthood. An adoption announcement would read, "Mr. and Mrs. Russ Lewis are happy to announce the adoption of Sarah Beth, July seventeenth, 1999, age three months." Or you might use the phrase, "welcome into their home" in place of the phrase about adoption.

A little caution, and then a great celebration

Modern healthcare has made infant mortality rare, but throughout much of human history, the first days of a baby's life were uncertain ones. Among the more interesting customs that grew out of a cautious approach to celebrating births are the Jewish *Bris* and the Chinese First Laugh celebrations:

✔ Jewish tradition calls for a baby boy to be circumcised on the eighth day following his birth, and that the new parents throw a party at their home to celebrate the occasion (even if the procedure is done at a clinic).

✔ The Chinese First Laugh tradition waits for the baby's first laugh (it can happen as early as the baby's first month) to signal the start of a community-wide celebration.

Both customs accomplish the same end: They delay the celebration until the baby's first precarious days are over and the baby seems certain to be healthy and happy.

The traditional gift for a Jewish baby is 18 coins, 18 dollars, or 18 other trinkets, because the eighteenth letter of the Jewish alphabet is understood to mean "life." Chinese tradition is remarkably similar: You give the baby gold coins suspended from a fine chain.

Making any reference to an adopted baby's birth mother (or either of the biological parents) is inappropriate. If the adoptive parents want to discuss the details of the adoption with you, by all means be a good listener, but don't press for details.

Discussing adoption with a child is the parents' responsibility. No matter how tempted you are, stay out of the conversation if you aren't the child's parent. It's not unusual for adopted children to develop a curiosity about their ancestry as they mature, and it's up to their parents (sometimes with the help of professional counselors) to help them resolve those questions.

When baby isn't well

Every parent hopes for a healthy infant. Although medical care gets better every year, some babies come into the world with health problems, and the sad truth is that some don't survive. If you have a close relationship with parents who are facing such difficulties, lend as much support as you can (unless the parents clearly express that they want to be left alone). Ask what you can do to help. Parents with a hospitalized newborn spend a lot of time at the hospital, and you may be able to help by watching their other children at home, doing household chores, providing transportation, running errands to the grocery store or pharmacy, or doing whatever else needs to be done.

Sometimes parents of infants who aren't well will not want to talk. Sometimes they will, and when they are ready, your job is to be a good listener. Don't pry or ask too many questions. Simply listen to whatever the parents want to tell you, offer your sympathy, and continue to be present whenever they need your help.

Children with disabilities

Parents suffer special anguish when their newborn is diagnosed with some sort of physical or mental abnormality. To deal with the challenge, the family needs a sense of community, and the baby needs love. The family will deeply appreciate your support in the form of a visit, a gift, an offer of assistance, or, above all, an ear. Don't worry about etiquette; just try to be a good friend.

For more information about interacting with people who have disabilities, see Chapter 22.

When a child is given for adoption

If a female friend or family member gives her child for adoption, your best display of good manners is to stay in the background until the birth mother is up and around, and then resume normal social contact. In this situation, you can be a good listener if she brings up the subject; otherwise, don't initiate the discussion yourself.

The advice in this section also applies to voluntarily terminated pregnancies. Sometimes the best display of good manners is respectful silence.

Attending a baptism

Baptisms (also commonly called "christenings," although the proper term is "baptism") usually take place in a child's first six months. Catholic children are sometimes baptized very early, within the first six weeks of life. Protestant children are usually baptized during their first six months, although baptism can take place at any age.

Notices/Announcements/Invitations

Invitations to a baptism are usually issued over the telephone. Usually, the parents or grandparents have a small gathering afterward. Invitations to a baptism should be informal, such as, "Jill's baptism will take place at St. Luke's Church at three o'clock on Sunday, February 16th. Will you and Peter come to the ceremony and join us afterward for a reception at our house?"

Who attends/Who's invited

Close family members attend the baptism, as well as the godparents, if there are any. Godparents should be intimate friends of the family, as their role is primarily a spiritual one. Godparents are meant to see that the child is given religious training and is confirmed at the proper time. The godparent is also expected to take a special interest in the child, as a close relative would do. This includes sending Christmas presents and a gift on the child's birthday, until he or she becomes an adult. In the Catholic faith, godparents must also be Catholic. In certain Protestant religions, godparents are not required.

Dress

Dress for a baptism as you would for a religious service.

Flowers/Gifts/Donations

Gifts are usually brought by the guests for the baby, as the guests are presumably very close relatives. For a girl, godparents might give a small piece of jewelry to be worn when she is older, or an engraved silver frame, small cup, or baby spoon. Other ideas include picture frames, a baby book, music box, or a gift certificate to a children's clothing store.

Attending a B'rith Milah

A circumcision and naming ceremony takes place eight days after a Jewish baby boy is born. The boy is also given godparents at this time. The ceremony can take place in the parents' home or in a special room in the hospital.

For a girl, there is a naming ceremony on the first Sabbath after she is born, in a service at the temple. Her father is called up to the Torah, where he recites a short prayer and states his daughter's name. The rabbi then recites a special blessing. A reception is hosted afterward by the baby's mother.

Notices/Announcements/Invitations

Invitations are usually issued over the telephone.

Who attends/Who's invited

Only a few family members and close relatives attend the ceremony.

Dress

Dress as you would for a religious service.

Flowers/Gifts/Donations

Gifts are sometimes presented for the baby on the occasion.

Becoming an Adult

Bar and bat mitzvahs, confirmations, and graduations confer grownup status on the young people whom they honor. Your responsibility as a close friend or relative is to attend the ceremony, join in the celebration, and offer an appropriate gift that is within your means. This section covers the particulars of each of these ceremonies.

Virtually all rites of passage include refreshments following the service. Enjoy the food and fellowship as you would at any other party (see Chapter 14 for tips on being a gracious guest), and don't forget to bring a gift. If you're in doubt about an appropriate gift, remember that young people always appreciate cash gifts, regardless of the occasion.

Bar and bat mitzvahs

Jewish tradition celebrates the attainment of age 13 for boys (bar mitzvah) and age 12 for girls (bat mitzvah). At this milestone, the community considers the young person to be capable of participating in religious observances as an adult. To commemorate this event, families usually allow the celebrant (the boy or girl) to lead the congregation in a regular weekly prayer service, including the reading of a passage from the Torah in Hebrew.

After the ceremony, the immediate family may gather in a private room in the temple to greet members of the congregation who want to offer congratulations. Often, this is followed by a lavish reception, which may be held in a temple reception room or a hotel or other public hall. The reception often includes a seated luncheon or dinner and may include dancing, flowers, and decorated tables.

Notices/Announcements/Invitations

If the reception is to be a large one, issue written invitations (see Chapter 15 for more instructions on how to do so). If it is a small affair with family and a very few friends, you can make your invitations by telephone.

Who attends/Who's invited

Proud parents invite friends to participate in and witness the proceedings. Non-Jewish well-wishers may also be invited to sit among the congregation. All congregations welcome non-Jews and don't expect them to know the details of the ritual. What counts is your presence. Just make sure to stand when everyone else stands and sit when everyone else sits. After the ceremony is over, generously congratulate the celebrant and his or her parents.

Dress

In some congregations, men are asked to wear a small, symbolic head covering. In Orthodox congregations, women also cover their heads and sit apart from the men. Otherwise, wear whatever types of clothing you would normally wear to attend a religious service.

Flowers/Gifts/Donations

Gifts are very important on the occasion of a bar or bat mitzvah. Gifts should not be brought to the temple or the reception, but sent to the child's home. Gifts are wonderful, but most children also appreciate checks. Gift ideas include a good book, a magazine subscription, or a gift certificate to a music store, video rental shop, or electronics store.

Confirmations

Confirmations are a rite of passage for Christians that means the confirmands are capable of participating in the religious life of their congregation as adults. The ceremony usually takes place when the child is in the seventh or eighth grade.

This is usually a quiet family occasion, with only the godparents and close relatives present. If there is a social gathering after the confirmation ceremony, it is appropriate to bring a small gift — a book that is inspirational in some way would be a very appropriate gift.

You should dress as you would to attend a service in a house of worship. The confirmand is usually dressed in his or her very best clothes.

Graduations

High-school and college graduations are some of the proudest occasions in a young person's life — and in the life of their proud parents. They mark completion of a stage of life, and the start of an exciting new life, whether it's moving on to college or their first job. Friends and family who have supported the graduate throughout their schooling look forward to graduation day as a way of celebrating the graduate's accomplishments.

Notices/Announcements/Invitations

Graduation ceremony invitations and announcements are normally given out by the school, which means immediate families only are able to attend. Parents usually plan a party or afternoon reception after the graduation ceremony. It can be elaborate or simple, and depending on the nature of the party, invitations can be printed, handwritten, or telephoned. Again, the larger and more formal the party, the better it is to issue a written invitation.

On the other hand, if the celebration is a backyard barbecue for family and a few neighbors and close friends, you may telephone the invitation. Often, graduates spend time at their own party, and late in the day begin circulating among their friends' houses to greet them and visit their graduation parties as well.

Parents often mail out announcements of a child's graduation, especially to out-of-town friends. (This announcement differs from an invitation to attend a graduation ceremony or reception.) The announcement should be mailed two weeks prior to graduation. If you receive a graduation announcement, you are not obligated to attend or send a gift. A note of congratulations or a graduation card should be sent.

Who attends/Who's invited

If you've attended a high school or college commencement recently, you know that seating is always limited and that parking can be a problem. Tickets to graduation exercises are rationed among the participants, so if you're invited to attend a graduation and you accept the invitation, *go*. Others are sitting at home pouting because there weren't enough tickets to go around. Usually, there are just enough tickets for the parents and siblings of the graduates, and the grandparents. If you are allowed to invite more guests, other close relatives or family friends should be invited. If you cannot invite everyone you'd like to the graduation ceremony, this should be explained to them. Most people will understand. However, everyone should be invited to a gathering honoring the graduate after the ceremony.

One tradition of graduation day is photos, and lots of them! It can be stressful for the graduate, who, in addition to the usual obligations of politeness and graciousness, must pose for photographs with assorted relatives and friends while clothed in cap and gown. Graduates should remember that no matter how awkward posing feels at the moment, doing so is an ordeal that all class-mates share (and the photos will come in handy years later when your own children doubt that their parents know anything!).

Dress

A graduation ceremony and party are an opportunity to look your festive best. Suits and ties for the men and nice dresses or long skirt and matching tops for the women are in order. Graduates often wear a new outfit, whether it's a suit or a special dress, which they can then use in their new life at college or out in the working world.

Flowers/Gifts/Donations

Gifts are de rigeur at a graduation party. Even if you are unable to attend the party, as a close friend or relative, it's thoughtful to send a gift to the graduate. Depending on your preference and price range, welcome gifts might include the following:

- ✔ Stereo equipment

- ✔ A book

- ✔ An atlas

- ✔ A dictionary

- ✔ An accessory for a bicycle

- ✔ A diary or journal

- ✔ A calculator

- ✔ Pair of tickets to a sporting event, rock concert, or play

- ✔ Gift certificate to an electronics store or clothing store

Don't plan on handing a wrapped present to the graduate at the ceremony — it would only get lost in the confusion. Send your gift to the graduate's home or if the party is at the parents' home, bring it with you.

Dealing with a Truly Wrenching Loss

Most cultures and religions have some type of memorial when a person passes away. These services provide a sense of completion, a process for mourning, and comfort for the living. The outpouring of grief and support for the family enables them to eventually go on with their own lives.

Notices/Announcements/Invitations

Notices should be placed in newspapers where family and friends of the deceased person live. The notice should be hand-delivered to the newspaper's editorial office. Notices can also be placed in cities where the departed previously lived, if family members and friends are there.

A notice can include the following information:

- ✔ Name and address of the person

- ✔ Date and place where he or she died

- ✔ Cause of death

- ✔ Name of spouse

- ✔ City of birth and date of birth

- ✔ Company where the person worked and their title

- ✔ Education, military service, or major awards or distinctions

✔ Names of survivors and their relationship to the deceased

✔ Information on the funeral or memorial service and whether it is private or for the public

✔ Where to send donations as memorials

Who attends/Who's invited

A funeral or memorial service may be a very public event, attended by family, friends, colleagues, neighbors and even acquaintances. The gathering held after the event usually includes only family members, the minister or priest, ushers and pallbearers, close social and business friends, and anyone who came from out of town for the service. If the service is private, those attending will be notified personally, usually by telephone.

Attending the events

In many cultures, the first event that follows a death is a *visitation* — a courtesy call at the funeral home prior to the funeral. The casket is present (open or closed), with flowers on display, and the family receives visitors who come to greet them and offer words of comfort and support. (This is a modern version of a very old custom that gave the family a day or two to socialize prior to the burial, to be absolutely certain that the deceased was truly dead and not just in a deep coma. Although no such uncertainty exists today, the custom persists.)

Funerals are often held in a chapel or a house of worship, and they may draw a very large congregation. Because the immediate family may be overwhelmed, you need only to greet the mourners and briefly offer condolences. Most important for the family is the knowledge of your presence.

Burials usually follow funerals. Some cultures consider it a sign of respect to deposit a ceremonial shovel of earth into the grave. This ceremony is initiated by a member of the family and followed by others. If you were close to the deceased, you may take your turn.

You usually exchange expressions of support at the residence of the deceased, a reserved social hall, or a room at the house of worship immediately following the burial or memorial service. In almost all cultures, taking a meal in the company of friends and family is a symbol of the continuation of life and a moment of separation from the intense details of the death, funeral, and burial. Recalling fond memories of the deceased may inspire smiles and even laughter at this gathering — this behavior is perfectly acceptable.

In the days immediately following a funeral, custom calls for neighbors and close friends to visit the bereaved family on a daily basis. Bringing prepared foods that the mourners can eat and share with visitors is a nice gesture.

Expressing your condolences

Most people are at a loss for words when it comes to comforting someone who is grieving. If you don't know what to say, try by starting with these thoughts:

- You are so sorry to hear this sad news.
- The deceased will be sorely missed by friends and colleagues.
- How much you loved this person and how bereaved you feel.
- You know how much the deceased loved and cared for the people who are left behind.
- The grief you feel for the person who is left behind.
- What a wonderful person the deceased was.

It's kind to recount anecdotes, warm remembrances, and stories about the deceased. Remembering the person's accomplishments and all that person meant to you and did for you, and sharing that with the family, is very important and much appreciated.

The etiquette of consoling a dear one is the etiquette of genuine affection. Do what you can to comfort and assist the survivors, and be alert for an indication that your attentions have been gratefully received and are no longer necessary. Sometimes people need to work things out for themselves.

Dress

Black has long been the traditional color for mourning. However, it is not required any longer. It is not a sign of disrespect to wear a color other than black, as long as it is not a bright color. Hats may be worn by women and at Orthodox Jewish services yarmulkes will be worn by the men. Dark suits and ties for men and dresses or suits for women are appropriate.

Some religions impose strict standards of modesty on women. When in doubt, ask someone. If you don't know whom to ask, make sure that the only skin you display at a funeral is from the neck up and the knees down.

Jewish mourning rituals

The Jewish faith marks a person's death with a seven-day period of mourning known as the Shivah. Condolence calls should be made during this time, which begins on the day of the funeral. An hour of the seventh day is counted as a full day. Visits should be made, therefore, within the six days after the funeral. Flowers should never be sent to a Jewish funeral, although it is a growing custom for close friends to send flowers to the family of the deceased sometime during the weeks following the funeral (except to Orthodox Jews).

Funerals are not encouraged in Orthodox synagogues. Therefore, Orthodox Jewish funerals are usually held in mortuary chapels or at home.

Among Orthodox and Conservative Jews it is customary for the immediate family and friends to return to the home of the mourners immediately following the interment of the deceased. Friends in the community come to the home of the mourners at evening time for seven days thereafter, for the purpose of participating in a worship service.

Reform Jews return to the home of the mourners immediately following burial for a brief worship service. This religious service in the home is optional, and is conducted by the Rabbi or a layman at the suggestion of some member of the family. Reform Jews refrain from business and social contacts for a customary period of at least three days following the death of a loved one.

Flowers/Gifts/Donations

During this period, you may send flowers to the funeral home. Donations may be made to the house of worship or made in the deceased person's name to a designated charity. Out-of-town friends and relatives who are not able to attend the funeral may send flowers and messages of condolence to the funeral home, the place of worship, or the family home.

When in doubt, go

Funerals can be difficult occasions. Many otherwise well-mannered people avoid funerals because they're sad and often emotional. The same goes for visiting a hospital patient who is seriously ill and may be connected to monitoring and life-support equipment.

As a general rule, you can assume that the more difficult the situation, the more the family will appreciate your presence and your words of support. You don't need to remain on the scene for a long time; hospitals may limit visits with patients to just a few minutes. But your willingness to go out of your way to say a word or two of comfort will be very much appreciated.

Chapter 20

I Do, I Do! Engagements and Weddings

In This Chapter
▶ Announcing your engagement
▶ Setting the wedding date and making the arrangements
▶ Composing your invitations
▶ Enjoying your big day

*B*ack in the dim reaches of history, a wedding was society's way of gathering together an audience to hear a man promise to take care of a woman. She, in turn, promised to obey him. You may hear faint echoes of those long-ago attitudes in the wedding vows that couples recite today, but the nature of a wedding has changed significantly over the years.

Sure, you can still have a traditional ceremony, where the bride glides down the aisle of a huge cathedral on the arm of her tuxedoed father and meets the groom at the altar. But nowadays, a wedding can be as simple as filling out some paperwork at the county courthouse or running off to get married on the beach in Jamaica. Your wedding can take place in a shady glen with your favorite folk singer officiating, if that's the kind of ceremony you prefer. However you do it, your wedding allows you to declare your love for one another in the company of the people who are most important to you.

One of the little luxuries of the modern wedding is wedding consultants (think Martin Short in *Father of the Bride*). These helpful people can handle everything from the announcements and invitations to the catering and flowers. However, many couples handle the details themselves. Some simply can't afford all the fancy touches. Others prefer to skip some — or even all — of the formalities. Divorced people who are giving marriage another chance face complications that the authorities on marriage often overlook. If you fall into any of these categories, you can find a lot of help in this chapter.

Note: Weddings are complicated business. For more in-depth information about weddings and wedding etiquette, see *Weddings For Dummies,* by Marcy Blum (published by IDG Books Worldwide, Inc.).

Getting Engaged

Getting engaged may be one of the most significant moments of your life. At the time, it may seem as though you and your beloved are the only two people on earth, but the reality of it is that a wedding is typically a uniting of families, not just a uniting of two people. Therefore, you need to know a few things about engagements to ensure that everyone involved feels nothing but joy for you and your spouse-to-be. This section tells you what you need to know about getting engaged and announcing to the world that you plan to wed.

In the past, a man would ask the woman's father for her hand in marriage. That custom has slowly passed into history, and many people now decide to get married without asking anyone's blessing. However, it still is a good idea to speak with both sets of parents immediately upon engagement to share the joyous news (more on this subject later in the chapter).

Selecting an engagement ring

The diamond industry may insist otherwise, but an engagement does not require a diamond ring. Neither is the man required to have purchased a ring before asking the woman of his dreams to marry him. (These days, it's perfectly acceptable for the woman to propose!) In fact, it may be wiser to wait and shop for rings together, letting the bride-to-be select the ring that she likes best. If you do want to present a ring when you pop the question, however, make sure to quiz your beloved on her engagement ring preferences and find out what she prefers in terms of size and shape of the stones, settings, and precious metals. This way, you're much more likely to choose a ring that she'll love.

If you receive an engagement ring that you're less than thrilled about, good manners require that you voice appreciation and admiration for the ring anyway. Many women have learned to love the rings their fiancés gave them. If you really would prefer something else, you can tell your fiancé that a day or two later and go back to the store together to select something that better suits your tastes.

Financing an engagement ring under terms that require payments during the early months of a marriage, when you never seem to have enough money for your needs, is no favor to you as a couple. If you can't afford what you think is the ring of your bride's dreams, select a ring that you can afford and promise to add to it in later years, when fortune smiles upon you.

A brief history of the engagement ring

The wedding ring's origins go back to ancient times, when a groom would wrap braided grass around the bride's wrists and ankles to prevent her spirit from leaving her body. The grass later gave way to leather, carved stone, metal, then silver and gold. The diamond engagement ring had its genesis in medieval Italy. The Italian custom called for a groom to give the bride's family precious stones as a sign that he was serious about marrying her.

The wedding ring is worn on the third finger on the left hand because centuries ago, there was thought to be a vein in that finger that led directly to the heart.

Announcing the engagement to family and friends

Congratulations! The two of you have agreed to marry and live happily ever after. What do you do next? Tell your parents as soon as possible. It's preferable, etiquette-wise, to tell the bride to-be's parents first (if her parents are divorced, you should tell the mother of the bride-to-be first) and then the prospective groom's parents. Next, you tell your closest family members (grandparents, siblings, aunts and uncles) and friends. After you have announced your engagement, both sets of parents should get in touch by phone immediately to offer joint congratulations. It doesn't matter who phones whom, as long as they reach each other. This is an important step in establishing cordial future family relations.

If you anticipate that the wedding will be small, you may want to mention this fact when calling family and friends. That way, you'll avoid disappointing people if you aren't able to invite everyone.

What often follows an engagement is a formal or casual engagement party, which is traditionally hosted by the bride-to-be's family or a close family friend. Traditionally, the announcement of the engagement is left as a surprise for the assembled guests. The family makes an excuse to host a party for relatives and friends and, during the party, drops subtle hints of an announcement to come. When the time is right, the bride-to-be's parents call for order and express great pleasure at their daughter's intentions to marry her beau. Then they propose a toast to the couple's future happiness. The groom responds with a toast of his own, praising his future in-laws for the warm welcome they have given him and saying how much he looks forward to becoming part of the family.

You aren't required to have an engagement party, however. You may live 1,000 miles away from your parents, which would make a party difficult to arrange. In that case, you may choose to announce your engagement informally, either by telling friends and family members individually or by having the bride-to-be wear her new engagement ring to work, in which case everyone will know that she's engaged by lunchtime.

If the bride has been married before, or if the couple is living together, it is not necessary to announce the engagement formally. It makes more sense for the couple themselves to announce their intention to marry.

Putting the news in print

After you inform your families and friends, you may want to put an announcement of your engagement in the local newspaper, either right after you get engaged or closer to the wedding itself. Submit a nice photo of the bride-to-be or a portrait of you as a couple, along with a brief caption that identifies you, your parents, and other important information. (If you're not sure what information to supply, call the newspaper and ask. Most newspapers send you a form to complete and then write the announcement for you based on the information you supply.) Your engagement notice should read something like this:

> The engagement of Laura Smith to Mr. William Rivera, a son of Mr. and Mrs. Harold Rivera of Los Angeles, has been announced by Dr. and Mrs. Gordon Smith of Highland Estates, parents of the bride-to-be. Ms. Smith is a graduate of Yale Law School and a member of the Jefferson County public defender's staff. Mr. Rivera is an airline pilot. The couple plan an autumn wedding.

Breaking up

If you break off your engagement, call your family first and tell them. Then tell your friends. Keep your explanation brief, and remember to be fair to your ex. You wouldn't want that person saying awful things about you, so don't you say awful things about the person you previously thought you wanted to marry. It's most fair to simply say that the decision to break off the engagement was mutual, even though that is rarely the case.

If the woman breaks the engagement, she should return the ring to the man. If the man breaks the engagement, she may keep the ring, although she often returns it bacause she doesn't want the reminder of the relationship. However, it may be possible for her to exchange the ring for a beautiful piece of jewelry.

FAUX PAS

Offering proper congratulations

Proper etiquette forbids you to congratulate a woman on her engagement. To do so implies that she scored a remarkable achievement in snagging a man — a very outdated idea. Instead, merely wish her all the happiness in the world.

The couple must return any engagement or wedding gifts they received. The easiest way to handle returning gifts is to mail them back (thus avoiding a personal visit and lengthy discussion of the breakup) and enclose a note expressing gratitude for the gift, but saying that it is being returned because the engagement has been cancelled.

If formal wedding invitations have been sent, you need to send a written cancellation to every invitee with words to this effect: "Mr. and Mrs. Gordon Schlessinger announce that the marriage of their daughter Angela to Rupert Harris will not take place."

Setting the Date and Making the Arrangements

After you get engaged, you are launched into a wondrous — and sometimes stressful — world of booking bands, selecting invitations, perusing menus, and trying on dress after dress after dress. Whether you enjoy this process or pull your hair out depends on your attitude. I hope that I can help keep you in a positive frame of mind with helpful information on the etiquette of handling the arrangements that contribute to a beautiful wedding.

Making financial arrangements

First things first: Before any monetary deposits are placed, and before anyone writes a single check, both families should agree upon who is paying for what. Tradition calls for the bride's family to pay for the majority of expenses. The groom's family, traditionally, pays for the rehearsal dinner the night before the wedding, the purchase of the wedding license, the clergy fee, the bride's bouquet and ushers' boutonnieres, and the honeymoon trip. The rest is left to the bride's family.

Today, with people getting married older, and divorcing and remarrying more frequently, these traditions are often altered. Also, more families are taking each other's financial situations into account. For example, if the groom's family is wealthy and the bride's is not, the groom's family often pays the majority of expenses, even though the invitations are sent out in the bride's family's name. In the case of a couple who are in their thirties and beyond, the bride and groom often pay a significant amount of the cost, depending on their parents' circumstances. In second marriages, the cost is often split between the bride and groom.

Whatever the case, it's is a good idea to write down who agrees to cover what item, and make a copy for both the bride's and groom's families to refer to throughout the wedding planning process.

Deciding when and where to get married

Do you have your heart set on a favorite hotel for the dinner reception you've dreamed of since you were 12 years old? If so, prepare to be a bit flexible when you try to set a date. Top hotels are booked long in advance, and you may find yourself going down a long list of possible places and dates before you find a site that can accommodate you, even ten months or more into the future. For many brides, the availability of a place for the ceremony and reception is the item that determines the time frame for the entire wedding.

Even if you can arrange something sooner, etiquette calls for you to allow the following amount of time for completing these wedding planning tasks to enable everyone to do their jobs properly:

- ✔ **Selecting, writing, and printing invitations:** Allow at least six weeks for printing after placing your order.

- ✔ **Mailing invitations:** Drop the invitations in the mail six to eight weeks before the ceremony.

- ✔ **Selecting the bridal party:** Give your party the glad tidings at least four months before the ceremony if you're having a formal wedding.

- ✔ **Outfitting the bride and bridal party:** To have a gown made and tuxedos ordered, allow at least four months' time.

Of course, you can manage to put together a wedding in whatever amount of time you have. If it's a month, given a willingness to make certain alterations to the traditional wedding expectations (for example, buying a wedding dress off the rack instead of ordering one and undergoing a series of fittings), you can certainly pull it off. For most weddings, though, you want to allow a minimum of five months to accomplish all the wedding details.

Planning the reception

Only you know the perfect way to celebrate your wedding. You may be able to use a church's social hall for an informal reception featuring hors d'oeuvres and nonalcoholic beverages; you can ask the whole gang back to your place for a barbecue; or you may invite guests to a cocktail party and a fancy sit-down banquet at the best hotel in town.

If you're having a religious ceremony, when you're booking the reception location, make sure to coordinate the date with your house of worship. There's nothing like patting yourself on the back after grabbing the only free Saturday in June at your country club only to call your church to find out that they've already booked two weddings for that afternoon.

You'll discover soon enough that a catered reception in a nice setting is a very expensive proposition. You may want the entire world to share in your happiness, but when you're paying anywhere from $50 to $150 a person, you may need to limit the number of attendees.

Your family's ethnic traditions, your position within your community, your financial resources, and other factors all play a part in deciding how you celebrate your wedding. Use the following paragraphs only as examples, because there are a virtually unlimited number of ways to share your happiness.

- ✔ **Three meals plus entertainment:** If money is no object and many honored guests are coming in from out of town, you can follow a morning wedding with a wedding luncheon that includes everyone who attended the ceremony, and then host an invitation-only dinner for selected guests at a hotel or restaurant, perhaps with live music and entertainment. Finally, you can host a brunch the next day to send your out-of-town guests home on a full stomach.

   Multiple-inning celebrations, where the guest list is different for each event, require separate invitations to each party and separate RSVP indications.

- ✔ **After the wedding, a buffet for everyone:** With an after-wedding buffet, both your budget and the number of guests you want to invite will affect your specific plans. Whether you use your church or synagogue's social hall for a modest selection of desserts and punch or you invite all the wedding guests to a hotel for a lavish buffet, you're guaranteed to have a great party.

- ✔ **A small wedding with no crowd:** Not everyone gets married in a big ceremony attended by dozens of well-wishers. Some folks run off to a judge or justice of the peace to say their vows. Sometimes, only the parents of the bride and groom are present.

In such situations, invitations are out of place, but wedding announcements are a nice touch. A couple who's been married in a small ceremony may tell the world of their marriage with this sort of wording:

Myra Macapagal
and
Henry Donald Jackson
were married on Saturday, September 20, 2000
in the chambers of The Honorable George Flagler
Judge of the Sixth Circuit, Orlando, Florida
Now at home and looking forward to greeting you at
1234 Elm Street
Oviedo, Florida 32765

Accounting for the time between the wedding and the reception

Weddings are rare occasions when all family members are present and formally attired. Therefore, they are an excellent opportunity to capture the formal portraits and photographs that live forever in family albums.

Immediately after the ceremony and before everyone starts to wilt, an extended photography session often occurs. The bride and groom and their respective families seldom notice the time passing, but the assembled guests who are waiting to toast the new couple and kiss the bride may need some sort of activity to pass the time.

To help your guests with the wedding-to-reception transition, designate a person to round up the guests, escort them to the reception site, and encourage them to take some light refreshments in advance of the wedding party's arrival. A time lag of as much as an hour isn't uncommon.

Selecting your wedding party

The etiquette of selecting a wedding party is very personal and subjective. Only you know, for example, that your sister Christina has been your closest ally since childhood and has been looking forward to your wedding day since age 3. On the other hand, a groom might have a very close group of male friends who have always assumed that they would take turns being best man at each other's weddings. Whatever your circumstances, think carefully about what you are asking of the people you invite to be in the wedding party.

Although being asked is a very special honor, being in a wedding involves many responsibilities and often a considerable financial cost. If you have your heart set on inviting someone who you think might have trouble meeting the costs, you would be kind to offer to cover the person's lodging or plane fare, for example.

Other questions you want to ask yourself when determining the wedding party include: Where is the wedding going to take place? Is the altar big enough to fit the number of people we want to involve in the ceremony?

It's not a rule that you must have the same number of bridesmaids as groomsmen. The bride and groom should each make a list of who they want in their party. If the number is not even and you want it to be, you can assign other jobs to some of them, such as usher or reader.

You should give party members at least four months' notice, and understand that some of them may not be able to accept. Give yourself ample time to ask alternates, just in case.

Understanding the traditional roles of the wedding party

Sure, you have a vague idea that the wedding party is supposed to support the bride and groom, help organize showers, and host the bachelor and bachelorette parties. But you may not know in detail what the real responsibilities of each member of the party are. In this section, I detail each person's job.

Maid or matron of honor and bridesmaids

The bridesmaids, along with the maid of honor, were historically the women who helped the bride sneak away from her overprotective family in order to be taken away by the groom.

The maid (if the woman is unmarried) or matron (if she is married) of honor and the bridesmaids have many traditional duties. Before the wedding, the bridesmaids arrange the bachelorette party. On the wedding day, the bridesmaids are meant to help the mother of the bride with whatever needs doing, to assist the bride in getting dressed, and to be gracious to all the wedding guests. After the wedding, the bridesmaids help the bride get changed and see that the wedding dress is returned to the bride's home in good condition.

In addition to those tasks, the maid or matron of honor has pre-wedding responsibilities of helping the bride with invitations, arranging the bridal shower, and keeping a record of shower and wedding gifts. During the ceremony, she arranges the bride's train and veil at the altar, gives the bride the groom's ring at the appropriate time in the ceremony, and holds the bride's bouquet while the bride exchanges rings with the groom. After the wedding, she signs the wedding certificate with the best man as a witness.

Best man and ushers

Historically, a man would sometimes have to capture his bride from a protective family — and sometimes a family might have many big brothers. The man would have to bring his "best men" along with him to help him kidnap the bride from her family's house. Today, the groom has only one attendant — the best man — although he may try to match the bridesmaids with the same number of ushers.

The best man should organize the bachelor party (and make sure that the groom makes it through the evening in one piece!). He should also check that the ushers have their tuxedos fitted and ready to go.

The best man has a myriad of responsibilities at the wedding and should be ready to offer assistance to anyone, from the mother of the bride to a guest who may be unwell, or to run a last-minute errand. The best man drives the groom to the ceremony. During the ceremony, he gives the groom the bride's ring. He is also responsible for giving the payment check to the officiant either just before or just after the ceremony (the groom's family traditionally pays for this expense), as well as giving payment to the other service providers such as chauffeurs and reception coordinators. The best man also returns the groom's attire if it is rented.

Ushers should arrive early to the hall in order to help set up the room, especially with last-minute little touches such as candles and ribbons. They escort guests to their seats, meet and welcome guests of honor (such as grandparents), and help straighten up after the ceremony. During the reception, the ushers should make sure that all the wedding gifts are put in a secure place and help decorate the newlyweds' car.

Important roles for little people

If you're looking for wedding party roles for the special little ones in your life, there are several roles that are traditionally filled by children.

Girls younger than 8 are usually trainbearers or flower girls. The flower girl is the last person down the aisle before the bride. She carries a basket of fresh petals and sprinkles them on the ground for the bride to walk on. Girls older than 8 can be junior bridesmaids. They get to stand with the wedding party but have none of the responsibilities of the other bridesmaids, and they may wear a different dress.

Young boys can be ring bearers or pages (although pages can be boys or girls). The ring bearer walks down the aisle before the flower girl carrying a satin pillow with two fake wedding rings sewn into it. The maid of honor and best man have the real rings. The pages/train bearers walk behind the bride and carry the train of her wedding dress. You can have pages even if your train is not that long if there are children you want to include in the ceremony. Usually there are two pages.

Designing the ceremony

When you're deciding on the marriage ceremony, the first issue to decide is whether you want a religious or a secular wedding. If you opt for a religious ceremony and you do not belong to a house of worship, give yourself plenty of time to find the right place and the right officiant. Some congregations won't allow a guest officiant to perform a wedding or won't marry people who are not members. Also, make sure to give yourself time to fulfill any premarital requirements of your house of worship. Some churches and temples require a program of premarital counseling or preparation, which can last from weeks to months.

Within the marriage ceremony, there have been shifts in etiquette. For example, the traditional question in Christian marriage vows of "Who gives this woman in marriage?" is rarely asked anymore. Today, when it comes to vows, the bride and groom are increasingly likely to make the same pledges. The traditional vow that the woman takes to "obey" is used very rarely, except in a conservative tradition.

When you meet the clergy member, that person will direct you in the traditions of that place of worship and on the parts of the ceremony that you are able to decide, such as readings and hymns. Today, you can write your own vows and still retain the traditional readings and rituals of your faith in the ceremony. You are also able to select your own readings, often one from the scriptures and a poem, for example. And, from a selection given by the musicians, you can choose your own music.

Choose a style of music that reflects the surroundings. For example, if you are getting married in a cathedral in front of 200 guests, don't choose a folk guitarist. Likewise, if you're getting married in a chapel with a piano, it's best not to invite the Mormon Tabernacle Choir to sing Handel's Hallelujah chorus.

Check with the church about the use of flower petals, as well as the throwing of birdseed after the service; either practice may be disallowed. If you use floral decorations in the sanctuary, many places of worship appreciate the donation of some of the flower arrangements from your ceremony for use in their regular worship service.

Some places of worship have a cost attached to the use of the facilities for the wedding. If there is no such charge, it is appropriate to make a donation to the work of the congregation. In addition to paying the clergy person's fee, it's appropriate and thoughtful to give a small gift and a note of thanks to your officiant, such as a gift certificate to a bookstore or restaurant.

Making a Guest List

In order to assure equanimity between the families, it's wise to set a maximum number of people and then divide the amount evenly between the prospective bride's and groom's families. After each side completes their list, they should compare notes if there is a possibility of duplicates (particularly if the prospective bride and groom are from the same hometown, for example). Although you should plan on some people declining the invitation, don't assume that too many will. There's nothing like a wedding to bring people in from all corners of the globe!

Issuing Invitations to a Wedding

Designing the invitations for your wedding can be one of the more fun parts of the wedding-planning process. In the old days, you had one choice of wedding invitation: black type centered on the front of a folded card of white or ivory paper. Although you are certainly still free to opt for this traditional, formal invitation style, you are no longer limited to only one choice. Today, stationery companies offer hundreds of different styles, so you and your fiancé can choose an invitation that reflects your personalities and the style you have chosen for your wedding.

Your invitation is the first clue that your guests get to the style of your wedding. If you're not having an ultra-formal wedding, you don't need an ultra-formal invitation. If your wedding has a theme or is more informal, you can go with something that reflects that taste.

This section gives you some guidelines for designing, wording, and sending out your wedding invitations and all the elements they contain. Have fun!

Formal invitations

The most formal invitation is on ecru (cream) or white, heavy paper stock engraved with black or dark gray ink. It is folded in half, with the text of the invitation on the front outside panel. A less formal invitation can be printed on an unfolded ecru or white card. Either of these papers may be plain or paneled.

The proper wording of a formal invitation is as follows:

> *Mr. and Mrs. Peter Sun*
> *request the honour of your presence*
> *at the marriage of their daughter*
> *Lily Yuh*
> *to Mr. Terry Fischer*
> *on Saturday, the seventeenth of September*
> *at five o'clock*
> *Fourth Presbyterian Church*
> *Chicago, Illinois*

If the wedding is to take place at a hotel or some other non-religious place, word your invitation as follows:

> *Mr. and Mrs. Richard Kaufmann*
> *request the pleasure of your company*
> *at the marriage of their daughter*
> *Denise Elizabeth*
> *to*
> *Mr. Albert Jay Friedman*
> *on Saturday, the eleventh of October, two thousand*
> *at noon*
> *Balmoral Hotel*
> *500 North State Street*
> *Omaha*

A word on interfaith weddings

Interfaith weddings are becoming common these days. An interfaith marriage can be a beautiful celebration of diversity and unity. Some religions allow officiants from other faiths to perform ceremonies in their houses of worship. Many people have two ceremonies of different faiths back to back. Consult with your house of worship to see what its policies and requirements are.

Many interfaith weddings take place in a beautiful setting such as a garden, country club, hotel, or country inn. The melding of two people from different traditions can create a wonderfully meaningful ceremony and a wonderful reception in which those traditions are both in evidence.

If the reception will be held in the same place as the ceremony, word the invitation as follows:

> *Mr. and Mrs. Richard Kaufmann*
> *request the pleasure of your company*
> *at the marriage of their daughter*
> *Denise Elizabeth*
> *to*
> *Mr. Albert Jay Friedman*
> *on Saturday, the eleventh of October, two thousand*
> *at noon*
> *and at a luncheon*
> *immediately following the ceremony*
> *Balmoral Hotel*
> *500 North State Street*
> *Omaha*

If you're putting on your own wedding instead of asking your parents to pay for it, you can make the invitation even less formal:

> *Denise Elizabeth Kaufmann*
> *and*
> *Albert Jay Friedman*
> *cordially invite you to attend their wedding*
> *(and so on)*

Less formal options

If your wedding will not be formal, you want to take a less formal approach to your invitation. You might have your invitation printed rather than engraved or use a colored paper. You might also alter the wording of the invitation. For example:

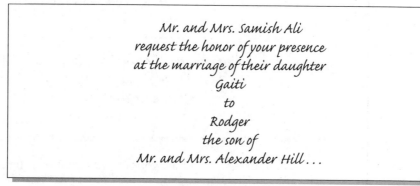

> *Maria Anne Rosati*
> *and*
> *Ian Johnston*
> *request the pleasure of your company*
> *at their marriage*
> *Friday, December 17, 2000*
> *St. Peter's Lutheran Church*
> *New York, New York*

Or, in another less traditional approach, the wedding might be hosted equally by the prospective bride and groom's families. In that case, you can word the invitation as follows:

> *Mr. and Mrs. Samish Ali*
> *request the honor of your presence*
> *at the marriage of their daughter*
> *Gaiti*
> *to*
> *Rodger*
> *the son of*
> *Mr. and Mrs. Alexander Hill . . .*

Because you need to mail the invitations six weeks in advance, leave yourself plenty of time to check them over, have them reprinted if anything is incorrect, and then address them (or send them out to be calligraphed by someone else). Make sure to find out from the stationer in advance of ordering how long it will take for the invitations to be printed so that you can account for that time accordingly.

Complicated family situations

How do you word the invitations when faced with circumstances like the following, in any combination: the bride's and/or groom's parents are divorced, some or all of the parents have remarried, one (or more) of the mothers/stepmothers goes by her maiden name, some or all of the parents/stepparents are hosting?

Note that it helps to simplify the wording if you can exclude the groom's parents' names. If they aren't helping to host the wedding, there is no need to include them; in many cultures, the groom's parents are not included in the wedding invitation in any case.

Including reception cards with your invitations

If you're holding your reception at a different location than that of your wedding, you should include a reception card with your invitation. Doing so is helpful in a couple of ways: First, it does not crowd the text on your invitation. Second, if you are inviting only some guests to the reception, it is convenient to simply add a reception card to the wedding invitations of those guests. The card should include the name and address of the establishment with "Reception immediately following the ceremony" at the top of the card, as follows:

> *Luncheon reception immediately following the ceremony*
> *The Atrium at Swan Lake*
> *4200 Lake Street*
> *Oakville*

Note that your invitations should tell your guests whether you're having a meal by indicating "Luncheon reception" or "Dinner reception," or, if you're not planning a meal, by using wording such as "Cocktail reception."

Requesting RSVPs

Weddings are among the very oldest of social customs. People getting married naturally assume that everyone in the world wishes them happiness and wants to be on hand for the big event. Within families and circles of friends, hard feelings can arise from someone's absence, and a failure to show up may be misinterpreted as a negative comment on the marriage. To reduce the risk of hurt feelings, you may want to consider including a response card with your invitation.

As a guest, you simply check the "regret" or "accept" space on the reply card and return it in the envelope provided. If no reply card is included in the invitation, give a formal acceptance or regret, carefully handwritten and centered on nice stationery. The text of your reply should read as follows:

> *Mr. and Mrs. Bernell Ramlo*
> *accept with pleasure*
> *Mr. and Mrs. Robert Reitan's*
> *kind invitation*
> *for Saturday, the thirteenth of April*

or

> *Mr. and Mrs. Bernell Ramlo*
> *sincerely regret*
> *that their absence from the city*
> *prevents them from accepting*
> *the kind invitation of*
> *Mr. and Mrs. Robert Reitan*
> *for Saturday, the thirteenth of April*

One word of caution here: Weddings can be complex events. Some folks may be invited to the ceremony but not to the luncheon or dinner reception. Study your invitation to make sure what is involved, and if you have any questions, telephone the person who issued the invitation and get things straight.

I can't overemphasize one rule of etiquette for guests: You must respond to the invitation promptly and as directed, and you must attend if you accept the invitation (unless you have an emergency, in which case you should notify the host by telephone). Caterers and hotels usually charge per table setting. If you say that you'll be there and then fail to show up, the bride's family may have to pay more than $100 for the meal you didn't eat and the drinks you didn't drink. Being a no-show after you've accepted the invitation is terribly rude.

Similarly, neglecting to send an RSVP and then appearing at a dinner is thoughtless. Yes, they'll seat you, because caterers always save the day, but you could've made the couple's life easier if you had signaled your intentions with an RSVP.

Assembling, addressing, and mailing your invitations

Many of the accoutrements of the formal invitation had their start many decades ago. The double envelope, for example, has its origins in the days invitations were delivered by hand. Upon reaching his destination, the footman would remove the clean invitation from its well-traveled outer envelope. Today, the outer envelope is sealed, the inner unsealed and placed with the guest's name face up.

Tissues are another item that had a practical use in the past, when inks took a longer time to dry. Printers placed a tissue over the ink so that it would not smear. If you choose to use a tissue, it is the first sheet of paper that covers the printed text of your invitation. The large sheet of tissue is for your invitation, the small one for your reply card and other small enclosures. Place the items in the inner envelope in order of importance, beginning with the invitation, then the reply card tucked under the flap of the reply envelope, a reception card, and any other card (such as one for directions or accommodations).

In addressing your envelopes, spell out all Avenues, Roads, Streets, Boulevards, and so on. Use the complete name of the guest: for example, Richard, not Rich. Write out numbers one to twenty; larger numbers can be written numerically. Junior, Senior, and such should be stated on the outside envelope, but not the inner.

Never assume that you know what the postage will be. Take a sample invitation to the post office and have it weighed so you know that you are using the proper amount of postage. Again, four to six weeks before the event is the general rule for mailing your invitations to ensure your guests receive their invitations and are able to respond in sufficient time. All invitations should be mailed at the same time to avoid potential hurt feelings (if your high school English teacher receives one and calls your Aunt Betty, who hasn't yet received hers, for example).

Sending out wedding announcements

Some couples can't afford to invite everyone they know to their wedding. Many times, doing so would be impractical (with acquaintances who live far away, for example). In these cases, you might choose to send wedding announcements. An announcement simply tells the recipient when and, if you wish, where you got married. Typical wording is something like this (follow the rules for wording invitations given earlier in this section):

> *Mr. and Mrs. Constance Avecilla*
> *have the honour of announcing*
> *the marriage of their daughter*
> *Michele May*
> *to*
> *Mr. Alfonso Natarelli*
> *on Sunday, the twentieth of September*
> *two thousand*
> *Holy Trinity Cathedral*
> *Vail, Colorado*

Usually, you order announcements that look very similar to your wedding invitations. Arrange for someone to mail them on the day of the wedding. Recipients of announcements are not expected to send gifts (as people who accept invitations are), although it is proper to send a note of congratulations.

No, your uninvited children may not attend

Doting parents may have every good reason to show little Donna and Charlie how people get married, but if the invitation doesn't mention your children, assume that they're not welcome.

Questions regarding the attendance of children at formal catered occasions have triggered legendary family feuds, so think about the implications of the invitations you send. If you want the kids to attend, address the invitation to Mr. and Mrs. William Birkholtz and Susan Camille and Sidney Jones. In extremely formal situations, address boys as "Master" (if below age 8) and the girls as "Miss." However you word it, mention the children if you want them to attend.

Be aware, too, that a failure to invite the children may cause their parents to turn down the invitation. If you sense the possibility of bruised feelings, you might look into the availability of child care and try to ease the tension with a personal phone call with an offer of arranging a sitter (whom you know or who has sat for friends of yours, of course).

Dealing with Difficult or Unusual Circumstances

If you read the advice columns in your daily newspaper, you're sure to notice that weddings inspire many questions. What begins as a simple plan for a man and a woman to marry rapidly inspires some of life's most difficult controversies. You may need a little help standing up for your own thoughts. Some of the following discussions may serve that purpose.

Handling divorced parents

Your parents are divorced and now married to other spouses. Even if the bride's father is paying for the festivities, the bride's mother needs to be involved in planning the wedding day. However, say she is close to her daughter, but she feels shut out of the whole thing, and she really doesn't want to have anything to do with her ex-husband or his new wife.

If ever an ideal situation existed to hire a professional wedding consultant, this is it. As a disinterested third party, the consultant can determine the wishes and inputs of everyone involved and suggest compromises. Best of all, the consultant can keep everyone apart until the actual day of the wedding, when civilized behavior is the rule of the day.

In the absence of a wedding consultant, however, the best solution is for everyone to behave as adults. That means putting others' needs before their own desires. Both of the newer spouses should try to stay out of the fray and let the bride's and groom's mother and father run the show. The wedding day is for the bride and groom, and everyone needs to cooperate to bring off the wedding without conflict or strife.

If the bride and groom sense family discord that can't be set aside temporarily, getting married in a way that does not involve a lot of ceremony may not be a bad idea.

Dealing with a family who objects to the marriage

Yes, people fall in love and get married even when one of the families voices strong disapproval of the match. If a parent is not happy with the news, he or she should keep the disappointment hidden until there is an opportunity to discuss the engagement privately with the son or daughter. Hopefully, with a good, open conversation, the son or daughter will be able to bring the parent around without too much difficulty.

If the parent still disapproves, even after the best efforts of the son or daughter, it is the parent's duty to hold his or her peace and go along with the wedding. It's better to allow a child to make what you view as a mistake than to create a breach in the relationship that might alienate the child from the parent for a long time.

Planning to say "I do" after you already did

Proper etiquette dictates that a second marriage ceremony should be a small affair, including only your family and closest friends. The ceremony is followed by a reception, and that can include just about anybody and encompass any type of affair you want. The bride can certainly wear a white dress, although it's considered more appropriate to avoid wearing a long white bridal dress with a train and veil, and to avoid having a large wedding party.

If the bride and groom are in their thirties or beyond, they usually extend the invitation to the ceremony themselves, either with a personal note or a telephone call. The written invitation to the reception would be worded as follows:

> Barbara Lynne Brickson
> and
> Keith I. Johnston
> request the pleasure of your company
> at dinner
> following their wedding
> on Friday, June 7, 2000
> at six o'clock
> National Arts Club
> New York City

As far as gifts are concerned, most people who are remarrying are more established than first-timers, and you could consider putting a "No gifts, please" clause in the invitation. If it's the first time for either of you, however, or if you would appreciate some help starting your new life together, gifts are appropriate.

If you are having a religious ceremony for a second marriage, consult with the officiant to make sure that you fulfill any special requirements.

After the Ceremony

The ceremony has taken place, and now it's time to celebrate! While you're having fun, don't forget your manners. To make it a wonderful celebration, I've outlined some traditional courtesies.

Knowing what to say in a receiving line

The receiving line is an opportunity for the bride, groom, and key members of the wedding party to meet and greet every guest on their way out of the ceremony. These days, most people do away with this ritual, which allows everyone to proceed to the reception that much quicker. As an alternative, some weddings have the receiving line in place as guests enter the reception.

If there is a receiving line, remember that the radiant bride and her adoring groom will be overjoyed and potentially overwhelmed by greeting dozens and dozens of guests. "Congratulations" or "I wish you happiness forever" is enough of a speech for a receiving line. And the only permissible gift in a receiving line is an envelope, handed to the bride. (Send your packages earlier or deposit them on a table set aside for such things.) Bridal parties that anticipate the presentation of envelopes to the bride should designate a person to stand at the side of the bride and hold the envelopes after they are handed over to the bride.

Toasting the bride and groom

There is a very specific etiquette to toasting, and if you follow it, you will find that it brings warmth and humor to a wedding. Toasts give people at the wedding an opportunity to put their feelings into words, and to express the collective feelings of everyone there. Toasts also allow a segue from the formal to the informal at the reception and allow the bride and the groom, and the friends and relatives who have contributed to the day's success, to relax and enjoy themselves.

The order of wedding toasts is as follows:

1. The first toast at the reception is given by the best man, after everyone has found their seat and has been served Champagne. The best man makes a toast to the bride or to the bride and groom. The bride and groom remain seated during the toast.

2. After the best man's toast, the groom stands up and thanks the best man for his toast and then toasts the bride, both sets of parents, and the bridesmaids. After that, the bride may make a toast if she wishes.

3. The best man responds by thanking the groom on behalf of the bridesmaids.

4. An usher or a particularly close friend might say a few words.

5. The father of the bride offers a toast. On behalf of his wife and himself, he can thank everyone for attending and indicate that the festivities may now begin.

Understanding the Rules of Wedding Gifts

When it comes to weddings, the gift-giving process can seem complicated. This is one case where gifts are generally expected, but you may not know when to deliver your gift or how much to spend. This section covers the basic "rules" of wedding gift-giving, and it also provides advice to the bride and groom on how to keep track of all those gifts and acknowledge them appropriately.

Giving wedding gifts

Although in the past bringing gifts to the wedding reception was common, today wedding gifts are more commonly sent to the bride's home. This practice frees members of the wedding party and family from the worry of transporting gifts (which might be breakable) during the reception, when they should be enjoying the party.

Although the historical purpose of wedding gifts is to help the new bride set up a household, guests have one year to send a wedding gift.

Be alert for the family tradition that calls for cash gifts for the bride. The usual practice is to hand an envelope to the bride as you go through the receiving line after the ceremony. If the family expects this sort of giving, the bride designates a member of the wedding party to take the envelopes as they are given to her and to mark the envelopes with the name of the giver. Accounting figures importantly in this tradition, where sums of money go back and forth within large families, more or less balancing the families' books on an ongoing basis.

Note that different families have different wedding-gift customs, so you need to check with your relatives when a wedding in your extended family occurs.

You may be expected to give a certain type of gift, or a gift of a certain value, so you want to know this ahead of time.

Make your wedding gift purchases in time to have the gift delivered at the bride-to-be's residence *before* the wedding date. If the gift is delivered after the wedding, there might be a problem if the couple is out of town traveling on their honeymoon.

Registering for gifts

Although you may think that registering for a large number of wedding gifts is a selfish act, doing so actually does your guests a great favor. Registering at large store chains helps well-wishers who otherwise wouldn't know what to give you for a wedding gift. It also ensures that you will like the gifts that they give you, so everyone ends up happy.

Many stores with wedding registries now have Web sites. Williams-Sonoma, for example, has a wonderful site that allows guests to click on their wedding registry, find the couple's name, pull up their list, and see what's already been purchased for them. You click on the item you want to purchase, denote who it's from, give your credit card information, and bingo! The wedding gift is shipped immediately. You never need to leave your home or office.

When making selections for your wedding registry, take care to include a wide range of items at a range of prices. Although some of your guests may want to give you lavish gifts, others will only be able to afford gifts of modest value, and you want to accommodate all parties.

It is perfectly acceptable to tell someone where you're registered if they ask you what kind of gift you'd like, but mentioning gifts in any way on your invitations is in very poor taste. I have received invitations to weddings in which a "We're registered at . . ." card was enclosed, which is an absolute no-no.

Keeping track of gifts and sending thank-you notes

When you're planning a wedding, you have to take care of many, many details, so don't trust yourself to remember who gives you what. Instead, keep a gift log and write down what gifts you receive from whom and when. Also note when you send out the thank-you note to ensure that no gift gets overlooked.

You may want to designate someone other than yourself to receive and log in every gift that arrives.

How did the cash gift tradition get started?

Here's a bit of ancient legend and the way that guests figured out how much money to give the bride as a wedding present, in families where cash gifts are traditional.

In villages where nobody was extremely wealthy, the father of the bride would host a huge celebration, with feasting for everyone, including wine, music, and dancing. Such a celebration used up all the financial resources of the father and prevented him from sending his own daughter off with a nest egg of her own. So the guests surveyed the party, made their best guess as to the cost on a per-person basis, and used that figure as the starting point for the value of their monetary gift. Often, they would add a little money as a gift for the bride.

Today, however, this method for figuring out how much to spend on a gift has gone by the wayside. Family members and friends should consider how close they are to the bride and groom, how much they have to spend, and how much help the couple needs in furnishing their household. Never overspend your limit on a wedding gift — remember that the truly meaningful part of the gift is the note you attach offering your congratulations, best wishes and personal thoughts for the couple.

Writing and mailing thank-you notes as soon as the gifts arrive is perfectly acceptable — there's no need to wait until after the wedding to do so. You should send out your thank-yous within four to six weeks of receiving a gift, although not everyone agrees on this time frame. Remember, too, that *written* thanks are in order here. Even if you thank Aunt Enid on the phone for the lovely serving dish, you must follow up in writing.

No one expects you to offer lengthy, eloquent expressions of gratitude, but do mention the gift and its intended use in a note like the following:

Dear Aunt Jean and Uncle Ned,

Thank you so much for the four place settings of our formal china. Jim and I look forward to welcoming you into our new home and serving you a meal on those beautiful dishes as soon as we are settled. We really appreciate your thoughtfulness.

Love,

Amy and Richard

Traditionally, the bride always received the gifts and issued the thank-you notes. The practice of sending gifts only to the bride is a faint echo of the idea of a dowry, which gives a woman a few possessions with which to enter her marriage. Today, this practice no longer continues (because the bride may be a business professional who earns as much as her adoring husband does!). The bride and groom can share equally in the task of writing the thank-you notes and sign them as a couple.

Imprinted thank-you cards are a nice touch. They can carry the imprint of your first names, such as "Amy and Richard," which sidesteps the question of whether it's bad luck for the bride to use her husband's last name for any purpose before the wedding.

Giving gifts to the wedding party

When a couple gets married, they don't just receive gifts; many times, they give them, too. It is customary for the bride to give a small gift to each of her bridesmaids and for the groom to give a gift to each of his groomsmen to thank them for participating in the wedding and for their continued friendship. You can give the maid or matron of honor and the best man a modestly more expensive gift, or you can give them the same gift that you give the other attendants — it's up to you. If you have a bridal shower, you can give the bridesmaids their gifts at that time; otherwise, present them at the rehearsal dinner. The same goes for the groomsmen.

The bride and groom may also choose to give gifts to each other. Customarily, each buys the other's wedding and engagement rings. Because the groom doesn't get an engagement ring in return, the bride may want to give him a gift to honor the engagement in order to even the score, so to speak. The couple may also give each other wedding gifts of their choosing to commemorate the occasion.

Exchanging or returning gifts

What do you do if you receive a gift that you either have a duplicate of or just plain don't like? You can certainly exchange duplicate gifts for something else, and the person who gave you a duplicate should not take offense. However, the issue of returning a gift you don't like is a somewhat touchier subject. If a gift is given by a family member or close friend, you simply must keep it and display it when the person comes into your home. Returning or exchanging such a gift is not worth the hurt feelings you may cause to someone who truly loves you. After a year or two, you can certainly "retire" the gift to the back of a cupboard or closet. Who knows? In 20 years, it may look quite chic!

Chapter 21

Good Manners for a Good Trip

There's no tougher test of your manners than traveling. When you travel — whether your destination is the beach or the boardroom — you'll no doubt see other people displaying very bad manners and even unbelievable rudeness. Yes, travel can put people under tremendous stress. But being away from home does not give you permission to abandon politeness. On the contrary! Particularly when you're a guest in another state or another culture, you need to be *extra* mannerly.

Unfortunately, though, traveling can make you feel weary and out-of-sorts, and you may be tempted to do some teeth gnashing and fit throwing. That's where this chapter can help. Here, you can find ideas to help you keep your manners in good shape as you travel. I cover travel in general, international travel, and business travel, so whatever your circumstances, you should be able to find the help you need.

Planning a Trip: Know Your Travel Personality

When you're considering a pleasure trip, take your travel personality into account and plan your itinerary accordingly. (Unfortunately, this doesn't apply to business trips, because you don't have much of a choice about where you're going!) What do you enjoy doing? Are you a beach and warm weather person? Do you need lots of activity or just relaxation? What age group do you want to be around? (If you're over 30, you may not enjoy Cancun during spring break.) Do you like traveling alone or with a companion? Do you prefer big cities or small villages? What can your budget handle?

It's essential to take all of these details into consideration before you leave. What does that have to do with etiquette? The better prepared you are for a trip, the better your experience will be, and the more likely you will be a kind and courteous tourist.

Flexibility is key when you're traveling. Remember to be as tolerant and adaptable as possible.

Getting There: Planes, Trains, and Automobiles

There's not just one way to see the world. Whatever your mode of transportation — be it plane, train, ship, car, bus, camel, bicycle, elephant, rickshaw, or space shuttle — the rules of travel are practically the same.

Getting from one place on this planet to another can take a very long time. You have to include the time it takes to get back and forth from airports, train, stations, and the like, as well as the time it takes to board the plane, train, or bus, and, at the other end, the time it takes to pick up your luggage — and that's assuming your journey goes smoothly and everything's on time!

The basic rule of travel etiquette, as with any other form of etiquette, is to respect others. In the often cramped and uncomfortable quarters that modes of transportation offer, etiquette infractions that may be slightly annoying in everyday life can escalate into tense situations while you're traveling.

Whatever you do, avoid provoking strangers. Generally, people who are traveling are under a lot of pressure and stress, and they may not respond as reasonably as they might otherwise.

To make your trip as safe and pleasant as possible, here are some guidelines for travel:

✔ **Double-check schedules.** Is it possible to wait at an airport gate for two solid hours, only to discover that your plane to Marseilles has been canceled due to a strike? Yes, it's possible. Moreover, it's not uncommon. The scene at any big-city airport is confusing enough when you speak the language, but it can be a nightmare if you're struggling to understand the various schedules and information displays.

Play it smart by using the services of a local travel agent. If you're away from home and you don't know where to find a travel agent, ask the concierge at your hotel.

✔ **Allow plenty of time; then allow more.** The best way to keep from suffering stress and anxiety while waiting to check in at an airport, railroad station, or bus terminal is to allow about twice as much time as your first impulse dictates. If you normally allow an hour at the airport, give yourself two hours — particularly when traveling abroad. You can always use the extra time, if there is any, to shop or grab a snack.

Use that same expansion of time at the other end of your journey. It can take a lot of time to gather your belongings and leave an airplane. If you're traveling internationally, clearing immigration and customs may take longer than you expect, and you may find yourself caught in unexpected rush-hour traffic.

✔ **Dress for a long journey.** If you're fated to spend many hours in the same outfit, wear casual, comfortable clothes that you can layer up and down as your environment gets warmer or cooler. It's possible to look neat and well put-together while being practical about travel. Women might try wearing knits, such as a long knit skirt or pants, plus a T-shirt and sweater. Carry a cozy wrap and an extra pair of socks in case the airplane is chilly. Men can wear loose, comfortable pants such as khakis, and layers on top. Wear shoes that you can easily loosen or tighten, because feet tend to swell during long flights.

✔ **When checking in your bags at an airport skycap, make sure to tip $1 per bag.** You want to make sure your luggage gets onto the airplane, right? Besides, these people work hard, rain or shine, to make it easier for you to get to your flight.

✔ **When traveling with children, do your best to keep them happy and occupied.** Let's face it, you can't control your child's behavior at a young age. But, you can bring along enough distractions in the form of toys, books, crayons, games, stuffed animals, dolls, and the like to keep them busy. Snacks and drinks are also a good idea because the food service can be slow. Try to be considerate of passengers around you. Don't let your child run in the aisles, crawl around the row, or be careless with food and drink.

✔ **When boarding or exiting the aircraft, be considerate of the people you're passing.** Walk through the aisle carefully, keeping your baggage either directly in front of you or holding it behind you. Anyone who's ever been hit in the head with a suitcase, purse, tote bag, laptop, stroller, baby seat, or any other of the myriad of items that people bring onboard knows the importance of this rule! If you happen to bump or stumble into another passenger, apologize and smile. And don't fight your way through the line to get to your seat first — or, in the case of unassigned seats, to get a better seat.

✔ **Once you're seated, share the armrests.** Each passenger should have one.

✔ **Avoid moving about the plane as much as possible.** Doesn't it seem that the people sitting in the window seats always need to get up the most? If you have that tendency, please book an aisle seat! Have your books, snacks, or papers that you need easily accessible — this way, you won't have to get up to rummage through the overhead compartments or disturb your neighbors.

✔ **Be aware of the airline's rules when it comes to baggage.** If you're uncertain, call ahead. Do not wait until you're at the airport to discover that you won't be able to check in two suitcases, a golf bag, and four huge boxes. If you have carry-on baggage, be considerate of the other passengers when placing it overhead or under your seat. You should try to limit yourself to one carry-on — two if you must, and if it's allowed. And, it's best to keep your carry-on under the seat in front of you or in the overhead bin directly above your row. Try to assist those that may not be able to reach the overhead bins.

✔ **Mind your own business.** If your neighbor is reading or working on a laptop computer, don't intrude by asking, "What are you doing?" Don't talk if your neighbor is trying to rest. If you're talking with a neighbor and you receive one-word comments or answers, take the hint and end the conversation.

✔ **Try to sleep, especially on longer overseas flights.** But be a conscientious sleeper! If you're lucky enough to be able to sleep on the plane, try to sleep with one eye open (so to speak). Don't lean beyond the boundaries of your seat, and do your best not to drool or snore.

✔ **Avoid calling the flight attendants if possible.** Their job is to make every passenger happy and comfortable while on the plane — not an easy task with a couple hundred anxious individuals onboard.

After you've finally made it to your destination, show your gratitude for a good flight by smiling and thanking the flight attendants and pilots as you leave. When retrieving your luggage in baggage claim, help others if they need assistance, and always make room for others to reach their luggage while you're standing at the conveyor belt waiting for your own.

Arriving at Your Destination and Enjoying Your Stay

Congratulations! You've survived the journey, and have successfully reached your destination. Now it's time for the real fun to begin. What follows are some suggestions for gracefully enjoying the sights and sounds of your travel destination, while being a credit to yourself, your fellow travelers, and if you're abroad, to your country.

Arriving at your hotel

You might take a hotel shuttle, a taxi, a bus, or train to your accommodations. If you are taking anything but a public form of transportation, make sure to tip the driver between 10 and 15 percent (see Chapter 25 for more in-depth information about tipping). If you are renting a car and take a rental car company shuttle to your car, tip the driver $1 per bag if he or she assists you. When you arrive at the hotel and the doorman assists you in getting into the hotel lobby, you should tip $1 to $2.

When you arrive, a bellhop might assist you with your bags. He or she should be tipped $3, or if there are a lot of bags, $5 to $10. If you decide to handle your own bags, make sure you can do so with ease. If you are struggling with a large suitcase or several smaller bags and refuse a bellhop's assistance, you might look cheap. (There's one exception to this, which is when you are leaving the hotel: If you are late for a train or airplane and think that the bellhop would only slow you down, then you are excused!)

As you step up to a hotel counter, begin by giving a greeting that's appropriate to the hour, such as "Good morning." Then state your business. You might want to carry a phrasebook so that you can communicate key words such as "check in," "one night," and numbers.

In many countries, the hotel must report foreign guests to the authorities. If the hotel clerk asks you to leave your passport at the front desk when you check in, don't worry. You're not surrendering your passport. An hour or so later, after taking care of the paperwork, the clerk will return your passport to you.

 When you head for a specific destination, write out the name and address of the place on a small card, or ask the hotel clerk to write it for you. You can then show the card to your taxi driver or to a helpful passerby on the street for help in heading in the right direction.

Tipping practices vary from country to country. In most European countries, tipping is built into the prices of items for sale or service. Taxi fares, for example, are adjusted for the number of passengers, the number of pieces of luggage, the time of day, and the neighborhood where you are picked up and let off. However, taxi drivers expect a tip in exchange for their skill in weaving through traffic and ignoring red lights. Hotel employees in every country appreciate tips. In some places, tips are their only source of income.

Coping with tourist attractions

It's likely that your travel plans will include some sightseeing, even if your trip is mainly for business. (The "Traveling for Business" section, later in this chapter, talks more about the specifics of business travel.) But even if you're enjoying a slow-paced, relaxed vacation, you need to do some planning of your itinerary. Museums, cathedrals, and other tourist attractions operate on schedules that may frustrate you. Call ahead to inquire or check with your hotel concierge on the hours of admission of the attractions you want to visit.

Long lines are a fact of life if you travel to a popular destination in high tourist season. Arriving early is the key to reducing your time in line. Show up about 15 minutes before the official opening time to be among the first visitors in line. Don't be surprised to find two lines — one for you and your fellow independent tourists, and one for organized groups under the leadership of an official guide. Guided tours are always admitted ahead of ordinary individuals.

Photography is a major etiquette issue in many museums. Generally, taking flash photographs isn't allowed, so you may want to leave your camera back at your hotel. In many cases, you can purchase photos in the museum gift shop that are far better than anything you could produce on your own.

When in Rome: Navigating Your Way through International Cultures

These days, tourists and businesspeople alike think nothing of jumping on an airplane to do business around the globe. The ease and speed of international travel, the ability to communicate instantly through satellite and computer, the interlocking and overlapping business interests in the Americas, Europe, Africa, and Asia mean that people are in touch with the world as never before. If you're one of those travelers, you need to know that the moment you set foot on foreign soil, the rules of etiquette change. Even if you're well on your way to bona fide expertise in American etiquette, practices that pass as polite in San Francisco may be deemed downright rude in Seoul or Sevilla.

When you travel to a foreign country, you can offend people through ignorance as easily as you can through bad intentions. Before your trip, take time to learn about the cultures you're going to visit. Although this chapter is a good start, you may want to consult a reputable guidebook for the country or countries you'll be visiting to learn more specific rules of conduct.

What you need to know before you go

You may be familiar with the golden rule: "Do unto others as you would have them do unto you." International travel puts a slight twist on that golden rule: "Do unto others as they would have you do unto them." When you step onto foreign ground, you can no longer assume that you know what behavior is acceptable. Your "normal" behavior may look completely different through the eyes of someone from another culture! When you're on foreign turf, try to see situations through the natives' eyes and respond accordingly.

Human nature being what it is, tourists are often judged by whether they behave like natives. But many customs are deeply rooted in history, culture, and temperament — something a recently arrived traveler couldn't possibly understand. Be unfailingly courteous and considerate while traveling. Good manners go far in creating good feelings and making new friends. If you happen to make an etiquette faux pas, don't panic. Most local residents are impressed by travelers who are as interested in their outlook and way of life as they are in their monuments and museums.

Conscientious travelers try to be at least twice as courteous and tactful in a foreign country as at home. Above all, that means respecting differences in culture. Be patient, practice good listening skills, and remain flexible. Perhaps most important, keep your sense of humor. If you can laugh at yourself in an awkward situation or alleviate a fellow traveler's embarrassment at making a mistake, people will appreciate it. Keeping your sense of humor is important at any time in life, of course, but even more so in international travel, when stress levels may be high and you may feel like a fish out of water.

Do's and don'ts for travelers

Use the following list to make sure that you display proper business etiquette when you travel outside the United States:

- ✔ DO observe local procedures and ethics.

- ✔ DO schedule your day to accommodate possible jet lag.

- ✔ If you attend a social event during your visit, DO send the host a thank-you note the next day.

- ✔ DO be aware of the country's current affairs during your visit, but DON'T bring up the taboo topics of politics and religion.

- ✔ DO be aware of local customs regarding alcohol, especially in Muslim countries, where drunkenness is not tolerated.

- ✔ DON'T use American slang and expect natives to understand you.

- ✔ If English is the native language in the country you're visiting, DO remember that words have different meanings. For example, in England, napkins are *serviettes,* an elevator is a *lift,* two weeks is a *fortnight,* french fries are *chips,* potato chips are *crisps,* and the bathroom is the *water closet.*

- ✔ When speaking to someone for whom English is a second language, DO speak slowly, but DON'T speak louder. Try to be patient and articulate clearly.

- ✔ DO remember that blending in and conforming are often a form of flattery.

The myth of the ugly American

"Ugly Americans" is an all-too-familiar term that refers to American tourists abroad. Fortunately, we know that Americans aren't ugly! This misperception stems from the fact that other nations, as a rule, are more formal than the United States. They base their manners on older cultures and a slower pace. Americans' casual behavior (the instant use of first names, the uninhibited questions, and the neglect of formalities), which we take for friendliness, is often mistaken for rudeness.

Fortunately, some of these misperceptions are changing. The jet age has brought about a fairly standard code of manners throughout Western society, so the manners that succeed in Indianapolis, for example, usually succeed in Jakarta, too.

Dressing appropriately

Clothing fashions change rapidly, and what's suitable one year may be hopelessly obsolete the next. However, you can utilize a few general guidelines when you pack for a trip and select your outfit for each day of travel activities:

- ✔ **Less flash is better when it comes to travel clothing.** Lean toward the inconspicuous instead of standing out in garish garb. Although college students on a backpacking tour can get away with more casual clothing, you should make an effort to look neat and well put together.

- ✔ **Your clothes should be natural to the surroundings you're visiting.** In other words, no sarongs and bikini tops on the streets of London, and no stiletto heels or black pantsuits at a Caribbean beach!

- ✔ **Skin can be a sin.** Religious establishments, in particular, impose strict modesty rules, especially for female visitors. Depending on the religion and the place, women may be required to cover their shoulders, arms, heads, legs, and/or feet. In general, dress rules are not strictly enforced for tourists, but you show your good manners when you show less of yourself.

- ✔ **Casual business dress doesn't translate.** Corporate officers may put in a productive day in California while wearing blue jeans, running shoes, and open-neck shirts, but the rest of the world hasn't quite caught up with casual business attire. When conducting business abroad, dress conventionally, conservatively, and appropriately.

- ✔ **Baubles inspire bandits.** You know how to avoid trouble when you're at home, but you may have no idea how criminals operate in other countries. Play it safe by leaving your precious jewelry locked up at home, and make do with costume jewelry and timepieces that you can bear to lose.

Communicating with the locals

The first thing you may notice upon arriving at your international destination, depending on the country, is that you can't understand a word of what people around you are saying. The language barrier is the biggest potential pitfall of etiquette-conscious travelers.

You can't be courteous if you can't communicate. If you plan to travel to — or through — a country where the language is not your own, learn a few of the most polite phrases in the local language. At a bare minimum, you need to know how to say hello, good-bye, please, thank you, where . . . ?, how . . . ?, when . . . ?, how much . . . ?, yes, and no. Every large bookstore sells small, pocket-sized phrasebooks and audio tapes in just about every language you'll ever need. You can learn at least a dozen words on the airplane as you fly toward your destination.

English is taught as a second language in many countries, and you may find your verbal exchanges easier if you begin a new contact by asking, "Do you speak English?" More often than not, the answer will be, "A little."

The following sections explain the particulars of various aspects of communication.

Remembering that English is not a secret code

You're thousands of miles away from home, surrounded by natives who speak a language that you don't understand. You may be tempted to use your native language, English, as a secret code to exchange private comments with your travel companion. However, this is almost always a mistake. Even when the people around you are conducting their conversations in Italian, French, or Hindi, you can bet that they know at least a few words of English.

Beaches

You may be surprised to discover that beach manners are generally more relaxed abroad than at home. Europeans everywhere are more casual than Americans about changing clothes and the size of their swimwear.

Beach rules can be completely different from one neighboring country to another. Regardless of how socially protected the women of certain countries are, as a visiting foreigner you can get away with wearing a bikini in most cosmopolitan resorts. To be on the safe side, pack a conservative bathing suit and check with your hotel's concierge about local customs and beach wear before venturing out.

Never say anything in English to your companion that you wouldn't want others around you to overhear. Your inability to speak the language of your host country is no excuse to abandon everyday good manners.

Fitting in with the natives by using polite expressions

You'll be welcomed into a country more easily if you learn a few commonly used expressions. This is particularly important because many cultures rely more heavily on these words than Americans do. "Good morning," "good evening," "please," and "thank you," when spoken in the native language of the country you're visiting, will go far in making you appear to be a polite and courteous traveler.

Europeans punctuate their conversations with "Thank you" and "Please" far more frequently than Americans do. Scandinavians, for example, are particularly effusive with polite expressions. During a meal, they give thanks each time a course is served, and they thank the host for the entire meal when they rise from the table. Scandinavians also exchange a round of thank-yous again before they leave. As a visitor, you're expected to follow suit. The British also use "Thank you" and "Please" more often than most Americans do. However, although the British say "Thank you," they don't say "You're welcome" as often as Americans might.

If you know the equivalents of "Please" and "Thank you" in the country you're visiting (and you should!), use them. Otherwise, say the words in English.

Gesturing

Contrary to what you may think, gestures do not have universal meanings. For example:

- ✔ In many parts of the world, a thumbs-up is an obscene gesture.

- ✔ People outside the United States, especially people from Asian countries, consider pointing the index finger rude.

- ✔ The American bye-bye gesture means "come here" to people from Southeast Asia.

- ✔ In Brazil and Portugal, the "okay" gesture that you make with your index finger and thumb is considered obscene.

- ✔ In Germany, you starting counting on your fingers with your thumb, not your pointer finger, so if you hold up your pointer finger to indicate that you want one item, you may end up with two.

Make sure to study a guidebook for the country or countries you're visiting to find out which gestures and body language to avoid while you're there.

Making physical contact

Your body language can say as much about you as the words that come out of your mouth. In addition to gestures, which I described in the preceding section, the appropriate level of physical contact varies greatly from culture to culture. For example:

- ✔ Japanese people don't approve of public body contact and thus have developed a complex system of bowing to express relationships. Touching a member of the opposite sex is particularly repugnant to Japanese sensitivities; consequently, they also consider kissing or any other form of body contact in public disgraceful.

- ✔ Many Asians believe that the head houses the soul. Therefore, if another person touches their heads, that action places them in jeopardy. As an outsider, avoid touching an Asian person's head and upper torso. Also avoid direct eye contact.

- ✔ Same-sex handholding between Asians, Middle Easterners, Latinos, and those from the Mediterranean countries is a sign of friendship. Walking with arms on each other's shoulders or with hands or arms linked also equates with camaraderie.

Keeping your distance (or not)

The need for some personal space is innate, but differences in how much space people from different cultures need can create uncomfortable situations. An American's personal space is much greater than that of an Arab or a Russian, but much smaller than that of someone from Great Britain.

Good manners dictate that whatever the social attitudes of the place you are visiting may be, you must try to follow them, even if they make you a bit uncomfortable or seem overly formal to you. Backing off when someone enters your personal space can send a negative message, just as stepping into someone's personal space can. Be wary of touching other people, too — even an arm on the shoulder or a pat on the back can violate someone's personal space.

Displaying emotion

Every culture has its own rules for how to show various emotions. Some cultures frown upon public expressions of sorrow or joy, and others encourage it. When you travel, understand what is acceptable by observing the natives. For example, the Japanese rarely express affection in public; the Chinese feel that emotional candor is rude; and showing your impatience is considered bad manners in the Middle East. On the other hand, people are very demonstrative in Italy, Spain, and some Latin American countries, for example. Italians might use elaborate hand gestures while talking, hold hands while walking, and show other forms of public affection for one another. You don't need to change who you are when you're traveling, but accept others' manners while you're among them and blend in.

Conversing

What is considered a polite topic of conversation differs from country to country. For example, most people in other countries find it strange when Americans speak freely about income and family matters — subjects they consider too private to share. Although Americans find it perfectly acceptable to ask what people do for a living and whether they are married, citizens of other countries often consider these questions rude.

When I was visiting Kenya recently on a sightseeing tour, one of the women in our group asked the male guide whether he was single or married. From his expression, we could see that he was shocked by her question. Although he answered reluctantly, we all knew that the question was probably a major faux pas in his country. Don't make this mistake yourself!

Unless you're speaking to a close friend of many years from another country, remember these rules when conversing with a person from another culture:

- Don't ask personal questions.
- Don't criticize the person's country or city.
- Don't compare the person's country to the United States.
- Don't mistakenly denigrate the country or city you're visiting by saying that it's cute, quaint, or old-fashioned.
- Don't discuss politics, local royalty, religion, or customs (although you should be prepared to discuss American crime, freedom of the press, political scandals, and the like).
- Don't tell jokes (they often don't translate well).
- Do pay compliments on the culture, beauty, and achievements of the country or city you're visiting.

If your conversation begins to lag, food, the arts, and sports are generally good, safe topics to introduce to revive talk.

Meeting and greeting

As they say, you get only one chance to make a first impression. Therefore, you want to behave properly when you meet someone for the first time — in a foreign land *or* on your home turf. Every culture follows its own particulars when it comes to meeting and greeting, so it's wise to consult a guidebook for specific advice. Following are some common forms of greeting that you may experience:

✔ The Japanese bow and smile when they greet others; handshakes are rare. The deeper and more numerous the bows, the greater the respect demonstrated.

✔ Indians and people from Buddhist countries lightly press their hands together as if praying and incline their heads at the same time.

As a Westerner, you are not expected to either bow or press your hands together. A Japanese or Indian person who knows Western ways may hold out his or her hand for you to shake instead. It's best to wait for that lead before offering your hand.

✔ The Chinese usually bow or nod their heads in greeting. If a Chinese person offers his or her hand, it's okay to give an American-style handshake, but don't judge the person by the handshake, because it may not be as firm as a handshake that you'd expect from a fellow American.

✔ Europeans, Latin Americans, and people who have been educated in Western countries customarily shake hands when they're introduced, each time they meet, and when they part. Even children follow this custom, and not shaking hands is considered rude.

✔ In many European and Middle Eastern countries, friends kiss each other on the cheeks when they meet. Business associates will most likely shake hands.

✔ In Austria, Germany, France, Italy, and Spain, a man may bow over the back of a woman's hand and make a gesture of kissing it — although these days, men shake women's hands more often than they kiss them. Because you never know which gesture a man may prefer, hold out your hand and prepare for either. If you're wearing gloves, don't bother to take them off, because the man doesn't actually kiss your hand, but instead raises it to within an inch or so of his lips.

Understanding the use of names

The American frontier left a strong tradition of being free and easy — including our casual use of names. Depending on where abroad you go, however, you may find that you have to make quick adjustments to the habit of automatically calling someone by his or her first name. Here are some points to remember about names:

✔ In Europe and South America, you should never automatically call someone by their first name. Use their "Mr." or "Mrs." and the last name unless you are invited to do otherwise.

✔ In Australia, Canada, and South Africa, the use of names (and titles, which are discussed in the following section) is similar to that in the United States. Although the rule against using first names is not as strict in these countries as it is in Europe or South America, proceed slowly and wait for permission before you use a first name.

✔ In the Asian tradition, the order of first and last names is reversed.

✔ In some cultures, people avoid using names entirely and describe their social relationships instead. People in many cultures believe that addressing someone by his or her first name is disrespectful. Younger people in particular must take special care to address older people by their titles (or as custom dictates).

To avoid offending someone, it's always safer to ask which name(s) a person prefers. If a name is difficult to pronounce, admit that you're having difficulty and ask the person to help you say it correctly.

Understanding the use of titles

We are rather sparing with the use of titles in the United States. This is not the case in other countries. In the U.S., physicians, dentists, and ministers are almost always addressed with their title, but you address almost everyone else as plain Mr., Mrs., Miss, or Ms. When traveling abroad, however, you might find that people normally address each other with a variety of elaborate and often descriptive titles.

It may seem daunting, but using titles is one of the things that makes travel a learning experience. Keep in mind that titles are either hereditary or professional. In the hereditary category are Prince, Duke, Marquis, Earl, Count, Viscount, Baron, Princess, Duchess, Countess, and so on. If you expect to meet titled people, you would be wise to study the correct use of hereditary titles.

Professional titles include the following:

✔ **Doctor:** A doctor can be a person with a Ph.D. or a person with a medical or dental degree. Follow the example of the natives closely when addressing a distinguished person. If you hear others calling that person "Dr.," make sure to follow suit.

✔ **Professor:** In the United States, this title means you have a Ph.D. However, in other countries, this title may be used as a way to show respect for someone's accomplishments. For example, in many countries, "professor" is used to address a businessperson who is known and distinguished in a certain field.

✔ **Name of profession:** People in some foreign countries address engineers, architects, and lawyers by the name of their profession. Examples include *Ingeniero Hernandez, Arquitecto Valenzuela,* and *Licenciado Santos.* You'll also see that Mr. will be added to the title, which when translated means Mr. Lawyer or Mr. Architect.

You might hear Latin American business people called simply by the name of their profession: Architect, Engineer, or Lawyer. Germans do something similar, but they add "Mr." or "Mrs." in front of the name of the profession. Even nonprofessional business people receive a title in Germany. The director of a hotel, government office, or a company, is

Herr Direktor. Germans may also address a civil servant specifically as *Herr.* The French have a word, *Maitre,* which they use as a title for distinguished male and female trial lawyers.

When in doubt, try to follow the lead of others. Don't panic even though you might be confused. Most people don't expect visitors to know all the intricacies of names and titles. If you make a mistake and are corrected, politely apologize and repeat the name correctly.

Eating and drinking

When the term "When in Rome" was coined, it not only meant to embrace the customs and culture, but it also included trying the food and drink! If you're adventurous, food can be one of the best parts of traveling.

Although you may love to try new foods and experience new flavors, you may long for the tastes of home after a few days away. And if you travel to a time zone that's many hours earlier or later your own, your body clock may be so thrown off that you don't even know when to be hungry. Then you have to factor in the differences in table manners and eating habits from culture to culture: How do you know what to do?

This section can help steer you around the gastronomical glitches that often trip up international travelers.

Adapting to the local foods and mealtimes

When making your travel reservations, take the trouble to ask your airline the exact details of food service for your class of ticket. Most international flights serve enough food to stave off starvation, but some economy flights are a little stingy when it comes to meals. If you have any doubts, pack some portable foods in your carry-on bag.

Some countries forbid the importation of food. Be prepared to discard any uneaten foods in your carry-on luggage.

Once you get to your destination, you have to adapt to the local ways of eating. Here are some points to keep in mind:

✔ Although it may come as a shock to Americans who were taught that breakfast is the most important meal of the day, the American idea of a hearty breakfast is virtually unknown in most foreign countries. Europeans tend to drink a glass of fruit juice, eat a croissant or roll with butter and jelly, and follow it with a cup of strong coffee. Some people even skip the bread. In most countries, you're unlikely to find fried eggs and bacon, pancakes with maple syrup, and hash-browned potatoes. You might try carrying a piece of fruit as a mid-morning snack on your first few days to get you to lunch.

✔ In some countries, all the retail stores close a few minutes before noon and don't reopen until mid-afternoon. Therefore, if you want to have an impulsive picnic, you must put your plans into action by 11:00 or 11:30 a.m. at the latest. Buy your sandwich makings and other goodies at a deli, pick up some nice, crisp rolls at a bakery, and head for a quiet spot.

✔ In many countries, restaurants use the same menu for lunch and dinner; there's no such thing as a luncheon menu. Especially in warm climates, the fashion is to eat a hearty lunch, take a nap, and then resume activity in mid-afternoon. In such societies, dinner is eaten quite late — 9:00 or 10:00 p.m. — by North American standards.

In order to acclimate yourself to unusual meal hours, carry snacks and use them to tide you over to the next meal. Crackers, trail mix, and high-energy bars are all easy to carry and are lifesavers when you're running low on fuel.

You will occasionally face foods that repel you in taste, smell, or appearance. Try your best to grit your teeth, swallow, and smile. You won't offend your host if you leave something on your plate because it disagrees with you, but you may offend your host if you don't try the food because it's strange to you. Do your best to be a good sport, and you'll be fine.

Adjusting your table manners

If you follow proper American dining etiquette, you'll do passably in most countries. However, there are a few notable exceptions:

✔ In China, eating is communal; you use chopsticks to serve yourself from a large platter. Don't cross chopsticks — leave them on the chopstick rest or place them parallel across the top of a bowl. If you have problems managing chopsticks, you may lift your rice bowl to your mouth to scoop with your chopsticks or ask for a knife and fork. (For more on using chopsticks, see Chapter 16.)

Asian restaurants provide toothpicks for you to use frequently and casually at the table. Just remember to shield your mouth with your other hand.

✔ In Europe, you find a slightly different table setting from the one that's common in the United States. For example, in France, the forks and spoons are placed upside down, the tines of the fork are down, and spoons turned over. Europeans eat their salad course last, so the salad fork is the one nearest the plate.

✔ Also, the European method of using a knife and fork differs from the American way (see Chapter 16). But both systems are correct, so you don't have to change your method if you don't want to.

If you don't want to stand out as an American, the first tip-off is your style of dining. Learn the Continental style, and you'll blend right in.

✔ In France, you rarely touch food with your fingers. French diners use their forks and knifes in creative ways to manipulate and eat various foods that Americans might pick up with their fingers.

✔ Some people in Middle Eastern countries and parts of India eat with the first three fingers of the right hand — never the left. Until you know the rules, keep your hands in your lap and watch the natives. Once you get a sense of how things are done, you can give it a try yourself. However, your host will probably be able to provide you with Western utensils if you ask.

Many other subtle differences in table manners exist. Ask your host what to do if you're uncertain.

However you eat it, remember that leaving food on your plate or refusing a second helping at a meal in a private home may be considered impolite. You don't want to imply that you don't enjoy the food that was set before you. In the Middle East, refusing cups of tea or coffee, which are offered endlessly in homes, shops, and offices, is also insulting to the host.

Playing it safe with beverages

When you eat, you drink, and in many countries, the drink you're served with lunch or dinner may well be alcoholic. Wherever your travels take you, being intoxicated is not good manners. In many places, intoxication is considered a sign of bad breeding. Be careful with beer as well as wine. American beer is limited, by law, to an alcohol content of 4 percent or less. Beer in other countries is much stronger, and a bottle or two can pack a punch that you may not expect.

Tipping

Tipping after a meal varies from country to country and is custom-tailored to each culture. In the Far East, tipping is done very discreetly, whereas in Arab countries, it may be done with great fanfare. In France, you leave a small tip at a café, but you don't leave a tip at many Italian espresso bars. Even in countries where service is included in the bill, leaving a small, additional tip is customary.

Restaurants often add on a certain percentage of the tab for service. If the restaurant at which you're dining engages in this practice, you'll see the charge itemized on your bill. When the tip is built in, you leave a small extra amount (somewhere between the foreign equivalent of $2 and $5) on the table.

Smoking

Although Americans have cut down on smoking and have outlawed it in many public places, the same rules do not necessarily apply in the rest of the world. Be prepared to find smokers in public, in private, and in transit. Smokers in public places in many foreign countries are within their legal rights, so you should either move away or put up with it. If you are highly sensitive to smoke, you should avoid bars and café areas that are frequented by smokers.

Handling invitations

Most countries handle invitations the same way we do in the United States. The exceptions are the Muslim countries of the Middle East and African countries, where an invitation is a sacred trust, and refusing an invitation (unless you have made a previous engagement) is considered an insult.

In many countries, being invited into someone's home is a great honor. As a guest to a private home in Russia, for example, you might be toasted to extensively with vodka and treated to an extensive formal dinner that goes on for hours. Offering a gift to your host is considerate. What should you bring? A flowering plant, a book about America, or a nice bottle of California wine could work. (When in doubt, chocolate is a favorite everywhere.) For specifics on gift-giving rituals in each country, you should ask someone who's visited there previously, speak with a native of that country, or consult a guidebook.

Be careful not to compliment or admire certain objects in a person's home. People in some cultures will feel obligated to give you the object, or something else, as a gift.

Traveling for Business

In today's multicultural and global business environment, you need to know proper etiquette in your own culture as well as international customs. If you travel abroad, you'll encounter more formality, the possibility of a language barrier, and customs that are likely to be unfamiliar to you. One benefit for Americans is that the global spread of American culture has increased the likelihood that your foreign host is likely to understand American customs and manners and make allowances for you.

When you're traveling domestically, you'll encounter cultural differences as well. Although the differences may not be as marked, you'll still need to follow the lead of people from that area. Don't be pushy or assume you know as much as those who live there.

Before you embark on an international business trip, you may want to consult a reputable guidebook on your destination to read up on the following essential information:

- ✔ Dressing properly
- ✔ Greeting rituals and key phrases (hello, please, thank you, and so on)
- ✔ Basic geography
- ✔ Gift-giving etiquette
- ✔ Climate
- ✔ Currency
- ✔ Beliefs and customs
- ✔ Religions
- ✔ Politics
- ✔ Cultural heritage — art, music, and so on
- ✔ Attitude toward Americans
- ✔ Potential social situations — bullfights, soccer games, parties, and bars

In any environment where you don't know the language or the rules, fall back on your host's assistance. Tell your host that you really don't know what you should do, and let him or her show you the way.

Interacting with overseas colleagues

You may never completely understand your colleagues in other countries, but you can come a lot closer to a mutual understanding by learning a bit about the other person's culture. Communication style can vary greatly, even among Asian countries or Western countries. Feeling completely comfortable in another culture can take months or years, but with just a little research you can lessen your chances of making a major faux pas and feel much more at home in another culture.

Americans are very direct. When we speak, we get right to the point. Usually, there are no double meanings, no hidden agendas, and no subtle hints. (Of course, there are times when this isn't the case, but generally, Americans are pretty up-front in how they speak.) Most of what Americans say is pretty much the way it is. Well, try that with an Italian! Because of our straightforward way of speaking, Latins (French, Italians, and Spaniards) often consider us somewhat uncouth and lacking in refinement.

Another unusual characteristic of Americans is a propensity to sing our own praises. In other cultures which aren't as individualistic, you can actually insult a person by singling him or her out for special compliments. This is especially true in group-oriented cultures such as Japan.

Many cultures closely observe volume, vocal quality, tone of voice, and posture, because they indicate good breeding. Therefore, don't speak loudly or monopolize conversations, and learn to listen more than you speak. When in doubt, modesty is the best policy.

Rank and status

Casual Fridays are a uniquely American phenomenon. In most cultures, what you wear is one of the best indicators of your rank and status in a company. So if you are an executive, you must dress the part. Outside the United States comfort is less valued than appearance by many businesspeople, who will wear their suit and tie no matter what the circumstances. Wearing khakis and a polo shirt to an overseas meeting may signal lack of respect for yourself, your company, and, most importantly, for the person with whom you're doing business. When in doubt, err on the conservative side by wearing a suit.

In a business meeting, the Chinese line up according to seniority so that you greet the most senior person first. American business people should line up the same way, so that the most senior American greets the most senior Chinese colleague, and the rest of the people in line then follow, greeting the others in turn.

Business cards

One of the most important aspects of meeting people is the proper presentation of your business card. Business cards are an important means of introduction around the world — particularly in Japan — because they list your name, company, and position within the company. When you receive someone's business card, don't put it in your pocket; doing so may indicate disregard. Instead, keep the card in front of you on the conference table and refer to it throughout the meeting.

The meaning of time

In the United States, people get down to business immediately. Once again, we're the odd ones out, because the only other countries that use this technique are the Germanic countries. Almost anywhere else — especially in Asian and Latin countries — you're expected to get to know the people you're dealing with first in order to build a bond of trust. Remember, America's fast-changing business culture, with people leaving companies and changing positions on a regular basis, is not the norm in most of the world. Most cultures see business relationships as long-lasting and, once formed, not easily broken.

Americans also think about time differently than many people in the world do. We demand promptness in appointments and expect speed in getting business done. Our focus is to use time efficiently and to get the maximum out of every minute of the day. That's not the way many other people in the world think about time. Every culture has different expectations about scheduling and appointments. How far in advance must you schedule appointments? Is being on time extremely critical or completely ignored? For an American who considers that time is money, facing a relationship-oriented Arab, Asian, or Latin can be extremely stressful. In those cultures, time is seen as flexible, and lateness and interruptions are accepted as a part of life. Americans who are brusque, rushing around, and cutting to the chase might not be successful in dealings with people from these cultures. To avoid problems, try to remain flexible.

Surviving business dinners

Everyone who has traveled to a foreign land to do business has heard stories about business meals where the host served "something terrible." In most cases, the food in question was a special delicacy that the host ordered at extra expense.

Good manners require gracious participation with such delicacies. If you find yourself absolutely unable to dig in, however, just eat what you can without comment. If a native chides you for leaving most of your raw yak liver on your plate, quietly explain that your doctor forbids you to eat raw yak liver.

Toasting

A business meal is seldom complete without toasts to honor guests and host. A few well-chosen words can help immensely in developing relationships with your foreign hosts, so give thought to an appropriate toast beforehand. Toasts don't necessarily translate well, especially if they contain a joke or are poetic. Stick to safe topics, such as friendship, the enjoyment of life, and health.

Was it something I said?

Some societies interpret the act of beginning to eat your food while you're engaged in a conversation as a sign of your displeasure with the conversation. Japanese etiquette, for example, calls for you to utter a simple phrase before you dig in. The rough translation is "Please excuse me. I am about to eat." Even if you don't know how to express this thought in the local language, you can say it in English. Adopt this foreign custom as an extra measure of politeness in all social dining situations.

In many countries, a host will begin the meal with a toast of welcome, in addition to the toasts that he or she offers toward the end of a meal. European and Asian countries all have a strong tradition of toasting. It's thoughtful to learn the local toast, whether it's "cheers" (Great Britain), "kampai" (Japan), "ganbei" (China), or "a votre sante" (France).

Remembering your table manners

Don't forget that, while all this entertaining is going on, table manners count. Unfortunately, what you consider polite may not be what your hosts consider polite — and eating with chopsticks or with your hands may be the least of the possible discrepancies. Likewise, slurping, burping, and drinking from each other's glass may be acceptable (or unacceptable) behaviors. In certain countries, silverware is used only for serving food. Therefore, you need to wash your hands thoroughly in the washroom or with the warm towel that your server provides before you begin eating.

Check a guidebook before you depart for tips on table manners. If you anticipate any difficulty, discuss your concerns with a contact who's familiar with the country or with a friend who has spent time there.

Reviewing Your Good Traveler Checklist

As you close your suitcase, review these simple tips for good behavior away from home:

✔ **Remember that lines are inevitable.** Allow enough extra time for waiting in line and wading through the details of travel. Be patient — everyone around you faces the same inconvenience. Take it as a personal challenge to deal with the delays graciously.

✔ **Don't be a target for thieves.** Leave your valuables at home in a safe. Purchase a slender wallet that hangs by a cord around your neck, under your shirt. Keep your passport, credit card, and large bank notes in that wallet, and go about your travels without worrying that someone may pick your pocket or steal your purse.

If you're traveling abroad, keep these additional points in mind:

✔ **Learn at least a few native words for polite exchanges with the locals.** The time it takes to fly to your destination is time enough to learn hello, goodbye, please, thank you, where is . . . ?, how much is . . . ?, my name is . . . , and the numbers from zero to ten. The more you learn, the more pleasant your trip will be.

You may want to carry a phrasebook or small dictionary. The time will come when you need to say a word or phrase in the local language that isn't on the list of words you already learned.

✔ **Learn the currency system.** Fumbling with a handful of bank notes and comments about funny money mark you as a poor traveler. Knowing your way around the local currency can help you avoid untrustworthy exchangers.

✔ **Learn the important points of local etiquette.** You can find local etiquette information in every up-to-date guidebook. Locals may excuse you as an ignorant tourist if you make a mistake, but why make the mistake? When in doubt, ask your hotel desk clerk or concierge for advice and guidance.

✔ **Be careful when taking photographs.** Ask permission before you take a picture of a local citizen. In some countries, taking pictures of military installations, airports, government buildings, power plants, and so on is against the law. This is especially true throughout Africa.

✔ **Don't say anything in English that you wouldn't want to be overheard if you said it in the local language.** Many natives understand and speak English.

✔ **Never accept a shopkeeper's advice on how to avoid U.S. Customs inspections and/or duty payments.** If you have to pay a customs fee on overseas purchases, the amount is likely to be modest and well within your budget. Don't join the ranks of travelers charged with smuggling.

Remember, the rules of how we act with others and how to behave in a polite and considerate manner out in the world are rules that have stood the test of time. And while we have relaxed some rules of etiquette in this century, it will never be in style to be rude or unkind. And always remember, when in doubt, treat other people as you would want to be treated yourself.

Chapter 22

Interacting with People Who Have Disabilities

*Y*ou're sipping your drink at a party. Your host introduces you to a man in a wheelchair and then moves away to greet another guest. How can you comfortably converse with your new acquaintance?

A woman who is deaf has applied for a position at your company. She arrives for her job interview accompanied by an interpreter of American Sign Language. Who should sit where during the interview?

You find yourself standing in line with a gentleman and his guide dog. You've always loved golden retrievers, and this one looks as if it could really use a pat on the head. . . .

More than 50 million Americans have serious disabilities — vision, hearing, speech, mobility, and developmental impairments. Millions more have hidden disabilities, such as heart disease or AIDS. These individuals come from every ethnic group, religion, economic class, and age bracket. They also pursue every hobby, profession, and dream you can think of.

People with disabilities are *people,* not statistics. Still, a few more numbers may be enlightening: A 1991 Harris poll found that 58 percent of Americans are uneasy around individuals with disabilities, and 47 percent experience some degree of fear. Imagine how it would feel — even if you knew that the unease stemmed from misconceptions — to sense discomfort from half the people you encountered in the course of a day! The frustrations and challenges that people with disabilities face are not limited to unseen obstacles and too-narrow doors.

How can you interact comfortably and considerately with these important members of society? Here are some general tips:

✔ Develop a vocabulary of respect — just because the blue signs all over town say *handicapped* doesn't mean that you should use the word, too.

✔ Take the time to learn appropriate etiquette for specific disabilities, just as you would for specific business or social encounters.

✔ Get to know the individuals with disabilities in your workplace and community. Get to know them as people — people who go to the movies, buy shoes, pay their taxes, get mad, and get married — and encourage your children to get to know them, too.

Using "People First" Terminology

If you care enough about social politeness to have purchased this book, you surely understand that certain expressions — "crip," to mention just one — are not respectful or acceptable. On the other hand, don't resort to euphemisms, either. Many disability groups consider terms such as "physically challenged" and "differently abled" patronizing.

A good general rule: Acknowledge the disability but place the person first. Simple as it may sound, if you use the term "person with a disability" rather than "disabled person," you're off to a good start.

Here are some further guidelines:

✔ Individuals and conditions are not synonymous; don't label a person with his or her disability. "A woman who has epilepsy" places the individual first; calling her "an epileptic" is judgmental.

✔ Refer to people without disabilities as "nondisabled" rather than "able bodied" or "healthy." Many people with disabilities are in excellent health.

✔ Don't tie yourself in knots over the literal meaning of common expressions. It's okay to say "Do you see what I mean?" to a woman who is blind or to invite a man in a wheelchair to join you for a walk.

✔ Avoid the words "handicapped" and "crippled." "Disabled" is the more respectful choice.

✔ Don't refer to someone as "wheelchair-bound" or "confined to a wheelchair." The chair, in fact, is a freedom machine, affording independence and mobility.

✔ "Invalid" implies a lack of validity. "Victim," "afflicted with," and "suffering from" carry negative — and often inaccurate — connotations. Even "courageous" and "inspirational" can seem patronizing to a person engaged in a normal, busy life — would you say "You're so courageous" to a person wearing glasses to correct poor eyesight? Try to focus on the interests and accomplishments of people with disabilities, distinct from their challenges.

✔ The preferred term for a person who can't talk is "without speech" — not "mute" and certainly not "dumb."

Understanding the Rules of Disability Etiquette

Certain rules of disability etiquette — such as never feeding a guide dog — are hard and fast. Others are more fluid, because the individuals involved don't always agree on what is offensive or correct.

In most encounters with a person with a disability, you behave exactly as you would with anyone else. Don't stare. Don't look away as if he or she didn't exist. Talk to the *person,* not to the companion pushing the wheelchair, acting as interpreter, or sitting in the adjacent seat on the plane.

People with disabilities have diverse personalities, just like rest of us. Some enjoy opera, and some prefer rock. Some love to be helped and fussed over, and others take fierce pride in their independence. Many have great senses of humor — one young man hangs a sign on his wheelchair saying "It's Okay to Stare, I Know I'm Handsome" — and wish that you'd just relax and laugh with them.

Offering to help a person with a disability is never wrong, but if the person declines your assistance, never insist. If he or she accepts, ask for specific instructions and follow them. Talk about the person's disability if the subject comes up naturally, but don't pry.

The guidelines in the following sections can help you behave graciously toward people with a range of disabilities. But the most important rule is this: If you ever have a question — what to do, how to do it, how to say it — the person with the disability is always your first and best resource.

Vision impairment

Not all people with visual impairments live in a world of total darkness. Those with tunnel vision can look into your eyes when they speak with you but see nothing in the periphery. Peripheral vision — the loss of central vision — is the reverse. Other people experience spotted, blurred, or double vision in the entire visual field.

Whatever the degree of disability, use common sense and empathy when you deal with people who have vision impairments. Remember that they often can't see your face well enough to identify you; they aren't aware that you've extended your hand for a handshake; and they can't perceive when you shrug your shoulders, nod your head, or raise your eyebrows in surprise. Remember to use *words:*

- ✔ Introduce yourself and anyone with you when you first approach. "Hi, Mr. Eliot. It's Daphne Jones. And I have Maria Perez here with me, to your left. Shall we shake hands?"

- ✔ Never leave without saying that you're leaving. The person may think that there was simply a pause in the conversation and start talking to thin air. Even if you only move from one end of the couch to the other, let the person know.

- ✔ Particularly in business settings or large groups, use names with every exchange so that the person with vision impairment knows who's talking to whom. "Valerie? John here. Can you give us the latest on the Mitchell account?" In a small group of friends, though, the person is more likely to recognize voices.

- ✔ Offer to read written material out loud. "This box has lots of instructions. Shall I read them to you?"

- ✔ If you see a person with a visual impairment in a potentially dangerous situation, voice your concerns calmly and concisely.

People with vision impairments use many tools to navigate smoothly in the world. Some carry canes. Others are accompanied by guide dogs (I discuss these marvelous animals later in this chapter). It's always appropriate to offer to help someone with a visual impairment. Do so politely, and don't be offended if your offer is refused.

Here are some types of help that you might offer:

- ✔ If you're asked to act as a guide, offer your elbow rather than grabbing the person's arm. He or she will probably walk slightly behind you to follow the motion of your body. Describe the route as you walk: "We have three steps coming up." Pause before the steps, but don't stop.

- ✔ If you lead a person to a seat, place her hand on the back of the chair. If you leave her standing in unfamiliar surroundings, make sure that she can touch something — a wall or a table, for example — so that she isn't left uncomfortably isolated.

- ✔ When giving directions, be as specific as you can: "You'll go 200 yards and then make a 90-degree turn to the left around the corner of the building." Detail any obstacles along the route.

- ✔ At a meal, relate where dishes and utensils are placed on the table. Use the face of a clock to describe the food on a plate: "You've got potatoes at 1:00, Brussels sprouts at 4:00, and turkey at 9:00. Do you need some help cutting the turkey?"

✔ Describe any item exchanging hands. If you're handing over several objects, describe their relationship to one other so that the person doesn't take hold of one item and drop the others: "Here's your costume for the play. The robe's on the bottom, and then the shoes, and the crown's on top."

✔ When exchanging money, separate the bills into denominations and hand over the stacks one at a time: "Here's four fives and two ones." You don't need to separate the coins, which are easy to identify by feel: "And 62 cents in change."

✔ When walking with a vision-impaired companion, describe your surroundings, not only to alert the person to obstacles but also to share the scene. Describe the layout of a room, the view out a window, and so on.

Give your descriptive powers free rein. A person of few words is not a good companion to a person who is visually impaired.

✔ If a person with a visual impairment needs to sign a document, guide his or her hand to the signature line and offer a straight edge — a ruler or a card — for alignment.

✔ Leave doors and cupboards either all the way open or all the way closed.

A final reminder: Never move items in the home or workplace of a person with impaired sight. Yes, that vase might look nicer on the mantle, but moving it is the equivalent of hiding it from a person who can see. And moving furniture can be downright hazardous.

Mobility impairment

Despite that universal sign of disability, not everyone with a mobility impairment uses a wheelchair. A man with rheumatoid arthritis in his hands has limited mobility. So does a woman weakened by a stroke.

Ideally, your behavior toward people with mobility impairments affirms their dignity. Here are some guidelines:

✔ Shake the hand that's extended to you. If you're offered the person's prosthesis or hook, shake that hand. If you're offered the left hand, you can shake it with your right. If shaking hands isn't an option, touch the person on the shoulder or arm as a sign of greeting and acknowledgment.

✔ When greeting a person in a motorized wheelchair, wait until he or she shuts off the power before shaking hands. You don't want to activate the controls inadvertently.

✔ Never move mobility aids, such as crutches, out of a person's reach.

✔ Don't push a wheelchair without offering first. If your offer is accepted, respect your limitations. If you don't think that you're strong enough to push the chair up a ramp or over a curb, let the person know.

✔ A wheelchair is part of its user's personal space. Never lean or hang on it.

✔ When speaking with a person in a wheelchair for more than a few minutes, place yourself at his or her eye level. Doing so is not only more respectful, but it's also easier on the person's neck. If you can pull up a chair, great — you'll both be more comfortable. You can also try squatting or kneeling if you have sturdy knees.

Hearing disabilities

"I've always loved Suzi's abstracts," you say to a man looking at a painting at the opening of a friend's show. The man doesn't respond. Your first assumption might be that he's rude. In fact, there's a good chance that he simply didn't hear you.

Hearing impairment can range from complete deafness to mild hearing loss, and unless you notice a hearing aid, the disability tends to be hidden. Be alert to the possibility of deafness when a person doesn't respond to audible cues.

To get the attention of someone with a hearing disability, tap him or her lightly on the shoulder or give a visual signal, such as a wave. Establish how you plan to communicate. Some people who are deaf can speak, and others cannot. Not everyone with a hearing impairment can read lips; even those who lip-read catch maybe four out of ten words and rely heavily on facial expressions and body language.

To facilitate lip-reading, do the following:

✔ Position yourself so that you're facing both the light source and the person you're speaking to. Don't walk around while you converse.

✔ Speak clearly, slowly, naturally, and expressively. Never exaggerate your lip movements; doing so makes lip-reading more difficult, plus you'll look *very* silly.

✔ Don't eat or smoke while you're talking. Gesture with your hands with abandon, but don't block your face. If you have a mustache, try brushing it away from your upper lip.

✔ Rather than repeating a sentence, try rewording it. "I'll scoop you up at six" may be hard to lip-read; "Wait for me after your meeting" may be fine.

✔ Never shout. If the person is deaf, shouting won't do a bit of good. If the person is hard of hearing — especially if he or she uses a hearing aid — shouting distorts the sound and can even be painful or dangerous.

✔ If necessary, write notes, but don't talk and write at the same time.

Many people in the United States use American Sign Language to communicate. ASL is not a universal language, although some signs are similar worldwide. If you know even minimal sign language, try using it. If an interpreter is present, observe the following etiquette:

- ✔ The interpreter should sit or stand next to you, facing the person who is deaf or hard of hearing.

- ✔ Maintain eye contact with the person with the hearing disability, even though that person will be looking between the interpreter and you.

- ✔ The interpreter may lag a few words behind you, especially when finger spelling. Pause occasionally so that he or she can catch up.

- ✔ In a business situation, never consult the interpreter — he or she is present only to facilitate communication. In a social situation, include the interpreter in a friendly manner, but remember to maintain eye contact with whomever you're addressing.

Speech impairment

A person whose speech is impaired due to cerebral palsy may pronounce each word with difficulty. Another person may speak flawlessly for phrases at a time and then block or stutter. Whatever the cause, and whatever the manifestation, the etiquette toward people with speech impairments remains the same:

- ✔ Give the person speaking your full, relaxed attention. Be patient and encouraging.

- ✔ Speak normally, without raising your voice. Most people with speech impairments have no problem hearing.

- ✔ Never supply a word unless you're asked to do so. Always allow the person to finish what he or she is trying to say. Your impulse will be to help, especially when you see how much effort the person is putting into the attempt, but be patient.

- ✔ Keep your questions simple. If possible, ask questions that the person can answer with short responses or with a shake or nod of the head.

- ✔ Never pretend that you understand if you don't. Repeating what you think you heard to make sure that you heard correctly is okay: "You'll be catching a 6:00 flight and need to be at the airport by 5:00. Is that right?"

- ✔ Pen and paper are wonderful inventions. Offer them to the person with a speech impairment in an encouraging manner — never as an act of impatience.

Guide and service animals

A guide dog leading a blind person is a familiar image in our culture. But did you know that carefully bred and trained dogs serve as partners to individuals with a range of disabilities?

Service dogs can conduct business transactions for people in wheelchairs, passing money to cashiers and accepting change and packages. They turn lights on and off, help their partners get in and out of bed, and even pick up the laundry — although, like many humans, they have to be told to do so.

A person who is deaf might wake up in the morning to a Corgi or Labrador jumping on his bed. His "hearing dog" will alert him with a gentle paw prod when he hears certain sounds — a smoke alarm, a doorbell, or even his handler's name spoken in the workplace — and then go sit by the sound.

Guide and service dogs make constant decisions that impact the welfare of their human companions. They have an important job to do, and frequently a hazardous one. Never distract them. Remember that your actions toward these dedicated animals are not just a question of politeness, but also of safety.

Here are some points to remember:

✔ Never touch guide or service animals unless the handler gives you permission to do so, particularly while it's doing its job in public. The rules may be more relaxed at home; still, always ask.

✔ Never call a dog's name or try to get its attention.

✔ Traffic presents particular hazards to guide dogs and their handlers. Streets are busier and wider than ever, and cars are quieter. You may think that honking your horn or calling out that the road is clear would be helpful, but it would only be distracting, so please refrain from doing so.

✔ Never, ever feed working dogs. Don't even offer them water without asking first. These animals have feeding schedules and relieving schedules, and disturbing their routine can be, at best, an inconvenience. If you sneak a guide dog a snack and the dog becomes ill, you could put the dog's handler in danger.

✔ Puppies in training, like their working counterparts, can go many places where pets cannot, accompanied by their nondisabled trainers. They usually wear identifying jackets. Treat puppies in training the way you would treat fully trained guide or service dogs so that they can learn their job.

✔ You may be tempted to ooh and ahh when you see a scene as endearing as a service dog carefully placing a package in its handler's lap. Go ahead and express yourself, as long as you don't distract the dog, but first make eye contact with the handler. As always, the first rule of etiquette toward people with disabilities is to put the person first — before the disability, before the wheelchair, and before the dog.

Dealing with Disability Issues in the Workplace

For all their recent gains in civil rights, people with disabilities are still greatly underrepresented in the workforce. According to the 1998 N.O.D./Harris Survey of Americans with Disabilities, only 29 percent of adults with disabilities work full- or part-time, compared to 79 percent of nondisabled adults. Most of those people who aren't working wish they were.

People with disabilities represent a huge, untapped talent pool, especially because advances in technology are breaking down physical barriers. These individuals have faced more challenges than many people and are a tremendous source of innovative and resourceful thinking. As the largest and most diverse minority group in the country, they are also a prime consumer market.

Whether you work with disabled people as coworkers or you interact with them as clients, you're likely to be in contact with people with disabilities in the workplace. If you combine the business etiquette pointers from elsewhere in this book with the guidelines in this chapter and throw in a healthy dose of common sense, you'll do fine. Here, however, are a few additional thoughts:

✔ Familiarize yourself with the location of accessible elevators, restrooms, and drinking fountains in your workplace.

✔ Learn about the assistive technologies that your coworkers use, and adapt your presentations and communications to accommodate them. People with vision impairments use scanners to move text from page to computer and screen-reading software to synthesize the words on the screen. People with hearing impairments use telecommunications devices for the deaf (TDDs) or similar tools. High-tech devices of all kinds are available to individuals with limited mobility. For an interesting primer on assistive technologies, check out Apple Computer's Disability Resources page (www.apple.com/education/k12/disability/).

TIP

The National Organization on Disability (NOD)

The National Organization on Disability (NOD) is a great place to start if you want to learn more about disability issues. On its Web site (www.nod.org) you can find Frequently Asked Questions, a summary of the Americans with Disabilities Act (ADA), findings of the NOD/Harris Survey on Americans with Disabilities, links to other sites, and more. Or contact the organization for information:

National Organization on Disability
910 16th St. NW, Suite 600
Washington, DC 20006

✔ If you own a business, make every effort to hire workers with disabilities and to implement Americans with Disabilities Act (ADA) requirements. You may be surprised how little it costs to fully accommodate a worker with a disability, and what a tremendous contribution that worker can make to your company. Make the effort to court clients who are disabled as well; doing so makes good business sense. A good resource is W. C. Duke and Associates (www.wcduke.com/training.html), which offers industry-specific "Opening Doors" seminars and videos on disability etiquette and ADA compliance.

✔ Consider creating a text-only version of your Web site. Complex formatting and graphics are difficult for screen readers to translate. Nondisabled individuals with slower computers will appreciate the version, too.

Talking to Your Children about People with Disabilities

Many children already know a person with a disability, perhaps a grandparent who has arthritis or uses a walker or a classmate at school. Use these experiences as a springboard for discussion. Explain that people of all ages have disabilities, and why: an accident, an illness, or simply the way the person was born. Let your children know that having a disability is okay, a fact of life. Point out all the things that people with disabilities can do.

Some children, if given inadvertent free rein, will walk up to a person with a disability, tug on his or her sleeve, and say, "You look funny." The proclamation isn't a so much a judgment as a statement of fact, a manifestation of the child's curiosity about the world.

Make sure that your child knows that saying or doing anything that might hurt a person's feelings is never okay. At the same time, don't discourage his or her natural curiosity. The worst thing you can tell a child — unless you first explain why — is not to stare. Doing so is as good as saying, "Let's pretend the person with crutches doesn't exist."

If your child is curious about a person's wheelchair — or her white cane, or his life — explain that asking questions is okay, but that it's also okay if the person doesn't really want to talk. If possible, make eye contact with the person who has the disability. If he or she seems receptive to your child, approach, let the child say, "Could I ask you a question?" and see what happens. Many people with disabilities are very willing to respond to children's questions, especially because a child's reaction to the answer is likely to be, "Oh, neat." No discomfort, no fear.

If children today feel at ease around people with disabilities, adults tomorrow will feel the same way. We want our children to be polite. If they happen to grow up to make the world a better place, that's okay, too.

Part VII
The Part of Tens

The 5th Wave   By Rich Tennant

JASON BREAKS CAMPFIRE ETIQUETTE BY INTRODUCING CONTRAPUNTAL HARMONIES TO LUKE'S HARMONICA RENDITION OF "THE COWBOY'S LAMENT."

In this part . . .

*I*f you're just looking for a quick etiquette lesson or two, this is the part for you. Here, you can find ten etiquette points to teach your children, ten ways to be a gracious guest (and get invited back again!), ten tipping situations and how to handle them, and ten etiquette mistakes to avoid.

Chapter 23

Ten Good-Manners Lessons for Children

In This Chapter

▶ Teaching your children respect

▶ Practicing etiquette with your children

▶ Praising your children's efforts

As you are probably aware, social graces at home and within the classroom are not what they should be today. Parents and teachers are constantly bombarded with rudeness from their children and students. And all too often, the students and children aren't even aware that they're being rude!

Although it's true that etiquette should be taught in the home, the sad reality is that it isn't. This creates a difficult situation within the home and classroom: How do you teach "the basics" when the students can't even behave in a way that is conducive to learning?

When it comes to teaching manners to kids, the phrase "monkey see, monkey do" says it all. Children learn by example. As adults, the way we behave around kids speaks volumes. This rule goes double for the youngest children, who may not yet understand verbal instructions — but believe me, they watch every move you make! Throughout my years of teaching, I've found that youngsters pay more attention than we give them credit for.

Inevitably, your child will ask, "Why do I have to learn about etiquette?" I usually respond by explaining that we show who we are by how we behave and appear to others. Behavior and appearance refer to the way we look, the way we talk, and the way we walk and sit and stand — just about everything we do!

Children can begin learning manners beginning at age 3 and continue learning through their teenage years. This chapter outlines the ten most important lessons to teach children regarding good manners.

Respect Yourself

As mentioned throughout this book, the rules of etiquette were created as a way to show respect for yourself as well as others. Living your life in a respectful way is the best way to teach your children respect. Be gracious and courteous in the way you treat your spouse, your neighbors, and even strangers, such as the checkout person at the grocery store. In this way, you demonstrate how your children should treat others. Make sure to include elders, people of other religions and cultures, and people with disabilities when you teach your children about respect. As I said, children watch their parents closely and begin learning from them at a very young age.

Children learn to respect others when they are respected as individuals. Make a conscious effort to respect your children's privacy and time. For example, don't just barge in unannounced if your child's bedroom door is closed — knock first! Show your child that you respect the need to have time alone.

Children must also learn that people treat you the way you treat yourself. Respecting, valuing, and looking after yourself are important. Others can then value you in return. For more on this point, see the section "Look Good and Feel Good," later in this chapter.

Put Your Manners Where Your Mouth Is

The fastest way to show your good manners is to say please, thank you, excuse me, and I'm sorry. (This rule applies to both children and adults.) You can begin teaching your children these simple words when they're toddlers.

What you say is important, but the *way* you say it is just as important. Again, teaching by example is the best way to show your children proper etiquette. Don't allow yourself to scream and yell around the house. Don't argue with your spouse in front of your children. Settle disputes quietly. If you find yourself in an argument with your children, have them go to their rooms to take a time-out before the argument gets too heated.

Take care to nip your children's poor conversation and listening habits in the bud. Bad listening habits include appearing impatient, completing other people's sentences, failing to respond, changing the subject, interrupting, neglecting to make eye contact, making wisecracks, talking back, and walking away during a conversation. The appropriate way to address your children's listening and conversation habits is to step in and correct the situation as it happens. For example, if Susie just jumped in and began talking over her younger brother, who was telling a story, you might say, "Susie, I believe Sam was in the middle of a story. Why don't we let him finish? When Sam's done, you can tell us all about your science teacher."

Get a Job!

Performing chores with patience and a light heart (in a happy mood, so to speak) is one of the biggest etiquette lessons that you can teach children. I always told my children that being grumpy doesn't make the chores go away; it just makes you feel bad while you do them. Doing chores with energy, on the other hand, makes you feel good — the work gets done quickly, and you can then enjoy other parts of your life.

Having your children perform jobs around the house teaches them to do things for themselves. Giving children tasks, such as setting the table, taking out the garbage, keeping their rooms clean, and feeding pets, gives them a sense of responsibility. Even at the age of 4 or 5, children can have chores, such as picking up toys when they're done playing or putting their clothes in the laundry hamper.

Taking on responsibility for the household is an important part of etiquette at home. As your children grow, give them slightly more complicated tasks and more responsibilities.

By keeping your home tidy, you show your children that it's important for them to keep their own space clean, too. Tell your children that having a neat, uncluttered home shows others that you respect yourself and your living space. (It also enables you to be ready to invite guests into your home at any time without embarrassment!) Nagging, threatening, or issuing ultimatums about housework rarely works. After a while, leading by example makes your message clear.

When my children grumbled about household duties, I told them that, although there are things that they'd rather not do, everyone must do chores, including Grandma, the President, and the richest person on Earth. All kinds of chores abound in life, and they never stop needing attention.

Learning to do chores without complaint isn't always easy for children. Not wanting to do chores is okay, but teach your children to practice enjoying their chores anyway, even when they'd rather be doing something else. The more they practice doing chores and taking care of other responsibilities, the more they'll enjoy all the parts of their lives. For example, it's much easier for your daughter to enjoy playing baseball with a clear conscience if she knows that poor Fido isn't sitting at home, hungry, because she already fed him as part of her morning chores!

When children keep busy with positive activities, their self-esteem grows. Doing chores around the house teaches children to be considerate of others in every aspect of life, and taking on these responsibilities builds character and makes them feel better about themselves.

Share and Share Alike

One manners mantra is to treat people the way you want others to treat you. What better rationale exists for sharing? Opportunities for teaching your children to share include sharing toys with friends and siblings and taking turns in the bathroom. These lessons can begin when they're toddlers (although they often take years to fully sink in!). As your children get older, you can take sharing to another level by showing them how to share their time and talents with others.

Practice, Practice, Practice

As with any performance, practicing before a big event, such as going out to a restaurant, is a good idea. I know of people who dress up their kids, sit them down at the family dining room table, and hand out homemade menus to practice eating out!

Children respond well to role-playing and can learn things sooner than you may think. When my oldest son, Stephen, was still in a high chair, I thought that letting him play with his food was okay. My husband thought differently, however. He made up a game that taught my son to keep his peas on his plate. Before I knew it, my son no longer smeared his food all over his tray.

Even if you don't do a full dress rehearsal before you go to a restaurant, teach your children the proper way to act at the table. No matter how rushed your schedule is, don't have pizza in front of the television all the time. A couple of times a week, make the effort to have a sit-down dinner so that your children can learn table manners. Start with the basics: Don't eat until everyone sits down, don't talk about unpleasant subjects, and don't grab for food — wait for dishes to be passed around the table. (See Chapter 16 for much more on table manners.)

Look Good and Feel Good

What's the use of having good manners if you have dirty fingernails, bad breath, or a shirt with holes in it? You can teach children that grooming and dressing properly show the world that you care about yourself.

Children need to learn to take care of themselves on a daily basis. Teaching your children to get enough sleep, exercise, shower or bathe, comb their hair, brush their teeth, and eat right gives them a sense of independence and responsibility that nurtures their self-respect. These consistent activities can become rituals, which provide a sense of security for children.

As kids get older, they sometimes experiment with hairstyles. Don't let your children's hairstyles alarm you — sometimes you have to let children have some freedom. I tell parents that even if a child's hair is purple, they can still insist that it be clean. This same principle applies to clothing. Children, especially as they become young adults, like to push the envelope by wearing outfits that adults might consider over the top. When it comes to school, though, children need to learn that dressing appropriately means wearing clothes that aren't too short, too long, too tight, too big, or too see-through. Children don't have to look dowdy or hide their bodies in sacks, but their appearance doesn't need to embarrass others, either.

Children should be taught that clothes say a lot about you, such as "I'm cool," "I'm sloppy," "I want to stand out," or "I don't care what people think of me." Because people judge you by your clothes and make those judgments within the first few minutes of meeting you, what you wear can help you or hurt you. Whatever your children wear, teach them that the most important thing is that their clothes are clean and neat.

As difficult as it may be for parents, when your children are old enough, you must allow them to select their own clothing, especially when they're with their peers. (If this advice seems a bit lenient, it may be that I became more liberal on this topic after raising two sons and seeing them go through every trend from surfer to hippie, punk and grunge!) If your children are attending an event with you or other adults, though, you can request that they conform to your standards of dress.

When children are young, you may want to try to set boundaries about dress that respects the views of both the parent and child. This stops you from constantly saying, "You're not really going out of the house like that, are you?"

Respect All Cultures

We live in a multicultural world, which creates the need for many new rules of etiquette. As an adult, you set an example for your children when you pay attention to your behavior and comments about others, especially when it comes to people of a different race or religion whose customs and cultures are unfamiliar to you.

I find that sitting down with children to explain child-rearing differences in various cultures is helpful. For example, some cultures give priority to family loyalty; therefore, their children may miss school to help support their families. Likewise, other children may celebrate holidays that your family does not. And some families practice customs that yours may not. For example, they might remove their shoes when entering a home. Tell your kids that if they notice shoes outside a friend's front door, they should remove their own shoes as well. (This goes for all types of customs — you should follow suit when you're in someone else's home.)

See Chapter 21 for more information about multicultural etiquette.

Be a Good Guest

Being a good guest is something that you can teach your children early. Kids can learn the importance of RSVPing promptly, bringing a gift to a party, and writing thank-you notes, for example. If the neighbor's 8-year-old son invites your 8-year-old son to his birthday party, for example, you can have your child call his friend to accept the invitation. He can then help you select a birthday present. With a little prodding, you may get him to write a thank-you note, too!

Teaching kids how to be gracious hosts is also a good idea. I learned this as a young child and have always been glad for it. My father was a Navy officer, so my family grew up with our own party protocol. Whenever my parents hosted a party, my siblings and I came down and were introduced to the guests. While we were at the party, we had a soda and a bite to eat and spoke with the guests before our parents sent us back upstairs. This brief exercise in proper party procedure helped us feel comfortable at parties. You can allow your own children to greet your guests, answer the door, take coats, and so on to teach them proper party etiquette.

Meet and Greet Properly

Remember the awkwardness you felt as a kid when you met adults? Even though meeting people seems routine to adults, kids wonder what they should say to someone they don't know. How do you find out who the person you're meeting is?

I teach kids that the best thing to do is to make it easy for the other person by talking about yourself. Tell your children to smile and then say in a clear voice, "Hello [or Hi], my name is _____, and I'm _____." For example, your child might say, "I'm a senior at Westmore High," or "I'm a freshman at Stanford this year," or "I live across the street." Kids should take their time, relax, and talk in their normal voice when they introduce themselves — tell them not to mumble!

As for the ever-so-scary handshake, I tell kids to extend their right hand in greeting and then shake hands with the other person while introducing themselves. Hold the person's entire hand, fingers, and palm to where the thumbs meet and cross over each other. Then squeeze firmly (not too hard!) and shake three times.

Tell your children to look at the other person's eyes when introducing themselves to a stranger. Direct eye contact lets the other person see that you are open, friendly, and genuine about getting to know him or her. It also makes it easy for the other person to respond.

Nobody's Perfect

Remember to correct your children's behavior without accusing, berating, or talking down to them. The point of teaching children manners is to build self-esteem and self-confidence. When a child does something correctly — such as holding a door for someone — make sure that you acknowledge the kind deed. However, if your child gets confused and makes a mistake, it's not the end of the world. I used to tell my boys that mistakes happen — life isn't perfect, and neither are we!

Let your kids continue through life, and correct and praise them when the opportunity presents itself. When children behave well, parents should acknowledge their good deeds, which reinforces good behavior. Tell your children that you love them and that you appreciate their courteous behavior.

Chapter 24

Ten Ways to Get Invited Back

- -

In This Chapter

▶ Arriving on time, properly dressed, and with an appropriate gift

▶ Being self-sufficient

▶ Practicing moderation in everything

▶ Making a graceful exit and following up with a thank-you note

- -

We've all heard horror stories about "nightmare" guests. You may have experienced one firsthand: a guest who shows up early, monopolizes your time while you're trying to make final preparations, stays too late, or possesses little of interest to add to the party's conversation. Follow the ten simple rules listed in this chapter to make sure that *you're* always invited back.

Stay Home If You're Sick

If you're sick, please stay home — the other guests will thank you for it. Simply call the host as soon as possible that day (or earlier, if you know that you won't be well enough to attend), explain the situation, give your regrets, and thank the host for the lovely invitation.

There are only two acceptable reasons for canceling after you accept an invitation: an emergency or an illness.

Be Prompt

Every invitation deserves a reply within 48 hours. Hosts are well within their rights to call you if you haven't replied by their invitation deadlines. If you don't know by the date specified whether you can attend the party, call the host and explain your hesitation.

Likewise, always be on time for a party, and don't arrive early. If the event is a formal dinner with no cocktail hour and the invitation says 7 p.m., arrive at 7 p.m. — no earlier, no later. If the invitation is for a casual dinner, arriving 20 minutes after the time stated on the invitation is acceptable. For cocktail receptions, the timing is even looser — you can arrive 30 to 45 minutes after the time specified on the invitation. If you think that you'll be late for a dinner party, call the host and explain your situation so that the dinner can proceed without everyone worrying about you.

Dress the Part

Wearing clothes that are appropriate to the occasion is very important. Don't dress casually when the host has made a great effort to put on an elegant party for you and the other guests. Underdressing for an occasion may insult the host and embarrass you. If you're unsure about what to wear, ask the host when you respond to the invitation. And remember: When in doubt, it's always better to be slightly overdressed than underdressed.

Here are some general guidelines regarding attire (see Chapter 7 for more on these distinctions):

- **Casual** for men means sport coats. Open-necked shirts are fine, as neckties are not required. Women can wear informal pantsuits or long or short skirts with blouses or sweaters. If the affair turns out to be more casual than you guessed, men may be permitted to remove their jackets.

- **Semi-formal** for men means a good-quality dark suit with a white shirt, dark tie, dark socks, and black shoes. Women should wear a ballet or cocktail-length dress in a nice fabric such as crepe, silk, or brocade; a dressy suit (sometimes called a cocktail or theater suit) that is made of wool or crepe with rhinestone buttons, for example, or satin or velvet; or a long skirt or long dress.

- **Black tie** indicates a tuxedo (dinner jacket) for men, with a white dress shirt, cuff links and studs, cummerbund, black silk socks, and black patent leather shoes. For women, a long, short, or three-quarter length evening gown with sheer hose and peau-de-soie pumps or evening sandals is appropriate.

- **White tie** means a tailcoat of black wool and silk with a white wing shirt, cuff links and studs, a white bow tie, a white cummerbund or white vest, black patent shoes or dress oxfords with black silk hose, white gloves (optional), and a black silk top hat (optional). Women should wear full-skirted grand ball gowns, sheer hose, evening sandals or peau-de-soie pumps dyed to match their dresses, long white gloves, a wrap (if the weather necessitates it), and lots of jewelry.

Give Thoughtfully

Gifts confuse many well-intentioned guests. You know that you need to bring something, but what? When the event consists of friends getting together for a casual dinner or barbecue, bringing food or drink as a gift is fine. However, in the case of a special occasion, gifts of food and drink are not appropriate, because the host may not know what to do with them. If you must bring wine or liquor to a special occasion, make sure to tell the host, "I thought you would enjoy this later," so that the host doesn't feel obligated to use your gift that evening.

You can take cut flowers as a gift if they're already in a vase. Bringing arranged flowers eliminates the host's need to take time out from greeting guests and making last-minute preparations to find a vase and arrange the cut flowers. If you want to give cut flowers as a gift, it's better to send them with a note on the day before or after the event.

Other excellent gifts include a book, a memento, something that relates to a hobby the host enjoys, or a flowering plant. Whatever gift you give, make sure that the host can set it aside and enjoy it later.

Be Self-Sufficient

A host likes nothing better than a self-sufficient guest — one who fearlessly makes introductions with other guests and mixes into conversations easily. How can you be one of those self-sufficient guests? Whether the event is business-related or social, paying attention to others is a great way to relax and make the occasion enjoyable. Listen to what is being said, enter into conversations wholeheartedly, ask questions, and really care about the answers.

People like to talk about themselves. Questions are a great tool to help quiet or reserved people open up. Just don't ask questions that are too personal! In the right situation, almost any question is acceptable, but in business and social dining occasions, where many people are meeting each other for the first time, avoid questions about religion, income, political preferences, and sex.

Make a Contribution to the Party

A host invites you to a party because he or she thinks that your presence will add something to the event. That means that the host expects you to contribute to the conversation and mix and mingle with the other guests.

No matter how awful your day was (even if your dog ran away, your kids threw temper tantrums, or you and your spouse had an ugly argument), never look downtrodden, have a dour look on your face, or act bored.

Inform yourself about current events before you go to a party. Read at least one newspaper and one news magazine, or at least scan the news headlines. Don't forget the sports and arts pages, too! Bring up current topics during the first conversational lull. The other guests will be grateful that you filled the silence, and they're likely to follow your lead. (Barbara Walters is a master of this simple technique; she's used it to open the mouths of many celebrities and heads of state.)

Drink in Moderation, If at All

Heavy drinking is out of style, and for some people, more than one drink can spell disaster! If you can't handle alcohol, you won't be able to handle the business or social situations you may find yourself in. Drinking too much undermines your reputation and, in business situations, your professionalism.

Even in social situations with close friends in which the purpose is to relax and have fun, you don't want to lose control. That advice may seem obvious, but you'd be amazed at how one cocktail too many can relax your tongue . . . and your manners. Don't embarrass yourself and someone else with rudeness. Limit your alcohol consumption to a reasonable amount, be considerate of those around you, and you'll behave well.

Be Considerate about Smoking

In many states, smoking laws greatly prohibit smokers. In areas where smoking is allowed, follow these guidelines:

- ✔ If you don't see an ashtray, don't ask for one.
- ✔ Never smoke at the table while others eat.
- ✔ Don't light up until after coffee is served and the other guests have finished dessert.
- ✔ When all else fails, use common sense. If you must light up, excuse yourself and go outside.

Don't smoke cigars anywhere unless the host offers you one. If you are offered a cigar, the same rules apply as for smoking.

Exit Gracefully

Before you leave a party, say good-bye to the host. It's important that you seek out the host to shake hands, hug, or kiss (depending on your familiarity with that person) and offer your thanks for the party. If there is more than one host, such as a husband and wife, seek out and thank each of them individually.

If the host is busy, wait until he or she has a free moment. If the host isn't available and you absolutely must leave without saying good-bye, make sure to call and say thank you the next day.

Send a Thank-You Note

After attending a party or other function, send a thank-you note within a week — even better, send it within 24 hours, while the event is still fresh in your mind. If you don't think that you can get a note in the mail, call the host. But thank-you notes make you look good and show the host respect. Simply *saying* thank you as you leave the event is not enough.

Writing a thank-you note takes only a few minutes at the most. Most thank-you notes contain no more than three lines (see Chapter 15 for more information about writing thank-you notes). Using the excuse that you don't have time to write a thank-you note is not acceptable — think of all the time and effort (not to mention the expense) that the host spent putting the party together!

Chapter 25

Ten Tipping Situations and How to Handle Them

The word *tip* comes from an old innkeeper's sign, "*To Insure Promptness.*" When patrons deposited a few coins, they received their drinks faster. Today, you give a tip to someone who performs a service for you. Learning how to tip (and especially how to figure the tip gracefully without involving others at the table) is an important skill. This chapter discusses ten situations in which tips are expected and helps you figure out how much to tip which people.

In general, you can tip less than is suggested in this chapter if the person providing the service performs that service in a substandard manner. You're justified in forgoing a tip if the person is hostile and rude.

Having a Drink at a Bar

If you sit at a bar and have a drink, tip the bartender 10 to 15 percent of the tab. If you sit at a table in a cocktail lounge, tip the cocktail waiter 15 percent.

Receiving Assistance in Selecting a Bottle of Wine

Give the wine steward or sommelier a tip that equals up to 10 to 15 percent of the cost of the wine. Give this tip *in addition* to the normal tip to your server of 15 to 20 percent of the cost of the meal, including wine. If you can't discreetly hand the sommelier a cash tip, you can simply include the amount on the bill as part of the entire tip. In most fine restaurants, the waiter shares the tips with the others who serve the table.

Being Attended to in a Restroom

Give a men's or ladies' room attendant 25 to 50 cents for providing a hand towel, which is a standard service. Tip another $1 for any additional service that the attendant provides, such as helping you remove a stain or providing hairspray or cologne.

Checking Your Coat with a Cloakroom Attendant

Tip a cloakroom attendant $1 per coat that you check. If you hang two coats on one hanger, add 50 cents for the additional coat.

Eating at a Lunch Counter or Buffet

If you eat at a lunch counter, tip 10 to 15 percent of the bill. (Be a little more generous if you just have a 95-cent cup of coffee.) If you eat a meal at a buffet-style restaurant, a 10 percent tip for the person who services your table is appropriate.

Hiring a Baby-sitter

Depending on your area, a baby-sitter customarily receives from no tip to a 15 percent tip. If you're unsure of what your sitter will expect, check with other local mothers.

TIP

Giving gifts as tips

Although people who expect a tip generally prefer to receive cash, on a few occasions you may give a small gift to express your appreciation instead. You may want to give a gift to the housekeeper or maid if you stay in someone's private home, for example. Giving a gift as a tip to the owners of a bed and breakfast, a hotel manager, or an official who has gone out of the way to assist you is also acceptable. An appropriate gift might be a gift certificate to a nearby restaurant or shop, a flowering plant, or an engraved item, such as a pen or business card holder.

Having an Appointment at a Hair Salon

Give your barber or hairstylist a 15 to 20 percent tip if you're having a cut, color, or perm. If you have a separate colorist and stylist, each person should receive 15 to 20 percent of the cost of the particular service that he or she provided. If you're having your hair set or washed and blow-dried, a 15 percent tip is sufficient.

If other people in the salon help you (for example, if a junior assistant washes your hair), tip each of them a few dollars for their services. If you have a manicure, tip the manicurist a minimum of $2 or 15 percent of the cost of the manicure. At a very modest hair establishment, tip 10 percent to the hairstylist, plus $1 to the shampoo person and $1 to $2 to the manicurist. If your hairstylist also shampoos your hair, add $1 to his or her tip.

Tipping a Takeout Delivery Person

Tip food delivery people a minimum of $1. If you ordered a large quantity of food, such as two large bags of takeout food or enough pizzas for a large party, tip $5. If the weather is inclement, be more generous — add $1 to the tip.

Taking a Taxi

A taxi driver who operates on a meter system should receive a 15 percent tip (with 50 cents as the minimum tip). For a $5 ride, tip $1. If the ride is a long one, pay 15 to 20 percent in tips.

In cities in which a zone system is in place, you tip for shorter rides by rounding up to the nearest dollar. For example, if your bill is $4.60, pay the driver $5. If the bill is much higher, again, tip 15 to 20 percent of the total fare.

You may alter your tip accordingly, depending on the circumstances. For example, if the driver takes the long route and runs up the fare, you can omit the tip. On the other hand, if you're caught in a traffic jam, you should pay slightly more than normal, because a driver loses money during the waiting period. If, say, you're stuck in traffic for ten minutes and the meter reads $10.50 when you reach your destination, you may want to raise your usual $2 tip to $3.

Utilizing a Bellhop's or Skycap's Services

Tip bellhops and skycaps at least $1 per bag. If you have a lot of luggage, you may want to add more. For three bags, for example, it would be courteous to give $5.

Every time a bellhop brings something to your room, tip $2. If the bellhop runs a special errand for you — to pick up a particular newspaper, for example — tip $5.

Chapter 26

Ten Common Etiquette Mistakes

The way you act in public and the way you treat other people say a lot about you. Remember that the real purpose of etiquette is to make others feel comfortable. Some etiquette mistakes are simply oversights; others stem from having a less-than-positive attitude and are more difficult to correct. This chapter points out ten of the most common manners mistakes and tells you how to avoid them.

Making Introductions in the Wrong Order

These days, introductions are more casual than they used to be, mainly because life is more relaxed. However, a few rules do persist:

- Always introduce the lower-ranking person to the higher-ranking person, as in, "Mr. Jones, I would like to introduce Robin, my administrative assistant." Introducing your boss to a junior colleague is a breach of etiquette.

- Always present a man to a woman. (In business situations, though, this rule applies only if she holds a more prestigious position than he does.)

- In the case of two women or two men, who is introduced to whom doesn't make a difference, unless one person is much older, such as an elderly grandmother. In that case, present the younger person to the older person, as above.

- Introduce the younger person to the older one out of respect.

The general rule is to be prepared to shake hands with anyone you meet. When it comes to shaking hands, the lower-ranking person generally extends a hand first. Remember to shake hands firmly — no fingertips, limp fish, or bone crushers, please!

A common mistake (although not a *terrible* one) is to say, "Pleased to meet you," when you first meet someone. The only correct way to acknowledge an introduction is to say, "How do you do?" Try *not* to say, "Pleased to meet you," "My pleasure," or "Pleased to make your acquaintance," because these statements may not be true after you get to know the person.

Showing Up Late for an Important Date

Be on time. Showing up late is disrespectful of other people's time. Our society is far too slack about punctuality, and arriving 45 minutes late for dinner doesn't represent good manners. Enough said.

If you know that you're running late because you're stuck in a horrendous traffic jam, for example, make every effort to call your host to explain. Apologize profusely, estimate when you might arrive, and insist to the host that the party proceed without you.

Resting Elbows on the Table

Never place your arms or elbows on the table while you eat. When in doubt about what to do with your hands, place them on your lap. When you're between courses and no dishes or food are on the table, or after you finish the meal, however, putting an elbow on the table is permissible. Just don't crowd the person next to you or use both of your arms for support.

Waving the White Flag: Improper Napkin Use

As soon as you sit down to eat, place your napkin, folded in half, on your lap. (If the event is very formal, wait for the host and guest of honor to place their napkins on their laps before doing so yourself.) Don't wave or shake your napkin like you're hanging out the laundry. Also, never use your napkin to wipe your face or your lipstick. Use it only to blot the corners of your mouth.

If you leave the table briefly, place your napkin on your chair. After you finish your meal, fold your napkin neatly and place it to the left of your plate. (See Chapter 16 for a complete listing of proper table manners.)

Explaining Too Much When Excusing Yourself

If you need to excuse yourself, you don't need to give a lengthy explanation about where you're going. Quietly say, "Excuse me," and don't make a fuss — don't announce a visit to the john or the powder room, the need to make an important phone call, or anything else. If an emergency comes up and you must leave for good before the meal is over, make a brief apology, indicate when you will next talk with important guests or clients, and leave with as little other interruption as possible. Proper etiquette for the remaining guests is to turn back to the meal and the conversation.

Drinking to Yourself

If someone makes a toast to you, never take a drink — not even a sip. If someone toasts you, simply acknowledge the toast by nodding and smiling.

You don't need to clink glasses after a toast, either. Raise your glass to the toast, lower it, and take a sip. Clinking glasses is an old custom that originated to ward off evil spirits, and it has no relevance today. Besides, it's hard on glassware.

Making Remarks That Embarrass or Offend Others

Avoid death, surgery, and illness as topics of discussion. Talking about your Aunt Martha's gallbladder surgery may fascinate you, but it may well nauseate your dinner companions. Other topics to avoid include religion, politics, salaries, and office gossip. Spare your companions the off-color jokes, too. Instead, turn the conversation to current events in the world or in your industry, mutual friends, hobbies, sports, or food — all of these topics make for good, non-controversial small talk. (See Chapter 10 for more on the lost art of conversation.)

Cutting in on Conversations

If you feel the urge to cut in on someone else's sentence with a fascinating tidbit of information that you think makes you look witty or erudite, sit back and wait a second. If a pause occurs, use it as your cue to talk. If a pause doesn't occur or the conversation changes course, be content with the thought that, although you may have missed a chance to contribute your wisdom to the discussion, you at least minded your manners.

Speaking Loudly

Speaking loudly in public, especially in restaurants, is common nowadays. But remember that it's not the loudest person who impresses his or her dinner companions; it's the person who has quiet confidence and good manners. Always use low, intimate tones when you're around other people.

If you're speaking loudly because you're talking into a cellular phone, shame on you! Cellular phones should be turned off before you enter a restaurant. Even if *you* don't mind your pleasant dinner being interrupted by a call, others in the restaurant might appreciate having their meal in peace. (See Chapter 9 for more on cellular phone etiquette.)

Flubbing a Phone Call

The impression you create on the telephone can be a lasting one, so make sure that your voice and manner show you in the most professional light. Callers base their opinions of you (and your company, if you're answering the phone in a business environment) on what you say and how you say it.

Answering the phone promptly is the first step. Treat every call that you receive as important. In business situations, try to answer the phone before the second ring, which shows your efficiency and makes the caller feel important. At home, answer the phone before the fourth ring so the caller doesn't assume that he or she has interrupted you in the middle of a task.

Whether you're the caller or the person answering the phone, always begin a call by introducing yourself and identifying your company (if applicable). While you speak, sit up straight with your feet on the floor and smile. Believe it or not, doing so gives you more energy, and that energy comes across on the telephone.

When dealing with two calls at once, remember that the person you called always maintains priority. If someone calls you while you're waiting for your first call to go through, tell the caller that you'll call back, such as with this script: "Hello, Bill. I'm on the other line. May I get back with you in just a few minutes?" Giving the first caller priority doesn't leave Bill listening to a dead receiver while you finish up on the other line.

If you reach a person's voice mail, state your name clearly (spell it out if it's difficult), slowly give your telephone number, and suggest a good time to return the call. If you're calling to answer a question that the person asked during a previous conversation, leave your answer on voice mail.

Finally, make sure to follow through on phone calls. If you promise information, try to call back promptly, or have someone else call back for you if you can't do so yourself.

Index